The Praxis of the Reign of God

The Praxis of the Reign of God

An Introduction to the Theology of Edward Schillebeeckx

Edited by
MARY CATHERINE HILKERT *and* ROBERT J. SCHREITER

Fordham University Press
New York
2002

Library of Congress Cataloging-in-Publication Data

The praxis of the reign of God: an introduction to the theology of Edward Schillebeeckx /edited by Mary Catherine Hilkert and Robert J. Schreiter. — 2nd ed.

p. cm.

Previous ed. published under title: The praxis of Christian experience.

Includes bibliographical references and index.

ISBN 0-8232-2022-2 — ISBN 0-8232-2023-0 (pbk.)

1. Schillebeeckx, Edward, 1914-I.Hilkert, Mary Catherine. II. Schreiter, Robert J. III. Praxis of Christian experience.

BX4705.S51314 P73 2002

230'.2'092--dc21

2001007185

Printed in the United States of America

02 03 04 05 06 5 4 3 2 1

Second Edition

CONTENTS

ABBREVIATIONS USED IN REFERENCES TO SCHILLEBEECKX'S WORKS

Christ	*Christ: The Experience of Jesus As Lord*
Church	*Church: The Human Story of God*
Interim Report	*Interim Report on the Books "Jesus" and "Christ"*
Jesus	*Jesus: An Experiment in Christology*
Ministry	*Ministry: Leadership in the Community of Jesus Christ*
Testament	*Theologisch testament*

PROLOGUE: HUMAN GOD-TALK AND GOD'S SILENCE

Edward Schillebeeckx

Religions are no longer primarily associations that endorse particular belief systems, but rather are traditions of religious experience (as I call them in several of my books). My assumption here is that any understanding of truth has a "tradition-conditioned" character, even in the matter of religious truth; hence we have "human traditions" (the term is Walter Benjamin's) and traditions of religious experience. No one begins at point zero, and if one does, one comes back empty-handed.

Religious by Nature?

The great world religions do not fall into the same genus, the genus of *religion,* like plants, animals, and people who, despite their differences, all are part of the genus of *living beings.* Of the many different kinds of religion, one can speak (with Wittgenstein) of family resemblances. If the world religions were to understand that, they would interact in a more friendly way—we would have basically a kind of "ecumene."

Personally, I would call the religions wisdom schools. They are schools that on the one hand, preserve us or liberate us from idolatry, that is, from the tendency to honor and adore something finite (this is something I learn from the Jewish school and the Christian school that emerged from it). On the other hand, they are schools that try to purify our cravings and desire (something I learn from the many branches of Hinduism and Buddhism). Religions are not systems of truth constructs; they try to trace a way of life, albeit not without truth and insights. The first name for the Christian Jesus movement was not

Christians or Christianity, not to mention Christendom. It was *he hodos,* "the way" (especially in the Acts of the Apostles).

Human beings are "religious by nature." This does not mean to imply that God exists; only that everyone (except perhaps for the cynical nihilist) has a kind of holy place somewhere in them, something that is unconditionally at their center. The question, therefore, is not whether we honor a god, but which god we honor and adore. This is the principal question, especially in a secularized culture. Secularized people will never call the gods they honor in their everyday lives (for example, mammon) their god. Everything but that. But that this is what they in fact do is craftily camouflaged. Human beings have no other choice than to set their hearts on something. They all have something sacred, unassailable, something worth living for, something worthy to engage their hearts, their minds, and all their senses. They commit themselves unconditionally to this. That's the way human beings are.

But if their god or idol is a creature, there can be destructive consequences that will consume human beings themselves. Think of the Holocaust, and the many new holocausts in the former Yugoslavia, in Rwanda, Burundi, Congo, Northern Ireland—one could go on and on. Unconditional surrender to nationalism, the state, mammon, the economy, whatever; to those who worship the left or the right or the middle, to those who regard opportunistic political parties as the goal or the summum bonum—all of this leads to catastrophe, to violence, to the loss of the other's sense of personhood, and even to genocide.

The same happens when the religion itself becomes an idol, albeit camouflaged and disguised, when it acts "in the name of the true God," in the form of unconditional struggle to maintain itself alone, when it will not relinquish positions of power, when it enriches itself financially at the cost of its own believers. When that happens, religious wars and inquisitions come about, and take up the use of force "in the name of JHWH," or Allah, or Christ the King. To be sure, some modern evangelists do the latter with charm, but with an all the more clever religious brainwashing.

The question as to which god you worship has to do with whether your heart is focused on the destruction of others, or on peace and freedom for each person; on solidarity, justice, and love; on friendship, gift of self, and the loss of self in the service of others, if necessary. We must be honest: being religious by nature, having a need for unconditioned commitment, can be extremely dangerous precisely when it becomes a human need and craving. Humans are, after all, also by nature idolaters. We cannot forget that human desire is a creature (and thus ambivalent), and whoever raises a creature to the glory of divine majesty is an idolater, certainly no servant of the divine mysteries. One can also swim in self-absorption in the "divine-sacred."

Let us not forget that when it is a matter of the true God, the living God of all human beings, believers cannot downgrade God to give themselves an unpaid upgrade. To adore God has its costs. If we do not pay the price of giving ourselves over, we run into all kinds of dangers at every turn. One of these, to my mind, is the much-heard appeal today to "the ineffable God of which (or whom) we must be silent." *Silence about God*: a slogan of postmodernism. Long before the term *postmodernism* was in fashion, the philosopher Wittgenstein wrote, "of that which we cannot speak we must be silent" (*Tractatus Logico-Philosophicus,* New York: Humanities Press, 1961, no. 7, 151). Elsewhere he added to this that it is precisely in that undiscussable zone that the deepest human problems of life are hidden, waiting for an answer.

THE DIALECTIC OF SPEAKING AND BEING SILENT

What is at play here is a dialectic of speaking and being silent. The question at the heart of religious experience can be formulated in this way: How can God be named? How can the ineffable be brought to words? The path of Christian wisdom is this: You must let go of your heart to the ineffable divine mystery, but in doing so at least some words must be spoken. Something gets the name *divine,* after all, if you honor it as that which, or who, is "the end" (the be-all or end-all). But it cannot be something or someone from our creaturely world, not even the totality of this finite world. Worship is proper to the concept God, it belongs to that concept; otherwise we are talking nonsense.

God is not God for himself. The mystery of God, at least for us human beings, is called God by those worshipping creatures who honor him—by us human beings. Jacques Pohier did not call his book (deemed heretical) *Quand je dis Dieu* ("when I say God") for nothing. Our enunciation of the name *God,* that is, "I say God," does not call the divine mystery into being. God's silence actually makes it possible that I sometimes have to cry out the name of God in tears. Without the worship of human beings, the divine mystery is never God.

But there is a lot of carelessness and lack of economy at play in much talk about God. God is, rather, the mystery with which no thing or person or image or power, nothing in this world, or even the world in its entirety, can be identified. On the other hand, the living God is transcendent to the degree that he dwells in the utmost depths of our selves, and we are like fish in divine water. He is more intimately close to us than we are to ourselves—*interior interiori meo,* as the Christian neo-Platonist St. Augustine put it. He was able to say that because of God's real transcendence. Zoologists have told me that fish, despite all the swimming they do in the water, are the last to discover that they are swimming in it—that it is the living source of their existence in which they live, move, and have their being.

But caution is advised here as well. The modern term *negative theology,* being silent about God, can be misleading. It is certainly not what the patristic period called apophatic or wordless theology, or what medieval (especially Thomist and Dominican) theology called the *via negativa.* At the heart of all the great world religions, there flows a mystical undercurrent of being silent about God. This is not not talking about God at all (although there are some interreligious differences here). Every serious religion has something like a ban on images (even if they also say that you may use images). All images are smashed. However necessary that may be, it becomes a purely hate-filled iconoclasm if you are not empowered to do this smashing of images—in other words, if all your denials do not find their power or springboard to negation in a positive recognition of God's untouchable holiness, or sacrality.

All denials presume an unexpressed but positive realization of what God is. Otherwise, you could not or even would not dare smash those human images of God. You know that they cannot be up to representing the reality of God, that is, that your human speaking about God does not make the grade at all. No single image, no single representation, no experiential or abstract concept is in a position to speak of God on God's level. Put another way, we have no concepts of God. Religious discourse is symbolic and metaphorical discourse. This is not a lower level of understanding, but precisely an awareness of a level higher than all rationality, a level that transcends our concepts, our capacity to form images and definitions. When we can no longer articulate something even while its name burns our lips, we poor, feeble beings do it with some artifice as the only way out.

The cognitive power of symbols and metaphors surpasses the assertive eloquence of all our concepts, and surpasses the theological concept (which some theologians use) of God as a human cipher of God, which can only be verified eschatologically, as the British theologian John Hick puts it. For it is only then that we shall "see," as Paul says, "face to face." Here on earth, it remains all artifice; even Paul had to use a mirror for it.

YET WE SPEAK OF GOD!

With all our awareness of the silence of God, we must have the courage to speak of God. The distinction between God and the world is from our perspective, not that of God. Thus the relation of dependence between the world and God is not mutual (as Thomas already had pointed out), but there is a mutuality of real contact between God and the religious person, at least in the mind of the Christian tradition of experience. A form of life that knows no form of responsive speech and, thus, always stops with silence is, in any event, not the form of life of Jesus of Nazareth, whom Christians confess as the God's first love and eschatological witness.

Without exception, there is an absolute priority of God's grace on all that human beings think, do, feel, and say. To speak as human beings is always a response. Playing around with being silent about God is, to my mind, not speaking about God at all and, moreover, being silent about Jesus of Nazareth as the dialogue or word of God. As mere creatures, we acknowledge the inadequacy of our discourse about God by speaking about God with economy and care. But if, following modern positivism, a literal, computer-like descriptive knowledge becomes the only paradigm of all human knowledge (and that threatens to become the dominant one in the positivistic West, even in some of the secular and Christian universities), then everything falling outside that paradigm is sheer nonsense, including every form of religion. Then the only voices we can hear on earth (since this makes nature mute) are the voices of those people crying in the wilderness, screaming in the cosmic darkness, who brought even a Blaise Pascal to fearful astonishment.

BEING SILENT ABOUT GOD AS COUNTERPOINT TO SPEAKING ABOUT GOD

Christianity is distinguished from philosophical agnosticism, and also from all postmodern silence about God, by the way it addresses—speaks to—Christian "unknowing." Christians speak to the Mystery right through the darkness. They respond surprised to the quiet that surrounds us, and that we allow to enter our interiority (for interiority is full of the exteriority from outside). This has to do with a silence that is recognized *as the voice of God.* God does not come "in storm, loud noise, and fire," as was the case in the first years of Israel, but in the lisp of a whispering voice. Thomas says: *Deus non est existens, sed supra existentiam* ("God does not exist, he transcends all existence," *Summa Theologiae* I, q. 12, a. 1, ad 3). Elsewhere he says, *De Deo scire non possumus quid sit, sed quid non sit* ("we cannot know what God is, but what he is not," *Summa Theologiae* I, q. 3–13).

But to say something like that, you have to know something positive about God; otherwise it is nonsense. We hear about the same thing from India: God is neither *sat* (not an existent being) nor *asat* (not stillness, not emptiness, although you must make yourself empty to receive it). God is neither of the two. We can correct the converse of an expression about God only by another converse expression (that is the tenor of Thomas's analogical speaking about God). But then you had better know what this divine mystery means regarding majesty and lure for people who maintain that God is ineffable. Because oscillating between "it is not this" and "it is not this either," and so on, is an endless dialectic of "warm or cold" that will never excite anyone.

I have already said that all great religions at their very best are schools of wisdom and freedom. In the first place, they want to protect us against the veneration of creaturely idols, against idolatry, against offering to a creature the worship that is only to be accorded to the divine mystery. Idolatry is a worship of an object upon which the glory of God has come down, or a thing upon which human beings project their own unsatiated desire and glory. I always think of the illuminating story of the burning bush (Ex 3:1–15), the place where God is present is not God. Where God is, is not God. If God is present in a person, in an event, in a dream or in a project, then we take off our shoes; we bow down and may well offer sacrifices, but that person, that event, that vision is not God. The sacrality of God's presence is never divine. God manifests himself in our acknowledgement of his holiness, that which lies behind our understanding, our control, our manipulating or our managing. It lies behind any knowing that wants to cast a net or a defining project over the mystery, in order to fish something meaningful out of it.

On the other hand, wanting to pause or stop by the dark night of the soul, the Cloud of Unknowing, the cloud of the ineffable, is itself also a form of idolatry. Then we are making an idol of the darkness. Medieval Flemish mystics (was it Hadewijch or Ruusbroec? It is still debated) tried to escape the idolatry of being silent in their via negativa by talking about something like a "dark light." A more paradoxical metaphor is unthinkable, but it does come near this reality, albeit from a creaturely point of view. The seductive power of idolatry also finds expression in various forms of worship of the void. But neither the darkness, nor even the gentle breeze is God: both merely point to the divine mystery that, in its quickly passing us, allows us only to see "its back," as it says in the story of Moses.

We may not make an object of the darkness or the silence before which we may pause to give our adoration. To do so is to make an idol of silence, like the neo-Platonic *Sige* (the Great Silence); the silence that, according to the fourteenth-century Byzantine Orthodox mystic and theologian Nicholas Cabasilas, the divine *ousia* (nature or substance) pushed deeper into the unknown. But then he had to admit that that hidden substance radiated a certain aura—he called them divine energies—that had to, as it were, bridge the distance between the unknown, deeper divine nature and the more external divine Triune Unity. There is a suggestion here that needs to be taken to heart regarding the Triune God. The one and only God is by nature (a nature that is pure, absolute freedom) such that he reveals himself in the economy of salvation as the one God—Father, Jesus Christ (the Son), and Spirit.

CHRISTIANITY AND THE DIALECTIC OF SPEAKING AND BEING SILENT

How does Christian faith see this dialectic of speaking and being silent? From a Christian point of view, the silence of the darkness (which we cannot deny) is nonetheless interrupted by a voice that speaks, to be sure a human voice, but as "the Word once spoken, the Life once lived, the Death once endured" (as I once heard in the Anglican liturgy). That is to say, Jesus Christ, a human being just like you and me, not an icon of himself, but pointing toward the one God worthy of our adoration, gate of our prayer to the Father, as it says in the Letter to the Hebrews: "Consequently he is able for all time to save those who approach God through him, since he always lives to make intercession for them" (Heb 7:25).

Dying on the cross, Jesus addressed him whom he called his loving Father: "My God, my God, why," but then, in spite of it all, "into your hands I commend my spirit, my entire being." To release oneself into the infinite divine mystery has, although in the tonality of a human response, the tenor of the voice of God himself. I would phrase it this way: God's silence becomes God's speaking, God's voice in the responding voice of a human being, a recognition of God's unassailable holiness. God's silence as anti-word (answer or counterpoint). It is not for nothing that the Jewish Psalms call God "the Holy One of Israel." No human voice can speak of "that which is from above," if it is not a counterpoint to what has been whispered from above. Not in storm, loud noise, or fire, but in the mute voice of a light rustle, in the silence and the loud cry of the one dying on the cross, who despite the darkness lays his all that he has and does, all his very being in the hands of the unknowable mystery.

DIALECTIC OF SUFFERING AND LIFE

Jesus' *paschal rising* appears to be God's confirmation of Jesus' faithfulness in the course of his life; that is to say, the Father stood with Jesus despite the murder human beings committed against him. The mission of the Holy Spirit equally can be seen as divine affirmation, but through the apostolic witness of Jesus' disciples, who were reminded by the divine spirit of their fidelity to the life of Jesus, and of their witness to

God's ratification of that life by God, the Living One, taking him to himself. Both salvific events are interpreted liturgically in two (or even three) different feast days (as Luke distinguishes them temporally). But they mark one and the same divine authentification of both Jesus' life lived consistently to the very end, and the apostolic witnesses to this divine ratification, thanks to the paschal gift of God's Holy Spirit to the disciples of Jesus.

All of this flows from the initiative of God the Father and points back, even in Jesus the anointed one, to the one God, the most holy mystery, who holds to his heart everything of life, from the heights to the depths, from ant and aphid to elephant and human being. He is a God of life, not of the dead, to whom he also gives a future.

Although it could be said that Christianity is the religion that least trivializes in its praxis the suffering of humanity, the Christian and the Christian mystic say: "Be not afraid: I am with you," or "I will be with you." This is the name of God, the name that the haggling Moses got out of God that God did not want to give to him. Shrewder than Moses, God did not let him check the divine passport, but gave him an honest answer, however evasive: "I will be there for you." The story suggests ironically: "You will have to settle for that name!" For God will, after all, also be there to judge the living and the dead. We will have to account for ourselves to the name of God. Christianity is above all the praxis of the reign of God, an entryway or pathway to the eschatological revelation of God's own name.

On the basis of the Jesus event, we can say that Christianity is about love as the way to God, but a love that is not silent about the price, the costs of loving. The disciples of the risen crucified one were inculcated with this: the light appears in the darkness. Matthew 25, in the Second or so-called New Testament, is the story in which it is most clear that the specific charge to Christians, as Christians, is to identify themselves with the least among human beings. That identification is the measure by which God, in Christ, will make the final judgment of human beings (whether or not they recognize Jesus as the Christ).

The trace of God is to be found especially in the face of the rejected and poor person looking at you. I would want to say to all future ministers of God's mysteries—faithful, deacon, priest, bishop, synod, or pope—that the church is not where you are, but where all the faithful, and especially the ministers of the holy mysteries, are, caring and helping, looking into the face of the poor. There is where you see the invisible God "as passing by." Yet be reminded that it was not the Jewish priest, not the levite, but the foreign Samaritan who did not pass by the wounded man, but rather took him in his care. And it was he who saw God as passing by!

Translated by Robert J. Schreiter

INTRODUCTION

Mary Catherine Hilkert

In an interview on the eve of his eightieth birthday in 1994, the Flemish theologian Edward Schillebeeckx noted that the following two biblical texts have sustained him throughout his theological career, which now spans more than sixty-five years:

> "Always be prepared to make a defence to anyone who calls you to account for the hope that is in you" (1 Peter 3.15b);
> "Do not quench the Spirit, do not despise prophecies, but test everything; hold fast [to] what is good" (1 Thessalonians 5.19–21).

Schillebeeckx describes himself as one who has tried to remain open to the God who is "new each moment." In living his life this way, Schillebeeckx has sought to bear testimony to others about the hope and joy within him. He attributes both the constructive-liberating character of his theology and its critical edge to the work of the Holy Spirit (*I Am a Happy Theologian,* 81; *Testament,* 173).

Pastoral and social concerns have been at the heart of Schillebeeckx's theological project from the beginning. His theological vision and method have developed in response to the questions and experiences of contemporary believers and all those searching for meaning and purpose in human life. Of particular interest to many were his efforts in the 1970s to rethink the story of Jesus *(Jesus: An Experiment in Christology)* and the Christian experience of salvation *(Christ: The Experience of Jesus As Lord)*, in the face of radical human suffering and the growing crisis of credibility confronting Christian faith in the modern world. Likewise, his investigations of the development of the church's ministerial structures and theology in the early 1980s (*Ministry: Leadership in the Community of Jesus Christ* and *The Church with a Human Face*) were prompted by concrete pastoral crises. Of particular concern were the increasing shortage of ordained ministers, the number of local communities deprived of Eucharist, and the forms of alternative practice emerging in a variety of communities of faith.

By the end of that decade, Schillebeeckx's theological work had caught the attention of scholars, ordinary believers, and others who confessed to curiosity about theology's contribution to the dilemmas facing the world at the end of the twentieth century. However, his work was not easily accessible, due to the length of his books, the breadth and detail of the scholarly research he included, and the inevitably technical theological language that his thought required. At that time, no single volume existed in the English-speaking world that provided a general introduction to Schillebeeckx's theology. In 1989 the authors in this book sought to remedy that lack, through a collection of essays that offered clear exposition of major theological themes that recurred in Schillebeeckx's writings on christology and ministry. That volume was published under the title *The Praxis of Christian Experience: An Introduction to the Theology of Edward Schillebeeckx*.

Because Schillebeeckx continued to explore new questions, to develop major theological themes that have engaged him throughout his career, and to rethink earlier positions in light of changing cultural and ecclesiastical climates, that introduction now needs to be revised and updated. In 1993 Philip Kennedy published *Schillebeeckx,* a work that provided an excellent analysis of the core of Schillebeeckx's theology, with particular attention to examination of his sources, the historical development in his thought, the core of his christological project, the centrality of creation in his theology, and the question of whether and how human beings can speak about God. But Kennedy never intended to offer an exposition of all the major themes covered in this volume, including some of long-term interest to Schillebeeckx, such as eschatology and sacraments. The addition to this book of Kennedy's chapter on Schillebeeckx's insights about God and creation has considerably expanded the scope of our introduction to Schillebeeckx's theology. Schillebeeckx's own previously untranslated prologue to this edition makes clear that the question of who God can be for human beings remains the central question at the heart of his diverse theological writings.

MAJOR DEVELOPMENTS SINCE 1989

A broad overview of the new topics and emphases in Schillebeeckx's theology since 1989 can help to orient readers, both those who are familiar with his thought and those who have turned to his work only recently. *The Praxis of Christian Experience* appeared the same year in which Schillebeeckx published the Dutch version of what was to have been the third and final volume of his christological trilogy. As he explained in the introduction to that work, however, it became instead a summary and overview of what he still views as the heart of the gospel and the Christian religion, an effort to express what God can mean for contemporary women and men. Written in a less technical style than the previous two volumes, *Church: The Human Story of God* (more accurately translated from the Dutch as "Human Beings as the Story of God") was intended to offer hope to ordinary believers. Schillebeeckx expressed concern that grassroots communities of believers were growing discouraged by the lack of implementation of the vision of Vatican II in a period of increasing polarization within the church, and noted that he wanted to address critical challenges to those in authority (*Church*, xiii).

Although the third volume for the most part summarized insights from the previous two parts of the trilogy, there were some important changes and developments. These included an explicit distinction between salvation and revelation, further clarification of the relationship between religious experience and ethics, a new approach to the question of the uniqueness and universality of Jesus, a more developed call for democratic exercise of authority in the church, and a growing emphasis on creation and ecology. As the title of his third volume suggests, Schillebeeckx's early focus on Jesus Christ as the sacrament of encounter with God has now shifted to humankind, and specifically to action on behalf of humankind and creation, as the central locus of encounter with God. According to Schillebeeckx, the entire human race constitutes the chosen people of God. In that context, he refers to Jesus as "paradigm of humanity" and "concentrated creation."

The explicit distinction that Schillebeeckx made in *Church* between salvation and revelation (discussed in chapter 4 of this book) prompted the change in the title of this revised introduction to his thought, from *The Praxis of Christian Experience* to *The Praxis of the Reign of God*. While

Schillebeeckx has written persuasively about "the praxis of Christian experience"—the living of the Christian life—he also insists that Christianity does not exhaust the mediation of God's reign. The "praxis of the reign of God"—fostering the well-being of creation and humanity—is not limited to Christians and cannot be identified solely with Christian experience.

Schillebeeckx's second collection of homilies and sermons, which appeared in English translation that same year under the title *For the Sake of the Gospel,* included several pieces that reflected his growing critique of official church structures that block, rather than foster, gospel freedom. In another section of that work, Schillebeeckx turned to believers' questions about the hiddenness of God (a topic to which he returns in the prologue to this book) and an issue of central importance in the postmodern world—the claim of God's omnipotence in the face of radical suffering. Moving beyond his description of God's power as "non-authoritarian, vulnerable, even helpless (*Church,* 221), he began to speak of God's "defenseless superior power over evil," both concealed and expressed in the life and death of Jesus (*For the Sake of the Gospel,* 97).

In other articles and chapters published since 1989, Schillebeeckx addressed the role of history in theology, the discontinuities in the living tradition of Christianity and explicitly in Christian doctrine, the mystical and political dimensions of theology, the uniqueness and universality of Jesus, a contemporary mariology, and creation theology. One valuable resource for an overview of both the continuity and the shifts in Schillebeeckx's theological concerns is *The Language of Faith: Essays on Jesus, Theology, and the Church* (1995). This is a collection of thirteen essays that appeared between 1964 and 1989, most of them in *Concilium,* the journal that he cofounded in 1965, along with Karl Rahner, Yves Congar, and Hans Küng, to help promote the theological dialogue and ecclesial reform that characterized the Second Vatican Council.

Although the essays were all published initially prior to 1989, several of them highlight key concerns that Schillebeeckx continued to develop in his later writings and unpublished lectures. Of particular importance are the essays on ecclesial critical communities ("Critical Theories and Christian Political Commitment," 1973), the teaching authority of all believers ("The Teaching Authority of All: A Reflection about the Structure of the New Testament," 1985), theological method ("The Role of History in What Is Called the New Paradigm," 1989), and the question of the universality of Jesus and Christianity in the context of religious pluralism and interreligious dialogue ("The Religious and Human Ecumene," 1989).

Schillebeeckx's long-term interest in the relationship between faith and culture took on a new focus as he turned to questions of religious pluralism, violence carried out in the name of religion, and a theology of forgiveness and reconciliation. In a recent series of essays on faith and culture, as well as in unpublished lectures, Schillebeeckx raises the question of whether religion is actually a threat to the well-being of humankind and the earth, in contemporary cultures. While insisting that violence is not inevitable in a pluralistic society, he nevertheless observes that historical evidence has made it clear that the claim of any religion to be the one true one has served as a virtual declaration of war on the others. For that reason, he argues, Christians need to rethink the claims of Christianity to universality and uniqueness.

In this same context, Schillebeeckx has proposed the necessity of a theology of forgiveness and reconciliation as a necessary step toward a new future for humankind and all of creation. In line with his most recent work on rethinking the sacraments "from below" as metaphors for human life, Schillebeeckx argues that remorse can be liberating, and that human repentance and forgiveness must be celebrated in their religious dimension as sacraments of God's forgiveness.

The purpose of this revised volume is to provide an updated overview and a reading guide to students, pastoral ministers, study groups, ecumenical audiences, and other interested adults who wish to explore Schillebeeckx's thought, but question where to begin. Since the book is intended to lead readers into Schillebeeckx's own writings, suggestions for further reading are provided at the end of each chapter. Serious students of Schillebeeckx's thought will want to consult the glossaries at the end of *Jesus* and *Christ* (titled "Technical Information") and the definitive *Bibliography 1936–1996 of Edward Schillebeeckx O.P.*, compiled by Ted Schoof, O.P., and Jan van de Westelaken (Baarn: Nelissen, 1997).

OVERVIEW OF THIS VOLUME

Schillebeeckx's prologue begins with a theme that echoes his recent interest in interreligious dialogue and his turn to human beings as the locus of encounter with God. Referring to human beings as "religious by nature" and to the religions of the world as "schools of wisdom," he reiterates a conviction that has been fundamental to his theology from the beginning: no human concepts can capture or exhaust the mystery of God. Nevertheless, Christians are called to respond to the God who has spoken in the economy of salvation, and preeminently in Jesus Christ. Stressing that the God of Jesus is a God of life, Schillebeeckx interprets God's name as revealed to Moses: "I will be there for you." He concludes with the central theme that recurs in each of the essays in this book, and from which it draws its title: Christianity is above all about praxis, the praxis of the reign of God.

The chapters that follow offer an overview of the development of and major themes within Schillebeeckx's vast and continuing theological project. In the opening chapter, William Hill provides an introduction to Schillebeeckx's "theology in transition," highlighting a primary theme that Schillebeeckx underscores in his prologue: God's cause is the human cause. Hill reviews Schillebeeckx's personal history and the roots of his theological development, from his Thomist origins through the influence of phenomenology and hermeneutics to his later understanding of theology as a critical and political task. In his *Theologisch testament,* Schillebeeckx describes his theological method as "critical-hermeneutical" (80). While Schillebeeckx has not directly engaged questions of postmodernity under that heading, his concern for radical suffering, along with his conviction that no grand narrative of history is possible in the face of radical evil, echo many of the claims of postmodernity. (Robert Schreiter points this out in his conclusion to this volume.) Throughout the shifts in Schillebeeckx's theological development, Hill identifies an underlying (Thomistic) conviction that pervades Schillebeeckx's varied writings: the absolute primacy of God and God's grace in history.

Developing the broad lines of Schillebeeckx's theological method outlined by Hill, William Portier in the second chapter situates Schillebeeckx's approach to the theological task in terms of both contemporary North American concern with theological method and the

Dutch Catholic context in which his theology was born. Portier underlines the necessity of theology's commitment to a historical praxis of mysticism and politics (another theme that recurs in later chapters) and concludes that for Schillebeeckx, "theology as interpretation entails concrete social dimensions with inseparable links to Christian life and worship." In addition, Portier notes a new emphasis in Schillebeeckx's writings on breaks or ruptures within the living Christian tradition. Because Schillebeeckx takes seriously the role of history in theology, he argues that Christian identity can be found only in and through cultural ruptures and shifts, including moments of discontinuity in Christian doctrine. As Portier notes, Schillebeeckx viewed the Second Vatican Council in precisely that way—as a break with the antimodern stance of the church in the first half of the twentieth century, precisely to ensure continuity with the larger Christian tradition. Because discussion of method in theology emerges only from reflection on the actual practice of the theological task, Portier's chapter, as well as Hill's, can be profitably reread after finishing the book.

In both his *Theologisch testament* and the more popular interview, *I Am a Happy Theologian,* Schillebeeckx comments that "faith in creation is the foundation of all theology" (*Testament,* 85; *I Am a Happy Theologian,* 47). But creation-faith *(scheppingsgeloof),* one of Schillebeeckx's frequently repeated terms, is possible only because of God's loving and free initiative, the absolute presence of creative love that sustains and empowers all that exists.

The one new chapter in the present volume is contributed by Philip Kennedy, an internationally recognized expert on Schillebeeckx's theology. He provides a much-needed review of Schillebeeckx's theology of creation and the Creator God. Kennedy demonstrates that the theme of creation, which is now returning to the center of theological discussion, has been a driving force in Schillebeeckx's theological project from the beginning. For Schillebeeckx, the theology of creation undergirds the very possibility of theology as human speech about God. Drawing from diverse writings throughout Schillebeeckx's career, Kennedy points to both the Thomistic grounding of Schillebeeckx's theology of creation and the startling breaks with Aquinas's insights, such as the assertion that creation is an adventure full of risks in which God remains defenseless. As Kennedy remarks, Schillebeeckx's theology of creation can be viewed as a reformulation of Irenaeus's declaration that the glory of God is humankind and all living creatures, fully alive. Stressing that for Schillebeeckx, creation faith has a critical and productive force, Kennedy explains how a theology of creation undergirds Schillebeeckx's understanding of ethics and the centrality of human praxis in mediating the reign of God. While many contemporary thinkers argue that christology is the necessary starting point for a Christian theology of creation, Kennedy notes that Schillebeeckx speaks of christology as "concentrated creation," a theme that recurs in chapter 6. In the final section of his chapter, Kennedy elucidates Schillebeeckx's descriptions of God as pure positivity, absolute freedom, constant source of future possibility, and more human than any human being.

The question of whether and how human beings can encounter the mystery of God is the focus of chapter 4, on "Experience and Revelation." While Schillebeeckx often used the terms *revelation* and *salvation* interchangeably in earlier writings, he made an explicit distinction between the two in the opening chapter of *Church*. The broader term, *salvation,* refers to the absolute presence of the Creator God and is mediated wherever good is done and evil resisted. As such, it cannot be identified with revelation—the experience, recognition, and celebration of the universal presence of God's saving grace. In chapter 4, I explore Schillebeeckx's claim that revelation occurs within, but cannot be identified with, human experience. I go about this by identifying crucial moves within Schillebeeckx's theology of revelation: the distinction between salvation and revelation; the relationship between experience and interpretation; the necessity of a faith horizon for the religious experience of revelation; the Christian claim that God has been revealed uniquely and definitively in Jesus; the historical transmission of the experience of revelation as a living tradition of faith through the praxis and words of the followers of Jesus today; and the need for a mutually critical correlation of contemporary experiences of faith with the original apostolic experiences of salvation.

Chapters 5 and 6 present the soteriological christology that Schillebeeckx identifies as his own personal theological project or research of choice (*I Am a Happy Theologian,* 44). His christological trilogy was occasioned by the widespread crisis in christology among both Catholics and Protestants. Locating Schillebeeckx within the broader discussion in contemporary christology, John Galvin, in chapter 5, emphasizes the uniqueness of Schillebeeckx's option for a narrative christology forged in the face of human suffering—a retelling of the story of Jesus as the story of God. Noting the breadth of Schillebeeckx's exegetical research, Galvin traces the main outlines of the *Jesus* book, highlighting the features of the "historical Jesus" that led to the later Christian confession of christological faith. Following a careful analysis of Schillebeeckx's unique and largely negative interpretation of the death of Jesus, his controversial theology of the resurrection, and his discussion of the development of early Christian plural strands of faith, Galvin concludes with important critical questions regarding Schillebeeckx's christology.

The soteriological focus of Schillebeeckx's christology, and specifically his attempt to provide a new focus for traditional Western christology in light of the ambiguities and paradoxes facing humankind at the end of the modern era, is developed further by Janet O'Meara in chapter 6. O'Meara explains how Schillebeeckx's move toward a contemporary soteriology in part 4 of the *Christ* volume is carefully interrelated with both the christology of *Jesus* (see Galvin's chapter) and the analysis of New Testament understandings of the experience of salvation, which continued in the earliest Christian communities in and through the power of the Spirit (the major portion of the *Christ* volume). After a brief survey of Schillebeeckx's theological synthesis of New Testament theologies of grace and his outline of the four structural elements that must undergird any current soteriology, the chapter concentrates on part 4 of *Christ,* where Schillebeeckx analyzes the contemporary historical situation, characterized by massive human suffering, as the context for any contemporary soteriology. O'Meara highlights Schillebeeckx's description of six anthropological constants as constitutive aspects of "livable humanity," and thus of human salvation. She then reviews Schillebeeckx's discussion of the problem of the relationship between human efforts towards self-liberation and the promise of final redemption by God.

O'Meara's chapter takes note of the increasing emphasis in *Church* and subsequent writings on the identification of salvation and God's absolute presence in creation. That is, God's universal salvific intention for creation is realized wherever good is done and evil resisted (see chapters 3 and 4). She also remarks on Schillebeeckx's new discussion, in *Church* and subsequent essays, of Jesus as universal, but not absolute, savior, and the responsibility of Jesus' followers to make the praxis of the reign of God a concrete possibility for all. Finally, she observes that while Schillebeeckx's emphasis is primarily on soteriology in relation to human history and the political relevance of the gospel, in the final section of *Church,* he also addresses the cosmic dimensions of redemption and liberation.

Underlying Schillebeeckx's theological writings is a profound Christian spirituality rooted in Jesus' "Abba experience" and the conviction that the Holy Spirit is the source and guide of the living Christian tradition. Donald Goergen, in chapter 7, shows the connections between the heritage of Schillebeeckx's Dominican tradition, which stresses a twofold "presence to God" and "presence to the world," and his christological project. Locating the foundation of Schillebeeckx's spirituality in Jesus as "parable of God" and "paradigm of humanity," Goergen shows how the spirituality at the heart of Schillebeeckx's theology calls for the "following of Jesus" in a "praxis of the reign of God" that is at once mystical and political. As the prologue to this volume makes clear, Schillebeeckx writes from the context of his own Christian tradition, while remaining fully aware that all great religions at their best constitute schools of wisdom and freedom.

In chapter 8, Susan Ross suggests that Schillebeeckx's theology of church and sacraments has not so much changed as intensified over the years, precisely because of his concern for human well-being and his attention to suffering. Ross reminds readers that from the time of his doctoral dissertation and his internationally acclaimed *Christ the Sacrament of Encounter with God* (1963), Schillebeeckx has stressed that God's presence is to be found in the concreteness of human history. His later writings, however, focus on God's presence as liberating and search for that presence not in human history in general, but in the history of human suffering.

While Schillebeeckx continues to locate God's definitive revelation in Jesus of Nazareth, he now argues that Jesus is not the only way to God, and that precisely as sacrament, Jesus both reveals and conceals the mystery of God. Likewise the church, as sacrament or "sign of salvation," conceals as well as reveals the work of salvation. Highlighting Schillebeeckx's approach to sacramentality as marked by ambiguity and tension, Ross shows how he can remain critical of aspects of the church's structures and governance as failing to embody the freedom of the gospel, while at the same time insisting on the necessity of Christian communities' practical embodiment of the reign of God.

Ross highlights Schillebeeckx's critical analysis of the concrete historical development of the church, and the role of critical local communities in preserving Vatican II's ecclesiological vision. Although Schillebeeckx continues to work on his new volume of sacramental theology, Ross identifies some of the traces of that project that have already appeared in his discussion of sacraments as "anticipatory signs" (*Christ*, part 4) and "metaphorical celebrations" of human life, in which the ongoing narrative of human history is interrupted by the narrative of the story of Jesus.

Schillebeeckx's sacramental understanding of church, when combined with his critical analysis of the historical development of ecclesial office, has serious implications for his theology of ministry, as Mary Hines illustrates in chapter 9. Tracing the main lines of *The Church with a Human Face*, Hines shows how the book serves as an excellent example of Schillebeeckx's theological method, which calls for a mutually critical correlation of present Christian experience and the past history of "the great Christian tradition." Noting that according to Schillebeeckx, the various cultural manifestations of ministry that have evolved throughout the church's history are "legitimate but not necessary" responses to various social and theological situations, Hines explains how, for Schillebeeckx, the present crisis of ordained leadership exists because of a failure to understand the implications of the sacramental nature of the church as the place where the Spirit dwells and moves freely.

Hines notes that the central conviction at the heart of Schillebeeckx's writings on ministry is that "ministry cannot be understood apart from community and there can be no community without ministry." The chapter concludes with a consideration of Schillebeeckx's recent work, in which he reaffirms his call for a more democratic church in today's social context, and for the exercise of ministerial authority in a way that is consistent with the liberating authority of Jesus Christ, in contrast to the present authoritarian exercise of governance by the Vatican and many church leaders.

In chapter 10, Bradford Hinze discusses the interrelationship of eschatology and ethics, two major concerns in Schillebeeckx's recent theological work. Hinze observes that Schillebeeckx's constant concern with history as the arena for human encounter with God has shifted from an early sacramental eschatology to a truly prophetic vision of history. He links that move to the development of Schillebeeckx's understanding of Jesus as "eschatological prophet," and to his increasing awareness of the dimensions of human suffering and oppression at the present moment in history.

Important ramifications for Christian ethics follow. While the call to the praxis of discipleship is a constant for followers of Jesus, all concrete ethical models throughout the history of Christianity—including those of the New Testament—remain socially and historically conditioned. As Hinze explains, for Schillebeeckx ethics maintains a certain independence from religion, yet the religious manifests itself in ethical praxis and transforms ethics. Christian ethics, the following of Jesus in our day, requires searching for contemporary possibilities for realizing the task and gift of humanity in solidarity with the marginalized and the suffering. The biblical narrative provides not concrete, unchanging moral norms, but rather the ongoing power to inspire conversion and commitment to the praxis of the reign of God. As Hinze's chapter makes clear and both Kennedy and O'Meara note, Schillebeeckx's ethical writings focus primarily on history, the *humanum*, and the social and political challenges of Christian ethics. Nevertheless, in sections of *Church*, particularly the epilogue, Schillebeeckx's long-term commitment to a theology of creation and his concern for the well-being of the entire cosmos are also evident.

In a final chapter, Robert Schreiter probes some of the foundational aspects of Schillebeeckx's thought, exploring especially some of those things that contribute to his enduring influence, especially among his North American and First World readership today. He identifies four such commitments: working inductively rather than deductively; the narrative character of experience; a concern for the mystery of suffering and the contrast experience; and the primacy of soteriology in the christological project. He indicates how some of these themes surface time and again in the contributions to this volume.

The authors of this book hope that this introduction to the thought of an important theologian will be useful to those encountering Schillebeeckx's thought for the first time as well as to those who are familiar with his work.

The Praxis of the Reign of God

1

A Theology in Transition

William J. Hill

FOREGROUND: THEOLOGY IN A NEW KEY

It has been said that the question of God is not one among several others or even the most important one, but the only question there is (Schubert M. Ogden, *The Reality of God and Other Essays,* San Francisco: Harper and Row, 1963, 1). At the beginning of the third millennium, this translates into the question of whether it is possible to believe any longer in the God of Christianity. Perhaps it is truer to see this as a crisis not of faith itself, but of culture. What is taken for granted in an age of secularity is not the demise of God in God's own reality, but of the cultural mediations of God. The latter, it is felt, have become archaic and "ideological"; they are obtrusions of abstract ideas upon reality that, in effect, distort life as we know it, offering to believers notions of God that are alienating and, in truth, sub-Christian. The agonizing question that unavoidably urges itself upon us is: Are we on the verge of ceasing to believe? Or have we come to the point where at last we are capable of becoming believers in an authentic sense? The frightening problem that can only be faced honestly is that of the credibility of Catholicism in the contemporary world.

It is this question that has centrally engaged the theological work of Edward Schillebeeckx, whose lifetime engagement has not been compromised in its critical force by the personal intensity he brings to the project. That faith in God is possible—even necessary, in the sense that human existence has no ultimate meaning without God—pivots on whether we truly believe and trust in the human as that which has been made one with God in Christ. Everything turns on acknowledging the truth of the incarnation (that is, of the hypostatic union that

Schillebeeckx prefers to call a hypostatic unity); namely, that the human as such is part of the object of faith, insofar as God has, in his unexacted love, made "the human cause to be his [God's] cause."

This is an uninhibited confirmation of the human as such, and as the locus of God's revelatory act, which latter thus acquires an experiential and self-authenticating character. It is in the immediacy of human experience that the transcendent is mediated to us, experience at once individual and social—that is, both personal and historically intersubjective. The Christian doctrines of creation and incarnation mean, respectively, that God does not wish to be everything in an exclusive sense, and that he wishes to be actively present to and involved in human affairs. Thus, one cannot love God otherwise than by loving humanity, and loving humankind is not loving the individual in isolation, but as he or she concretely lives within the structures of social existence. Christian love has thereby simultaneously a vertical (toward God) and a horizontal (toward humanity) dimension.

Needless to say, none of this emphasis upon present experience as disclosive of God is meant to minimize the other indispensable pole to revelation; namely, the sacred scriptures as the articulation in a normative way of the original and privileged experience of Jesus' disciples, and the continued mediation and interpretation of that experience by way of the living tradition of the Christian church. Revelation is, thus, a dialectical act in which past and present converge without priority being afforded to either. What is no longer possible in the modern world is to accept on no other basis than that of the unalloyed authority of others that God has drawn near to us in Christ. We can no longer abdicate our thinking to others irresponsibly, without some touchstone for truth in our own experience.

Secular experience in its very secularity must supply some "inner references toward an absolute mystery without which even secularity is threatened with collapse." Schillebeeckx himself has articulated this truth in a lucid phrase: "Christianity is not a message which has to be believed, but an experience of faith which becomes a message, and as an explicit message seeks to offer a new possibility of life experience to others who hear it from within their own experience" (*Interim Report,* 50).

What this makes clear is that all revelation from God occurs as experience; the full impact of that is furthered in the awareness that all experience, in turn, is interpreted experience. How this achieves a necessary universal character remains, of course, problematic. Schillebeeckx's explanation is that the universality is only that which is possible historically; that is, we experience the same reality and events as did the first disciples—the experience of God proffering salvation in Christ, but in the context of our epoch rather than theirs.

One difference, of course, is that they mediate our experience by what they have brought to language in the New Testament and what has been mediated further by living tradition. What is experienced in this interpreted way is not merely the message conveyed to us, but, through that, the phenomenon of the Jesus movement itself. In our own vastly differing cultural context and interpretative framework, we do not merely seek for historical reconstruction, but endeavor to experience for ourselves what the first disciples experienced. God's loving action toward contemporary humankind is, after all, not any less than it was toward those to whom it was first offered historically.

In an attempt to identify further the kind of interpreted experience that is in question here for believers, Schillebeeckx notes that it is more a matter of orthopraxis than of orthodoxy; it is more a matter of living out the truths and values of the gospel than of illuminating them theoretically. The Christian response to the gospel seeks not just to explain the world in one more way, but to change it by bringing it into the kingdom of God. Without neglecting the past (which would mean a total loss of identity), Christianity's present concern assigns priority to the future. Christian life practice cannot exist in isolation from theory, and without it would lack all criteria for truth. Still, it is the more fundamental dimension of human existing from which theories are reflectively derived, and is far more than the mere practical implementation of theory. Praxis means precisely this dialectical interacting of theory and concrete action.

There is, however, a dark specter that looms over this optimistic human posture. Christian praxis, which is by nature social and historical, finds itself confronted with overweening forces of evil and suffering (especially evil and suffering that are undeserved) that seemingly prevail in the end—unavoidably so in the case of death. Such negativity calls into question God's benign presence in the world. In the face of this consideration, some theologians have not hesitated to lay evil at God's door, making God at least its indirect cause in not precluding evil from the world. Others, wishing to absolve God of moral fault, have simply cast him in the role of a cosmic deity, finite in power and capable at the most of only mitigating the powers of evil that menace the world. Most influential at the moment, perhaps, is the position adopted by Jürgen Moltmann, for whom the origin of evil lies outside of God, but whose love nevertheless leads him to absorb it within himself (truly willing, then, to suffer in his very divinity) and, in the process, negate its power and draw from it positive values.

Schillebeeckx's thought, by contrast, takes a different tack, absolving God of all complicity in evil and rendering God ontologically impervious to any experience of it by virtue of his transcendence of all that is finite. The source of the evil that is human suffering lies with the finite and fallible freedom of humanity, which, in a memorable phrase of Yves Congar, possesses the one awesome power over God of being able to negate and shatter his loving initiatives. A classical expression of this view (though one that both Aquinas and Luther would find extreme) is to be found in the work of the fifteenth-century Italian humanist Pico della Mirandola, who has God say to humankind in the *Oration on the Dignity of Man:*

> We have made you a creature neither of heaven nor of earth, neither mortal nor immortal, in order that you may, as the free and proud shaper of your own being, fashion yourself in the form you may prefer. It will be in your power to descend to the lower, brutish forms of life; you will be able, through your own decision, to rise again to the superior orders whose life is divine.

Undergirding this abuse of freedom, however, lies the finitude of the cosmos itself, which, held out in existence over the void by God, is by necessity prone to the intersecting of opposing causalities that unavoidably give rise to physical evil. At this point evil becomes a surd, the ultimate meaning (or, perhaps better, meaninglessness) of which lies beyond our ken. With Wittgenstein, we must fall silent before that of which we cannot speak. Robert Butterworth has astutely observed here that we have no profounder guide than *The Book of Job,* which leaves the existence of evil as a mystery that gainsays all our efforts at explanation.

It has been a hallmark of Schillebeeckx's theology to proclaim the active presence and goodness of the transcendent against this all-pervasive phenomenon of evil, and to do so in the very face of the dark and demonic forces modern humans have called to life—science, technology, industrialization, the circle of poverty, terrorism in the interest of self-aggrandizement, and so forth. God manifests his presence not as one who permits such suffering, but as one whose will is set against it, as one who is aligned on the side of humanity against all forms of inhumanity. It is here in such "negative contrast experiences" that God manifests himself as with us in the very moment of what is otherwise human failure.

Schillebeeckx is able to illustrate this paradox with Christ's cry of dereliction from the cross—"My God, my God, why have you forsaken me?" (Mk 15:34)—interpreting it not as an abandonment of Jesus by God, but as Jesus' anguished cry of desolation at not being able to experience the succor of God in this moment of darkness, even as he trusts entirely in the nearness of God that is, in fact, his continuing saving presence. This is made clear in subsequent verses of Psalm 22 that Jesus cites, such as "[God] has not hid his face from him, but has heard, when he cried out to him" (Ps 22:24). Jesus entrusts to God what on the level of our history seems to be genuine failure, but in reality is no such thing. The resurrection, then, is the manifestation of this abiding real presence of God to Jesus, which remained hidden, however, throughout his passion.

But what justifies this interpretation in which, rather than being absent, God is present and active in a hidden way in the face of human suffering? Only the fact that for the believer, the interpreted experience, through scripture and tradition, of a revealing and saving God focuses on the meaning of the life, death, and resurrection of Jesus, which is first and foremost something negative; that is, an opposition to everything that threatens or diminishes the truly human. Whereas some ambiguity remains, even in an appeal to the gospels as to what constitutes positively the fulfillment of the truly human, no such hesitancy is felt in opposition to everything that dehumanizes and threatens humanity. If it be true that, in the unquenchable search for meaning, what is truly worthy of humankind is not something already given beforehand but something for which we strive, the Christian believer trusts that whereas "everything is decided in our history . . . the last word is not with history, but with the God who lives with us" (*Christ,* 831).

God's overcoming of human failure is not subsequent to that failure, but is being accomplished during and in the historical moment of failure itself—as was the case with Christ on his cross. Thus, our experience of redemption and salvation occurs only in passing and fragmentary ways, as we entrust our failures to God in hoping for the future that looks to the divine promises. Christianity thus acknowledges that God comes to us as we really are. God "loved us while we were still in our sins" (Rom 5:8)—and saves us for life as much as from our sins. Schillebeeckx's theology does not flee from a world where negative experiences abound; rather, it forcefully asserts a calm confidence in God as a God for humanity, and is marked by an unshakable joy in believing in this God "whose honor is the happiness of humankind."

A Christian orthopraxis, then, that "lives out" the doctrines is not at all individualistic; rather, with its new risks and ambiguities, it occurs only within the context of a concrete Christian community. Schillebeeckx himself has declared, "I do not accept the possibility of having a Christianity or a Christian community that is not ecclesial." It is the ecclesial community that is the bearer of truth, and the role of theology becomes that of a hermeneutics of Christian practice. Theologians bring this praxis to theoretical and technical language that the community then tests against the norms of its own experience. The teaching office of the church is not, then, a mere deposit of truths, a bureau of orthodoxy, but a genuine pastoral office that seeks the doctrines entrusted to the church in the gospel, in tradition, and in the lives of Christians.

The magisterium is not itself a theological locus, but the final judge of the truths found in the theological loci. It alone passes judgment in an authoritative way, because of its charism of being able to call upon the Holy Spirit "who will teach you all things and remind you of all I have said to you" (Jn 14:26). But it does so in a responsible manner, acknowledging that the Spirit continues to mediate truth through Christian lives lived in a history of which the magisterium must take note. Its all-important role is one of negotiating that delicate balance of language that distinguishes truth from its distortions—as it did at Nicaea in the fourth century, at Chalcedon in the fifth, at Trent in the sixteenth, and at Vatican II in the twentieth.

The specifically Christian contribution to this human solidarity against all forms of inhumanity lies in the acknowledgment that only God will give final meaning to history that will transform it into the kingdom. But it is *this* world that will be so transformed; eternity has already begun within the parameters of time. God's action in the world, moreover, is not in rivalry with that of humankind itself; human beings cannot expect to find God if they abandon the human condition. One of the richest of Schillebeeckx's concepts is that of "mediated immediacy," by which he means that while all contact with the divine is mediated through creatures, at the very heart of that mediation, God mysteriously gives us nothing less than God's own uncreated self.

BACKGROUND: A THEOLOGIAN'S JOURNEY

The above synthesis represents in a nutshell the itinerary of one theologian's lifetime journey. The respective details and their implications will be worked out in a more generous and discursive manner in the chapters to follow—all that has been presented here is an architectonic model of a complex whole. Its epicenter is surely the question concerning the historical mediation of the transcendent—one that successfully avoids the Scylla of deism on the one hand and the Charybdis of pantheism on the other.

As a hermeneutic of history and of Christian praxis, Schillebeeckx's theology views Christianity not as a privileged segment of universal history, namely, the chronicle of God's dealing with humanity through Israel and the Christ event, but of all of history seen from the vantage point of God himself as the Lord of history, as the one who ultimately gives meaning to history. The experience of our impotence in its negative way makes possible a positive experience, however fragmentary and provisional, of how God seeks lovingly to transform the world—bearing in mind that it is this world, shaped by the initiatives of our freedom, that is being so transformed. If we do not directly register this transformation, it is because it transpires in a dimension proper to God alone. God, after all, in his immanence to creatures cannot cease to be God, cannot surrender his transcendence of all that is creaturely and finite.

The most we are left with, then, is an analogous awareness of this transformation, to which we can look in faith and hope. And since its consummation lies in the future, it is not something about which we know in theory, but something for which we strive; it is more a matter of orthopraxis than of orthodoxy.

Family and Regional Background

What is now instructive and illuminating to ask is how Schillebeeckx has come to this theology in a new key. What a person is to become in the full maturity of life is determined by the myriad earlier influences that shape that becoming. But inversely, what a person ultimately makes of oneself sheds light on what was going on in the earlier formative processes.

Edward Cornelis Florentius Alfons Schillebeeckx was born on 12 November 1914 in Antwerp, Belgium, the sixth of fourteen children of a middle-class Flemish family. He grew up in the nearby village of Kortenberg. His secondary education was in the hands of the Jesuits at Turnhout. In his familial ambiance, Christianity was a pronounced formative factor, not at all a sanctimonious one, but a practical day-to-day personal appropriation of Catholic faith. Schillebeeckx recounts his father explaining that the child in the Christmas crib was indeed God. He was a father who insisted on saying grace before meals in his own house, even after the ordination of his son Edward. This perhaps explains, to a degree, Schillebeeckx's tendency to begin with the concrete and particular, deriving ideas and theories from life situations rather than vice versa.

This tendency is exemplified in the stress upon "orthopraxis" over "orthodoxy" that comes increasingly to the fore in his later theological writings. Dogmas are not only something that we confess in a cerebral way, but something that we do and so determine behavior. Schillebeeckx's emphasis upon the practical also owes something to his Dutch background (he is Flemish-speaking), though the other side of the coin is his exposure to French spirituality, the other cultural current in Belgium. At the risk of a vast oversimplification, the Flemish ingredient explains the social and political orientation in Schillebeeckx's Christian thought, while the French explains the leaning toward personal communing with God. His recent work has repeatedly emphasized two mediations of the transcendent to humankind: the political and ethical on the one hand, the mystical and personally prayerful on the other.

Thomist Origins

In 1934 when Schillebeeckx entered the Dominican order, whose demanding intellectualism tempered with a humanist spirit he found congenial, he found himself confronted with the neo-Thomist revival inaugurated by Pope Leo XIII in the encyclical *Aeterni Patris* (1879) and implemented to a considerable extent by Jacques Maritain and Etienne Gilson. This program was intensified considerably by the condemnations of modernism by Pope Pius X in 1907, in the decree *Lamentabile* and the encyclical *Pascendi*. The neo-Thomist revival was an attempt to confront modernity, but from the very start it engaged modern thought in the interest of refuting it on the assumption that from Descartes onward, modern thought had taken an erroneous turn.

Schillebeeckx's own theological nurture, at the French Dominican faculty of theology at Le Saulchoir, just south of Paris, took place in the general ambiance of this revival—but with significant distinguishing characteristics of its own deriving from the influence of Marie-Dominique Chenu and Yves Congar. Two lasting convictions from this experience were an understanding that God's self-disclosure is not a mere occurrence of the past but a continuing phenomenon mediated through contemporary cultural realities, and an awareness that the recovery of the thought of Aquinas meant a reconstruction of the historical context in which it came to birth. That historical approach to Aquinas's writings allowed his thought to reemerge in a way that challenged the rationalistic and conceptualist interpretation being put upon it by neo-Thomism. What has issued from this is a pronounced and perduring emphasis upon the primacy of God as Creator in the order of being and as Savior in the order of grace.

The former of these acknowledges that God is not homogeneous to anything that forms part of this world; God "lives" in a domain of intelligibility that is radically distinct from that of the thing-like entities of the cosmos. St. Thomas expressed this by naming God not as any sort of essence having existence (not even as the infinite and most perfect of beings), but as the sheer act of existing itself, which escapes objectification in any finite concept. For Aquinas, God subsists as Being. Grammatically speaking, God subsists in the participial sense of the verb. Thus it is less proper to say that God is in the world than that the world is in God, much as it is truer to speak of the body being in the soul than the soul in the body. God (so to speak) "empties out" himself to make room for a universe of creatures who possess, however, as their own the existence given them by God and sustained by him. The root explanation of the divine immanence to all reality is, then, precisely the divine transcendence; it is because God is the cause of the human creature's very act of freedom that such a creature can be free in the first place.

The primal sin is the denial of our creatureliness. Even in freeing us from sin, God does not enable us to escape the limitations that are necessarily inherent in our finitude. This explains that the first cause of our defects and failures lies with ourselves, with that weightiness of our being toward the nothingness from which it was called into existence. Evil arises from initiatives of our own that shatter, or at least neutralize, the divine initiatives toward being and goodness.

Implicit in this worldview is a quiet confidence in our ability to know God. However faintly, creaturely perfections mirror their creator, enabling us to know God in this indirect way—somewhat after the fashion in which a painting reflects the artist who painted it. It is not that God possesses these created qualities even to an infinite degree, but that they provide us with vectors from which we can name God in a vastly inadequate yet truthful way, one tailored to our humanity. The play of language, then, when it stretches out to the realm of the divine, engages a distinctive world of meaning, a second level of discourse. This rescues us from the silence of agnosticism in allowing us to speak of what remains shrouded in mystery, using concepts and images that name God but cannot represent him (see Schillebeeckx's prologue). We know God in a conscious unknowing, which means we are aware that we do not know God as he is in himself.

All of this, however, is a prerogative of humankind on the level of what belongs to it by nature, in the sphere of the relationship between creature and creator, leaving God in a certain anonymity that falls short of a deeply personal communion with him. Yet the latter is mysteriously desired and sought after (Aquinas speaks of a natural desire to see God), even as it remains impossible for us to implement—an ontological impossibility that is radicalized and ratified by our sinful alienation from God. But what is impossible to humankind in its natural constitution is made an actuality by grace, that is, by God's gracious summoning of us to intersubjectivity with himself. Our freedom, our subjectivity, is made into an orientation and an openness toward the absolute subject who is God. Human freedom (which belongs to us as "made in the image of God"), while first of all a horizontal transcendence, is rooted in a vertical transcendence that is, in turn, transformed into a genuine trans-ascendance toward personal intersubjectivity with God in faith, hope, and love.

Contribution from Phenomenology

Schillebeeckx's rediscovery of the authentic thought of Aquinas, his fixing from within of the spirit of that "metaphysics of faith," is of course an interpretation of Thomas. It is an interpretation dominated by the illuminating insights achieved in the twentieth-century philosophical movement known as phenomenology (among whose principal exponents were Edmund Husserl, Martin Heidegger, and Maurice Merleau-Ponty). Schillebeeckx was introduced to it by a fellow Dominican, Dominic De Petter, under whom he studied philosophy at the University of Louvain. Most influential here, perhaps, for the theology to come is the category of "encounter" as the fundamental mode of existing in the world proper to the existent that is human and personal. It is a structure of embodied consciousness focusing on the body as the point of insertion in the world. The body is not primarily an object among all the other things in the world, but rather a subject that gives rise to a unique mode of contact between consciousness and the world.

What is properly human, then, is an instance of incarnate subjectivity characterized by an awareness that precedes our objective and impersonal knowledge of things. Encounter is, thus, the ground of interpersonal awareness and of that openness of existence that is, in fact, coexistence. Bodiliness is the locus for the emergence and expression of meaning; it is the sacrament of the self.

Obviously, this has rich implications for Christian, and especially for Catholic, theology. The incarnation as God's assumption of humanity, and so of our human bodiliness, makes Christ the primordial sacrament of our encounter with God. As a man among men and women, Jesus renders the hidden God and his saving intentions manifest in our very midst and draws believers into a personal and intersubjective closeness with God, who offers to us his very self. At the juncture of this bodiliness in its spatiality and temporality—both in its natural and Eucharistic modes—there transpires the phenomenon of revelation as an intercommunion between God and humankind. Here phenomenological thought opens up an enriched understanding of the mystery of divine grace, especially in its modalities of revelation and faith.

The traditional Thomistic axiom that "grace presupposes nature" is newly illumined by this. Supernatural grace is not simply something superimposed upon nature from without, endowing nature with capabilities beyond anything for which it is capable by itself. Rather, the human being already stands before the face of God as a personal absolute in purely natural existence; this is a depth dimension to the concrete historical condition of being situated in the world, with other men and women. The concrete experience of existence is such that the objective and ontic dynamism of experienced reality carries the human—in a way as yet only implicit, prereflexive, and unthematized—to God as the personal ground of all reality in what becomes an act of implicit intuition.

This natural reference to an awareness of God belongs to the very being of humanity, and is an intrinsic condition for the very possibility of revelation. But it undergoes a transformation with God's loving and gratuitous offer of communion with himself, which is either freely assented to or freely rejected. Thus there is now no purely natural human life, because of God's universal saving will. God now gives himself directly to those disposed to believe. This is done not only through created realities of the world, even though awareness of this divine self-communication cannot be otherwise than in terms of those realities and the concepts, images, and narratives expressive of them. God, as he is in his inmost self, renders himself present to us in what may be called, paradoxically, a "mediated immediacy."

An important conclusion flows from this reconception of the nature/grace—or, more accurately, the reason/faith—problematic. If Christian faith terminates at the reality revealed (ultimately God himself), though necessarily in an unthematic way that can only be thematized inadequately in finite concepts and symbols directly expressive of created realities, then such thematizations, including those that acquire the status of dogma, necessarily and spontaneously are subject to a process of continuous reinterpretation. In short, all of this offers grounds for a theory of development of dogma.

From Dogma to Critical Hermeneutics

An important consequence of employing phenomenology as an interpretative key in theological reflection is the abandonment of a dogmatic starting point. Rather than starting with truths taken on faith as revealed by God and seeking to unfold their meaning, the theologian begins with an analysis of the subject to whom such revelation is made, that is, with reflection upon the mystery of human existence in the world. This gives a central role to hermeneutics, the science of interpretation that seeks to recover the meaning of the past for the present in a confrontation of Christianity with modernity.

Here the thought of Martin Heidegger became a dominant influence that was imported into Christian theology by Rudolf Bultmann: all understanding is self-understanding. The gospels, then, are not meant to convey otherwise unavailable information about God and his intentions vis-à-vis humankind, but to articulate the self-understanding of the first disciples made possible by their contact with Jesus of Nazareth. Theology as hermeneutics will then strive to reproduce that encounter with God through the life and death of Jesus, in such a way that God's revelatory word will be translated into contemporary culture and its meaning for us released.

The difficulty with this early phase of hermeneutics is that too much rides on the subjectivity of the believer, on a "decisionism" that is an interpretation of the *kerygma* rather than of the Christ event, which lies behind it and is its ground. The word of God is invested with an authority that is not established historically; indeed there is an escape from history, into the safe harbor of the decision of faith.

The corrective to this way of thinking was supplied by Wolfhart Pannenberg, in insisting that encounter with God does not occur other than historically, making it necessary to get behind the kerygma to the events that are its origin. Interpretation is not separate from the facts and superimposed upon them by the interpreter (a Kantian principle) but resident in the facts themselves, as understood in the movement of history (Hegel's alternative to Kant). Now it is understood not only that revelation is historical (Bultmann) but that history universally taken (which universality comes only from history in its consummation anticipated in the resurrection of Jesus) constitutes revelation (Pannenberg). The meaning and meaningfulness for us of the past events recounted in the New Testament do not reside in a structural commonality of consciousness (ours and that of the first disciples) that allows that the scriptures are directly inspired by God, but in the objective content of the events themselves when they are grasped in the context of a tradition that views the scriptures as only witnessing to such meaning. Theology now is no longer a hermeneutics of the word of God, but a hermeneutics of history.

So now the task of hermeneutics becomes not one of merely reinterpreting the past so that it might spring forth with fresh meaning for the present, but one of dialectically relating theory and praxis, so that the latter can be both the proving ground for the former and the matrix of a genuinely new and enriched understanding of theoretical truth. Orthodoxy and orthopraxis thus remain inseparable, but a certain primacy is given to the latter as transforming Christian existence, and thus opening the way to a new future.

But this awareness of the hermeneutical task of theology leads to another realization. If theology is charged with the task of reinterpreting and transforming the past (without doing violence to it), then it has to be aware that the past is mediated with the constant risk of some distortion. Theology, then, cannot neglect its critical function, both of discerning such aberrations and of disclaiming any absolute claim for present utopian projects. Followers of Christ cannot fail to strive after all that makes for human healing and renewal, with the political struggle for peace and justice in the world. But by the same token, we must be aware that none of the changes we succeed in making will themselves bring about the kingdom of God. Christianity cannot lay claim to knowing positively what is ultimately worthy of humankind and constitutive of its destiny, apart from the resurrection of Christ, which is in the mode of a promise to which believers look with hope. But it can know what threatens the truly human, and thus align itself against all forms of evil and suffering.

The positive contribution of Christianity toward the full humanization of humankind is the realization that critical rationality and humanism, however loftily conceived, are not enough. We strive for the truly human only in union with God, who has made "the cause of humankind to be [God's] cause" (*Christ,* passim). In the end, it is God who will establish the kingdom. Yet it remains true that our eschatological hope is not a flight from this world and its history, for they remain the stage whereupon the gradual fulfillment takes shape. Our striving under God is the anticipation of the kingdom to come; for now, we are a people in exodus.

Thus Schillebeeckx can write, "everything has been given to us and everything has yet to be done" (*Christ,* 514). Everything depends on God's free gift of grace, and yet grace is real only as implemented by human freedom in the response of faith. But God is already enlisted on the side of humankind against all that dehumanizes. This means that even in human failure and the suffering that comes in its wake, God remains at the side of men and women. It is not that God is absent now from human disaster, but will be present and active in the eschatological future to set things right. Rather, God is present precisely in failure. Christian faith is steadfastness in this conviction, in "this awareness of being grounded in God, of persisting when every empirical foundation and every guarantee have been removed and one weeps over the fiasco of one's life" (*Christ,* 815).

To the extent that one can be aware of this nearness of God, it can be experienced not only in the mode of positive support but also in the mode of absence, because this incomprehensible immediacy is the immediacy of God, which paradoxically is real only in its finite mediations. As soon as it is sought directly in itself, it vanishes, eluding finite attempts to grasp it. If this is so, it follows that " *ultimate* failure, *definitive* evil and *unreconciled* suffering have their real, final and terrifying form only in human reluctance and inability to love" (*Christ,* 831). What Christian faith confesses in all of this is "the continuity between the hidden dimension of what took place on the cross and its manifestation in the resurrection of Jesus, though we are not in a position to make a theoretical reconciliation of the human experience of failure and the religious experience of the redemptive triumph of God in this failure" (*Christ,* 831).

Not to be overlooked amid these academic achievements is a strong pastoral concern, a personal commitment that is intense and even passionate in kind, blending together theory and practice. Schillebeeckx was summoned to Rome to defend certain of his theological positions before church authorities. He did so in irenic fashion, without rancor, witnessing personally to his conviction that the mystery of salvation in Jesus is always mediated to us by the living tradition of the community of believers that is the church. Yet this was done without compromising the sense of how indispensable to the church is the role of the critical scholar, who must not only reverence the past but interpret it as well.

In all of this, we catch a glimpse of the deep simplicity and unpretentiousness that mark his own faith that "only truth can be the soul of a free community of men and women," especially the community that lives by faith in "the God who has made the cause of humankind to be [God's] own cause." Schillebeeckx's own life, even more than his work, has emphasized graphically that we wait for the future by shaping it now, and that believers live out in the present the promises of God, like a leaven that quickens and renews.

Thus, at the heart of the theology of Edward Schillebeeckx as it develops organically through a variety of methodologies, drawing richly but critically from all of them, there lies a manifest thematic unity, albeit one that lives and so grows. It is that of the absolute primacy of God and his grace, construed at first metaphysically, wherein God is the pure act of "to be"; then anthropologically, that is, with reference to humankind and its free future, wherein God is the redeemer of history; and finally in a strictly theological way, wherein God's primacy is that of uncreated and altruistic love—this God who is revealed in Jesus the Christ as a God whose honor is the happiness of men and women.

This primal theme is displayed by Schillebeeckx in countless books and articles on sacraments, faith, revelation, Christ, redemption, eschatology, Mary, the church, hermeneutics, the Eucharist, marriage, ministry, laity, and liberation theology. The chapters that follow single out these central concerns in an attempt to implement and clarify this suggestive theology in enriching detail.

SUGGESTIONS FOR FURTHER READING

Schillebeeckx's most recent review of his life and thought is to be found in the untranslated *Theologisch testament: Notarieel nog niet verleden* (Baarn: Nelissen, 1994), issued on the occasion of his eightieth birthday. A briefer version is available in interview format, in *I Am a Happy Theologian: Conversations with Francesco Strazarri* (1993, English translation New York: Crossroad, 1994). The earlier interview, *God Is New Each Moment: Edward Schillebeeckx in Conversation with Huub Oosterhuis and Piet Hoogeveen* (New York: Seabury, 1983) remains a valuable source of insights into Schillebeeckx's life and theological emphases as well.

Many of Schillebeeckx's key contributions to *Concilium*, the international journal he cofounded in the wake of Vatican II, are collected in *The Language of Faith: Essays on Jesus, Theology, and the Church* (Maryknoll, N.Y.: Orbis, 1995). For an overview and sampling of the wide range of theological topics Schillebeeckx has addressed, see Robert J. Schreiter, ed., *The Schillebeeckx Reader* (New York: Crossroad, 1984). A documented summary of Schillebeeckx's controversy with the Congregation for the Doctrine of the Faith can be found in Ted Schoof, ed., *The Schillebeeckx Case* (New York: Paulist, 1984). In *Theologisch testament,* Schillebeeckx claims his identity as a preacher as well as a theologian, and remarks that many of his theological insights come through in his own preaching. The two published volumes of his homilies and spiritual writings to date are *God Among Us: The Gospel Proclaimed* (New York: Crossroad, 1983) and *For the Sake of the Gospel* (New York: Crossroad, 1990).

An overview of the theological themes that Schillebeeckx pursued during his teaching career in Nijmegen is available in Ted Schoof's two-part survey, "Twenty-Five Years in Nijmegen," *Theology Digest* 37, no. 4 (1990): 313–32, and *Theology Digest* 38, no. 1 (1991): 31–44. The Dominican provincialate in the Netherlands has commissioned Erik Borgman to write a biography of Schillebeeckx, the first volume of which is now available in Dutch: *Edward Schillebeeckx: Een theoloog in zijn geschiedenis,* vol. 1: *Een katholieke cultuurtheologie, 1914–1965* (Baarn: Nelissen, 1999).

Other overviews of Schillebeeckx's life, the influences on his thought, and the main themes in his work include Philip Kennedy, *Schillebeeckx* (Collegeville, Minn.: Liturgical Press, 1993); John Bowden, *Edward Schillebeeckx: In Search of the Kingdom of God* (New York: Crossroad, 1983); Robert J. Schreiter, "Edward Schillebeeckx," in D. G. Peerman and Martin E. Marty, eds., *A Handbook of Christian Theologians* (Nashville: Abingdon, 1985); and Mary Catherine Hilkert, "Edward Schillebeeckx," in Donald W. Mussner and Joseph L. Price, eds., *A New Handbook of Christian Theologians* (Nashville: Abingdon, 1996). Of particular value in understanding the cultural influences on Schillebeeckx's thought and the shift in his work in 1967 is the article by Ted Schoof, "Masters in Israel: VII," in *Clergy Review* 55 (1970): 943–60.

2

Interpretation and Method

William L. Portier

THE APPEARANCE of a chapter on method near the beginning of this thematic introduction to Schillebeeckx's thought makes a statement about the discipline of theology in the contemporary Western academy. Among academic theologians, especially in the United States, the topic of "method in theology"—the question about what theology is and how to do it—is vigorously debated. The term *theological method* refers to the approach one takes to the task of theology. To discuss theological method is to give an account of the terms one uses in conceiving that task and to show what is required, for example, in the way of ancillary disciplines, to carry out the task of theology. The purpose of this chapter, then, is to explain the distinguishing features of Schillebeeckx's approach to the theological task. First, however, it is necessary to explain why method is an issue in contemporary Catholic thought.

Ever since the advent of the "new science" and its overthrow of the traditional worldview at the beginning of the modern period, Western thought has preoccupied itself with the question of method. René Descartes's *Discourse on Method* (1637) voices this concern in its classic form. As the church struggled with its response to modernity, modern thinkers not only questioned the value of monarchy in political life, but also the validity of appeals to authority as a way to truth in intellectual and religious matters. A major development occurred in 1879, when, with his encyclical *Aeterni Patris,* Pope Leo XIII launched a massive revival of scholastic method in philosophy and theology.

Unlike medieval scholasticism, which was an organic part of an emerging civilization, the neo-scholasticism of the Thomistic revival was self-consciously antimodern. Scholastic method emphasized logical relationships and metaphysical distinctions among the various truths witnessed to by the disparate array of biblical and patristic sources. Since the historical contexts of truth claims were considered logically and metaphysically irrelevant, historical concerns were systematically absent from scholastic thought. This rendered Leo XIII's renewed scholasticism singularly ill-equipped to deal with the nineteenth century's emerging sense of the methodological importance of considerations of time and place, that is, of history. With some notable exceptions, neo-scholastic method tended to dominate Catholic intellectual life from the time of Leo XIII until the "return to the sources" *(ressourcement)* that preceded and prepared the way for the Second Vatican Council in 1962.

After the council, many Catholic thinkers abandoned scholastic methodology, finding it inadequate to the needs of contemporary life and thought. With the collapse of the public language and common set of assumptions provided by scholastic method, the modern methodological problematic raised many troubling questions for ill-prepared Catholic thinkers: How should theology's proper field of inquiry be located and marked off? What should count as relevant evidence in theological argumentation? Should philosophy be the only mediating device for communicating the truth of Christianity to Westerners, or did it need to be supplemented by other disciplines such as history and the social sciences? Such questions underscored the range of possible theological methods and the necessity of identifying each theologian's particular approach.

During the period of renewal in theology that preceded Vatican II, two Jesuit thinkers who lived from 1904 to 1984 stand out as particularly creative and influential in their attempts to engage neo-scholasticism in a dialogue with modern thought: Karl Rahner and Bernard Lonergan. With greater or less appropriateness, and partly under the influence of Otto Muck's *The Transcendental Method* (New York: Herder and Herder, 1968), their thought has been lumped together and designated as "transcendental method" or "transcendental Thomism." In a very general way, transcendental method deals with the process of reasoning to the necessary conditions of the possibility, in the human subject, of whatever philosophical or theological issue is under discussion. The issue might be the phenomenon of human knowing, or the belief that humans have heard a revelation from God, or that God has become human in Jesus Christ. Rahner's early thought is preoccupied with questions about what kind of beings humans have to be for these beliefs to be true.

The voices of Rahner and Lonergan have shaped the discussion of theological method that emerged after the Vatican council. Lonergan's magisterial *Method in Theology* (New York: Herder and Herder, 1972) addresses the issue explicitly. The theological education of significant numbers among the present generation of professors in Catholic seminaries and graduate schools of theology includes a powerful dose of transcendental method. Consequently, the thought of Rahner and Lonergan, especially that of the former, has held a certain position of dominance in the Catholic theological academy in North America.

As a theology professor in the divinity school at the University of Chicago, David Tracy has developed Lonergan's thought in an attempt to ensure the academic legitimacy of theology within the American political framework of separation of church and state. In this context, the foundational question about whether confessional religious faith is a necessary dimension in theological inquiry becomes central. In his *Analogical Imagination* (New York: Crossroad, 1981), Tracy sketched what he called a "social portrait of the theologian." He argued that the answer to the question "what is theology?" depends in significant measure on the answer to the prior question "to whom do theologians think they are talking?" Tracy identified three possible reference groups or "publics" for theological discourse: society, academy, and church.

In these terms we could say, at the risk of oversimplification, that Rahner's primary public is the church, especially those groups such as clergy and religious, who have a deep interest in the maintenance and renewal of the church's present forms. Lonergan's focus is more directly on the academic sector of the church public, asking how theology can maintain itself as a discipline under modern conditions. Tracy carries this discussion into the academy at large.

In the context of contemporary Catholic theology, Schillebeeckx occupies a distinctive position in relation to the approaches of the other major theologians mentioned here. In this chapter, the question of his method—his understanding of what theologians do—will be addressed, as Tracy suggests, by first inquiring about the audience Schillebeeckx thinks he is addressing.

SCHILLEBEECKX'S PUBLIC AND THE DUTCH CATHOLIC EXPERIENCE

The Dutch Catholic experience during and after Vatican II has shaped Schillebeeckx's understanding of the public to whom his theology is addressed. Like Rahner, Lonergan, and Tracy, Schillebeeckx has spent most of his life as a theology professor, a member of a professional elite in both church and society. Strangely enough, however, he doesn't consider his primary public to be the academy. Nor is his intended public narrowly ecclesiastical.

In the one-page foreword to his *Jesus* book, Schillebeeckx makes an astounding statement about his intended audience. On the opening page of this more-than-700-page digest of, and theological reflection upon, the entire range of twentieth-century scholarship on Jesus in the synoptic gospels, the author dares to claim that the work is not addressed to the questions "that normally preoccupy academics," but rather to the questions "that seem most urgent to the ordinary Christian." The "ordinary Christians" among us can judge for themselves whether he has been successful. Schillebeeckx himself has acknowledged that *Jesus* and *Christ* are "hard to read" (*Church,* xv). In any case, this brief text reveals one of the most significant and distinguishing features of Schillebeeckx's thought—his intended public. He insists that in the *Jesus* book he has "tried to bridge the gap between academic theology and the concrete needs of the ordinary Christian." He claims that, although this task calls for a certain amount of "academically disciplined work," he has written the *Jesus* book with a minimum of theological jargon, and "in such a way as one might suppose would put the contents within reach of anybody interested."

Although Schillebeeckx brings considerable academic resources to bear on his work, he rarely addresses the methodological question that so exercises contemporary theology. He hardly ever uses the term *method* and probably regards the methodological problematic sketched above as abstract and rationalistic. He might insist, as he does in the preface to *Interim Report on the Books "Jesus" and "Christ"* that: "Methodology only becomes possible when one begins to reflect on the actual method of interpretation used in a particular study." Perhaps because of his long tenure in the state-supported Catholic faculty of theology at Nijmegen, he has not had to face the question of theology's legitimacy in the academy in precisely the terms posed by David Tracy.

He is therefore quite comfortable describing himself in traditional terms, as a believer who reflects. His methodological interludes often contain variations on the Anselmian *fides quaerens intellectum* ("faith seeking understanding"). He feels no need to offer a reasoned defense of faith's constitutive role in theology.

His public is, therefore, more the church than the academy. But it is the church conceived in a particular way, as a community of participating believers who are also part of society or the world—albeit a prophetic part—rather than ranged against society and the world in resignation and resentment. The church is not conceived in terms of "the elitist experiences of intellectual clerics" (*Interim Report,* 4), but as made up of believers who are also active participants in Dutch, German, or North American culture and society.

The experience of Dutch Catholicism has decisively shaped Schillebeeckx's understanding of the church to which his theological reflections are addressed. As theologian extraordinaire—first to the bishops, especially Cardinal Bernard Alfrink of Utrecht, to whom the *Jesus* book is dedicated, and the Dutch Pastoral Council; and then, later, to the so-called critical communities of Dutch Christians upon whose experiences his theology of ministry claims to be a reflection—he has served as a kind of theological midwife for a new way of experiencing the church in the Netherlands. Since 1971, he has struggled to keep this experience alive. This struggle has had a profound impact on his conception of theology. Schillebeeckx's theology is thoroughly "contextual," and its context is the Dutch Catholic experience since Vatican II. According to an arrangement known as columnization, the Dutch Reformed, Roman Catholics, and socialists each form one of the pillars, or columns, holding up the common arch of Dutch society.

This is, in a sense, a thoroughly modern arrangement, with each interest group guaranteed access to the public forum, in keeping with the modern values of democratic pluralism. At the same time, the traditional identity of each column is preserved by means of state support for its separate institutions, such as schools, hospitals, and media of mass communication. Pressure to introduce the democratic, pluralistic values of the public sphere into the Catholic column began to build up during the 1950s. This pressure to "break through" columnization coincided with the Second Vatican Council and produced the unique experience of Dutch Catholicism during the 1960s.

The parallels with the Catholic experience in the United States during the same period are striking. The immigrant church had produced a Catholic subculture, with its own network of institutions. After World War II, as later-generation immigrants assimilated to the wider culture, pressure built to introduce some of its values into the church itself. The Second Vatican Council's reforms coincided with a period of singular turbulence in society at large. In both countries, Vatican II reforms were followed by a period of polarization. A key difference between the U.S. and Dutch experiences of renewal after Vatican II is that, by means of state support, separate Catholic institutions in Holland were able to maintain themselves with relative ease, in spite of decolumnization. With their institutional maintenance guaranteed, Catholics like Schillebeeckx can afford to be somewhat more open to contemporary trends. The similarity between the two experiences helps to account for the continuing popularity of Schillebeeckx's books in the United States.

As the leading theologian in the Dutch Catholic church during the time of decolumnization, Schillebeeckx found himself cast in a quasi-public role as mediator or interpreter, whose task was to justify present experiments in church life on the basis of appeals to the historical tradition. He then found himself in the position of having to reflect theologically on these new experiences in the light of the tradition. He has mediated between the universal church, with its diverse tradition, and the Dutch church, as one of its contemporary localizations. In his two books on ministry, he tried to mediate between extreme elements in the Dutch church and the Roman authorities.

This role helps to account for Schillebeeckx's sense that his own public extends beyond the academy, and lends plausibility to his claim that he writes for the ordinary believer. In the years following the council, Schillebeeckx left his Dominican residence nearly every Sunday "to live liturgically with ordinary people." Such liturgical praxis has been a key source for his theology (*Testament,* 82). As polarization in the Dutch church has intensified, due in part to episcopal appointments by the Vatican, Schillebeeckx's role as mediator has become more of the painful struggle in faith that we see reflected in the foreword to *Church.* In 1989 he was one of the European theologians who signed the Cologne declaration protesting Vatican centralization.

THEOLOGY AS INTERPRETATION: FROM HISTORY TO HERMENEUTICS TO CRITICAL THEORY

Overview

Because his public is not limited to academic theologians but extends to ordinary believers as members of a secular society, Schillebeeckx's approach to theology has come more and more to center on the interpretation of experience, both past Christian experience and that of contemporary believers. He wants to assist in the creation of new forms and possibilities for Christian experience. His understanding of what theologians do is rooted in his own experience. A key term that he has used consistently to describe the theological task is *interpretation*. As his thought develops, this term takes on an ever more concrete meaning. Far from being a personal, theoretical activity, theology as interpretation entails concrete social dimensions with inseparable links to Christian life and worship.

This means that Christians don't simply have experience and then abstractly interpret it in Christian terms. Rather, Christians are people who actually *experience* life—and don't merely interpret it—in terms of the story of Jesus Christ. In keeping with this concrete sense of interpretation, Schillebeeckx has referred to theology as the mutually critical correlation between Christian sources and contemporary Christian experience and the critical reflection on Christian praxis. More recently he has spoken of "two stories converging," one the "story of the Christian tradition of faith," the other "the personal and communal story of our lives" ("Role of History," 314). Theologians investigate "the mystery of the reciprocal relationship between the living God and the men and women who live in and through him—God's story in human history" (*Church,* xvi).

For Schillebeeckx, human experience, and hence revelation as well, have a narrative structure. A helpful way to clarify his various descriptions of the theological task—for example, interpretation, mutually critical correlation, or critical reflection on Christian praxis—might be to place them in the setting of the story of his life as a theologian in and to the Dutch church. A brief summary of his movement from history in the form of a presentation of the results of ressourcement in the interpersonal categories of phenomenology (1957–66) to hermeneutics (1966–71) to critical theory (1971 to the present) will precede a more detailed account of how Schillebeeckx's understanding of the nature of theology has developed from the end of the Vatican council to the present, in dialogue with hermeneutic philosophy and the Frankfurt School's critical theory of society.

Each of these intellectual developments finds its concrete context in the Dutch Catholic experience. Pivotal dates are 1966 and 1971: 1966 marks the beginning of the Dutch Pastoral Council and efforts to bring modern values into the life of the church; 1971 marks the beginnings of polarization within the Dutch church, the rise of the critical communities, and the attempt to achieve some critical distance from modernity.

The path Schillebeeckx's thought has followed since Vatican II is representative of the personal and intellectual development of many other Catholic theologians. From the Thomism of his early training, he moved to the kind of existential phenomenology popular in post-World War II France, where he studied. In his *Christ the Sacrament of the Encounter with God,* he used the interpersonal categories of phenomenology to make available to a contemporary audience the results of his historical research on the sacraments.

Once within the orbit of the phenomenological movement, Schillebeeckx discovered hermeneutics and its promise for better understanding of the dogmatic tradition of Christianity. Hermeneutics, the art of understanding or interpreting another's meaning, with proper qualifications, can be used synonymously with the term *interpretation*. For Schillebeeckx, hermeneutics is not limited to interpretation. It also inquires "into the preunderstandings of each interpretation" (*Testament,* 80). Criticisms of hermeneutics as too theoretical by Jürgen Habermas (b. 1929) and other neo-Marxist social theorists led Schillebeeckx to "critical theory," with its focus on the unavoidable political or praxis dimension of all interpretation and experience.

Critical theory attempts to exploit one of the fundamental insights of the Marxist tradition—now a commonplace in a variety of forms of social thought—that the interpretation of any tradition likely involves systematic distortions of communication in the interests of those who have power and privilege. This discovery that communication or interpretation within a given tradition can be systematically skewed lies at the root of all present forms of "critical" or "local" theology, from feminist theology in the industrial West to liberation theology in Latin America. Thus Schillebeeckx now speaks of "hermeneutical theology in an anti-ideological perspective," even as he carefully distinguishes between positive and unfavorable senses of ideology ("Role of History," 314). His theological method is "critical-hermeneutical" (*Testament,* 80). This means that faithful interpretation becomes, in significant measure, a function of ethical and political commitment to act in a way that will minimize systemic distortion. As the Gospel of John points out, the truth is something we must do rather than simply know.

Throughout all of these developments, Schillebeeckx's abiding concern has been to make the experience of Christ more real for contemporary believers. "Tentatively and stammeringly," he has sought "what God can mean for men and women" (*Church,* xv). This overriding interest permeates his thought, from his early work on the sacraments to the massive christological trilogy begun in the 1970s and finally completed in 1989. The question about the experience of the reality of God, the presence of the absolute in finite forms in human language and history, has preoccupied him in various conceptual forms, from his earlier interest in the development of doctrine to his present concern with what might be termed the continuity of Christian experience. He has come to believe that this continuity "comes only through breaks" (*Testament,* 69).

1966–1971: Hermeneutics and the Dialogue with Modernity

But for the intervention of the Second Vatican Council, Schillebeeckx may have spent his life in relative academic obscurity at the University of Nijmegen. Instead he became a theological consultant to the Dutch bishops, a significant if unofficial presence at the council and, most importantly, a key architect of the experiment of Dutch Catholicism during the period of decolumnization and the council. During this time, Dutch Catholicism gave birth to a new sense of being the church, characterized by "grassroots" participation and "collegiality," and understood as the maximum lay involvement consistent with Catholic ecclesiology.

It began with a nationwide network of discussion groups early in the decade and culminated in the Dutch Pastoral Council, which opened in 1966 and held sessions between 1968 and 1970. The publicly supported resources of the Catholic column were put at the service of introducing the political freedoms of modern Western society into church life, insofar as this was judged to be theologically possible. Schillebeeckx has acknowledged that "the ordinary person" was not well represented at the pastoral council.

As did U.S. Catholicism during the same period, the Dutch Catholic experience of the 1960s doubtless produced excess and abuse. But it also generated an intense spirit of optimism and enthusiasm. Using the terminology of Emile Durkheim, sociologist John A. Coleman has described it as an experience of "collective effervescence." This spirit has left its permanent mark on Schillebeeckx's theological style. Apart from it, one would be hard put to account for the urgent tone, the hopeful spirit, and even the occasional nature of Schillebeeckx's theology. Likewise, it is difficult to avoid the conclusion that his theology has become the primary bearer or mediator of what Coleman calls "a new set of collective symbols for the church" (John A. Coleman, *The Evolution of Dutch Catholicism, 1958–1974,* Berkeley and Los Angeles: University of California Press, 1978, 164). Words such as *grassroots, collegiality, dialogue,* and *the future* are among these. Schillebeeckx's historical sense helped to set this experience in motion; subsequently, he would try to give it shape and direction. Until the polarization that occurred after the 1971 synod at Rome, in part over the issue of clerical celibacy, Schillebeeckx performed this mediating function for the Dutch church at large.

During the next decade, the experiences of those Christians he described in the *Ministry* book and in *God Is New Each Moment* as "critical communities" became the object of his theological reflection. More recently, he has felt that the Vatican has turned away from this new set of collective symbols for the church. In the process of assisting at the birth of new forms of Dutch Catholicism during the 1960s, Schillebeeckx began to experience his role as a theologian in a new way. The previous generation's emphasis on historical recovery of the sources of Christian doctrine and worship as a way of clarifying their present meaning gave way to deeper questions about the role of the present and the future, in the faithful interpretation of the past. With the contemporary setting changing so rapidly itself, its role in shaping our interpretations of the historical context of the tradition became more clear. Contemporary Christian experience would have to be located within a fusion of these two settings, or horizons, with the contemporary the only available medium for interpreting the past. Such considerations led Schillebeeckx from what might be termed "historical sense" to what David Tracy calls "historical consciousness" and Bernard Lonergan calls "historical mindedness."

Thus, by the mid-1960s Schillebeeckx had entered the universe of discourse of hermeneutic philosophy. This discovery of the historical interpreter's own historicity proved too heady for many during this period. But the move to historical consciousness need not end in an absolute and hopeless sense of historical relativity. First, absolute historical relativism self-destructs in inner contradiction, as soon as one proclaims that all truths are relative. As Lonergan has explained, truths are not absolutely or simply relative, but relative to a time and place. Times and places are connected, and the study of these connections is called history. The human act of interpretation or understanding is, therefore, profoundly historical. As Schillebeeckx would learn from critical theory during the next decade, the study of history or the interpretation of tradition opens out onto ethics and politics. Absolute historical relativism is nothing more than a form of ethical paralysis, whose only practical effect is to maintain the status quo.

At the very time when Dutch Catholics were trying to integrate the modern secular values of freedom and pluralism into church structures on a grand scale, certain theologians in the United States were elaborating a form of theology that now appears quite naive in its affirmation of modern Western culture. During an extended tour of the United States late in the decade, Schillebeeckx encountered the theology of secularization and the death of God, and found aspects of it congenial for interpreting the recent experience of Dutch Catholicism. This encounter set the stage for a serious consideration of the question of Christianity and culture in the early 1970s, and for the reconceiving of theology as the mutually critical correlation of Christian tradition and contemporary experience. At this point, however, contemporary experience, in the form of the theology of secularization, threatened to overwhelm the Christian tradition.

A group of young theological colleagues, students of J. B. Metz at Münster, challenged Schillebeeckx's brief flirtation with the theology of secularization, and the overidentification with modern Western culture it implied. Along with some of Schillebeeckx's students at Nijmegen, these "theologians of contestation," as he called them—his fellow Dominican Karl Derksen and the Belgian Marcel Xhaufflaire among others—forced Schillebeeckx to deal more seriously with critical theory. He was already familiar with Habermas, the chief proponent of critical theory, from Habermas's debate with Hans Georg Gadamer. But the challenge of these young theologians certainly accelerated his examination of this new movement. Denouncing the theology of secularization as an unquestioning capitulation to modernity, Xhaufflaire drew upon the resources of critical theory to call for a "critical theology" that would no longer be content to accept modern secularism wholeheartedly without protest. He argued that theologians ought to reassess their assumptions about the relationship between theory and practice. In response, Schillebeeckx reappraised as excessively theoretical the notion of interpretation he had learned from Martin Heidegger and the hermeneutic philosophers: "Our relationship with the past is never purely theoretical or hermeneutical" (*Christ,* 72). From this dialogue with critical theory has grown his present understanding of theology. Orthopraxis (right living) must be "an essential element of the hermeneutic process." In this conceptual framework, theology becomes reflective "self-consciousness of Christian praxis," or "the critical theory (in a specifically theological manner) of the praxis of faith" (*Understanding of Faith,* 132, 143–44).

The unfamiliar term *praxis* is used deliberately, to avoid the connotations of *practice.* The latter implies a prior pure theory that we then apply practically; *praxis,* by contrast, is understood as co-constitutive of theory likewise conceived. The ethical moment is, therefore, inseparable from theory or reflection. This is a contemporary rendering or recovery of the biblical and patristic truism that Christian thinking arises from and must return to Christian living.

1971–Present: Critical Theory and the Critique of Modernity

Critical theory arose in Germany during the Weimar years. It concerned itself with what Schillebeeckx might now call the "negative contrast experience" of a group of German Jewish intellectuals outraged by the ethical paralysis that afflicted traditional forms of theory in the German universities in the face of the obvious inhumanities of National Socialism. These victims of Nazi barbarism voiced their criticism of modern Western rationality in two key notions, both of which had considerable impact on Schillebeeckx's thought: the dialectic of enlightenment and the critical negativity of the negative dialectic.

In 1986, Schillebeeckx was invited to give the Abraham Kuyper Lectures at the Free University of Amsterdam. He began by noting the historical irony that the cultural forces of science and technology, widely hailed since the seventeenth century as liberating humans from bondage to nature, have succeeded instead in compounding human hunger and war, and in threatening the ultimate violence of nuclear destruction (*On Christian Faith,* 1). Since the history of reason began, with the Greeks, it has promised liberation from natural and religious forces only to deliver us into the bondage of humanly created forces. To this paradox of history, Max Horkheimer and Theodor Adorno, the progenitors of contemporary critical theory, gave the name "dialectic of enlightenment."

The dialectic of enlightenment means that any theoretician from any discipline, including theology, who dares to give an account of the necessary rationality and meaning of the present order makes a mockery of all those voiceless ones on the margins, all those who have suffered and died needlessly for what passes in traditional theory for the rationality of the present order. To those who look at it from the underside, to those who suffer and have suffered at its hands, the present order can never be completely rational. Needless human suffering, the history of the "barbarous excess" of human suffering, as Schillebeeckx names it in the *Christ* book, cries out against any premature attempt to close the account of the present order's rationality. In the name of those who have suffered needlessly and irrationally, critical theory must protest against any attempt to force an ultimate human solution or interpretation on the human condition. This is the critical negativity of the negative dialectic, the need to deny ultimate political and social solutions to the human predicament, as falling short of all inclusive freedom and rationality. As Horkheimer put it: "The whole is the lie."

In critical theory's concern for suffering humanity, Schillebeeckx finds resonances with Jesus' way of life. For the sake of the kingdom of

God preached by Jesus, whose eschatological promise relativizes all human attempts at peace and order, Schillebeeckx embraces the negative dialectic as a fitting contribution to theology. But he finds fault with what he judges to be its inability to provide a positive vision that can serve as the basis for what he calls "political love" in the present. He looks for this needed vision in the story of Jesus Christ, in whose death and resurrection the kingdom of God and the history of true human freedom have already begun. In his monumental christological trilogy, begun in the 1970s after his encounter with critical theory, Schillebeeckx presents to contemporary readers, in the form of a narrative of Jesus' life based on the best New Testament scholarship he can find, his vision of the specific contribution that Christians can make to the needed salvation of a suffering world.

Schillebeeckx's christology has made critical theory's sensitivity to needless human suffering its own. In *Jesus and Christ,* he has placed Jesus and his ignominious death on the cross among the numberless, voiceless victims in the long history of human suffering. God's saving presence and love need to be shown today as they were shown in Jesus' life and death and resurrection. Just as those who experienced Jesus experienced salvation from God, so Schillebeeckx thinks that today, we can experience God's salvation in a particular way, in "negative contrast experiences" that reveal our need for God's salvation, and in various short-of-ultimate liberations that reveal God's saving presence.

During the 1980s, Schillebeeckx often used the terms *mysticism* and *politics* to refer to such experiences, as well as to explain what theologians do. In 1982 the Dutch government awarded him, the first theologian so honored, the Erasmus prize for his contribution to European culture. Singled out for special notice was his critical posture toward the currently ambiguous and noninclusive functioning of Western values in the world. His remarks on this occasion dwelt upon the theologian's responsibility in such situations. Noting theology's past complicity, he wrote: "But whatever one thinks of contemporary theologians, one thing should be granted them: by means of a historical praxis of commitment to mysticism and politics, they are trying to discover the human face of God and, starting from there, to revive hope in a society, a humanity with a more human face." He went on to describe the main task of theology: "to preserve the transcendence of the God who loves humankind, hidden and yet so near, in the face of the idols which human beings set up" (*God Among Us*, 253).

In *On Christian Faith: The Spiritual, Ethical, and Political Dimensions,* the translation of his 1986 Abraham Kuyper Lectures, he treats mysticism and politics at length as historical developments of the two great commandments, love of God and love of neighbor. Mysticism and politics are the forms such love is likely to take among middle-class Christians, members of the relatively privileged classes in the dominant culture, citizens of nation-states that possess and threaten to use nuclear weapons. As one who reflects critically on Christian praxis, the theologian is sent to search this experience for the call and salvation of God. "Without prayer or mysticism," Schillebeeckx concludes, "politics soon becomes cruel and barbaric; without political love, prayer or mysticism soon becomes sentimental uncommitted interiority" (*On Christian Faith,* 75).

In addition to his introduction of the categories of mysticism and politics, the 1980s also saw Schillebeeckx approach the familiar question of Christianity's identity in history with the new category of the break, or rupture. In both personal and communal stories, some forms of continuity can only be reached thanks to breaks (*Testament,* 69). Schillebeeckx has used the concept of *break* to look back both on his own life as a theologian, and on the history of the church. Breaks are like hermeneutical negative contrast experiences. Schillebeeckx has long been concerned with the continuity of Christian experience in history. But events since the time of his formal retirement in 1983 have made him increasingly aware of the role of breaks in the experience of that continuity. The universal and transcultural gospel is found only in particular cultural forms. The continued life of Christianity through and across cultures means that Christian identity is often found precisely "in cultural ruptures and shifts" ("Role of History," 313).

For Schillebeeckx, the Second Vatican Council was one of those breaks necessary to ensure continuity. The rupture consisted in the church's break with its previously unambiguous antimodern posture. As polarization has intensified in the Dutch church, Schillebeeckx has become increasingly at odds with what he sees as backward-looking Vatican and papal policies that have failed to acknowledge the real break that took place between 1962 and 1965. He has called the polarization of the Dutch church between 1971 and 1994 "a sad and abnormal situation." The *Church* book's foreword conveys the impact of that polarization on the conclusion of his christological trilogy. Theological hermeneutics now more clearly involves conflict and struggle in faith. Interpretation doesn't go as smoothly as terms such as *dialogue* and *correlation* might suggest. Interpretation is, rather, "something of a culture shock," with the historical identity of what is permanent appearing only in what is transitory ("Role of History," 310, 312).

CONCLUSION

Schillebeeckx's theology is distinguished by its striking degree of intellectual depth and its authentic tone of moral urgency. His status as a quasi-public figure in Holland provides him with an opportunity, afforded only rarely to theologians, to practice the task of building bridges between Christianity and modern Western culture in the public arena. His abiding concern for contemporary mediations of the experience of God in Christ and his vision of the church as a participatory community of faith help to keep alive the hope that Vatican II inspired in many North American Catholics for a renewed church. He has reconceived theology as a form of reflection with intimate bonds to Christian worship and living, and dared to practice it that way on a scale unprecedented among male Catholic thinkers in the West. This approach to theology offers both a promise to ordinary believers and a challenge to theological colleagues in church and academy.

If such a theology remains sometimes more theoretical interpretation than historical praxis, or sometimes more political than mystical or vice versa, this should not appear unusual in a world that falls short of the kingdom of God. In the meantime, we who are both theologians and ordinary believers must have what Schillebeeckx calls the commitment to a historical praxis of mysticism and politics. In the midst of our daily tasks and our participation in the struggle for justice, we can remember liturgically the story of Jesus' life, execution, and resurrection, celebrate in thanksgiving the short-of-ultimate forms of salvation we have been given, and hear, not in morbid guilt but in resolute trust, what Schillebeeckx has called "the gospel of the poor for prosperous people."

SUGGESTIONS FOR FURTHER READING

Schillebeeckx considers the methodological question explicitly in the sections of *Jesus: An Experiment in Christology* (New York: Seabury, 1979) and *Christ: The Experience of Jesus As Lord* (New York: Crossroad, 1980) that reflect on interpretation and experience, and, in dialogue with his critics, in *Interim Report on the Books "Jesus" and "Christ"* (New York: Crossroad, 1980), and in his 1977 communication to the Congregation for the Doctrine of the Faith in *The Schillebeeckx Case* (Ted Schoof, ed., New York: Paulist, 1984). Required reading for anyone who would understand Schillebeeckx in his context in the Dutch Catholic experience is John A. Coleman's fascinating sociological study *The Evolution of Dutch Catholicism, 1958–1974* (Berkeley and Los Angeles: University of California Press, 1978), to which the above sketch is heavily indebted. The essays in *God the Future of Man* (New York: Sheed and Ward, 1968) show Schillebeeckx appropriating secularization theology and hermeneutics. *The Understanding of Faith* (New York: Seabury, 1974) chronicles his dialogue with critical theory. In his two books *Ministry: Leadership in the Community of Jesus Christ* (New York: Crossroad, 1981) and *The Church with a Human Face: A New and Expanded Theology of Ministry* (New York: Crossroad, 1985), we find him engaging in theology as the critical reflection on Christian praxis. Part 4 of the *Christ* book presents the most comprehensive treatment of Schillebeeckx's version of political theology. In *On Christian Faith: The Spiritual, Ethical, and Political Dimensions* (New York: Crossroad, 1987), he develops the categories of mysticism and politics. *Theologisch testament: Notarieel nog niet verleden* (Baarn: Nelissen, 1994) looks back on his life as a theologian. Part 2, chapter 1, 69–83, is especially relevant. In this section he treats, among other topics, the hermeneutical role of breaks. This is also addressed in "The Role of History in What Is Called the New Paradigm," in H. Küng and D. Tracy, eds., *Paradigm Change in Theology: A Symposium for the Future* (New York: Crossroad, 1989). Schillebeeckx's most developed treatment of that topic is found in "Breuken in christelijke dogma's," in E. Schillebeeckx et al., eds., *Breuklijnen grenservaringen en zoektochten. Veertien essays voor Ted Schoof bij zijn afscheid van de theologische faculteit Nijmegen* (Baarn: Nelissen, 1994). Chapter 4 of *I Am a Happy Theologian: Conversations with Francesco Strazzari* (New York: Crossroad, 1994), based on a 1993 interview, briefly covers some of the same ground as the above-cited section of *Theologisch testament*. Chapter 4 of *Church: The Human Story of God* (New York: Crossroad, 1990) gives his sense of Vatican II as a break that ensured continuity. The foreword powerfully conveys the complexity of Schillebeeckx's contemporary theological mood.

3

God and Creation

Philip Kennedy

WITHOUT OXYGEN, humans soon perish. Given its indispensability, it is surprising they take it so much for granted. They are aware of its significance, yet it rarely preoccupies their thoughts. Somewhat similarly, the idea of creation is the oxygen and lifeblood of Edward Schillebeeckx's theology. It is the cardinal motif and architectonic principle of his many and varied writings. How intriguing, then, that he has never devoted a book to the subject. He has written at length on sacraments, Mary, marriage, ministry, Jesus, and the church, but has not published a sustained and detailed elaboration of his theology of creation. Moreover, only intermittently do interpreters of his work name creation as the underlying foundation that supports all of his theological discussions.

The purpose of this chapter is to explain what Schillebeeckx means by creation, and to illustrate how pivotal it is to his thought. In his work, the theme of creation is inseparably entwined with a concept of God. Hence, to attend to creation in his writings is simultaneously to focus on his understanding of God. What follows falls into three main sections. The first dwells on what Schillebeeckx says about the significance of creation in his works. The second forms the main body of the chapter, and explains in more detail his essential interpretation of what Christian belief in creation entails. The third part concentrates on Schillebeeckx's understanding of God in the light of his theology of creation.

Before launching into these sections, a very general comment on the theme of creation in Christianity today would not be out of place. On the whole, Christians have never divided seriously over their belief that reality is a divine creation. Over the past twenty centuries they have argued bitterly, and even violently, over the identity of Jesus, the Trinity, the church, sin, salvation, nature, and grace. Even so, belief in creation has not proved to be a major schismatic stumbling block. Theologians certainly differed markedly over creation during the Middle Ages, but their doctrinal controversies, as in other epochs, never engineered large-scale ecclesiastical splits. In the latter half of the twentieth century, Catholics of the Roman Rite have fought over liturgy, and Anglicans have tussled about the ordination of women as deacons, priests, and bishops. Neither group has quibbled intensely over faith in a divine creation. All of which is to illustrate that twentieth-century Christians have been generally united in their profession that God creates, even as they bicker about the church, the significance of Jesus, feminist theories, and the status of Christianity in relation to other religions.

Throughout the past century or so, creation has clearly been a subject of anxious questioning for many Christians, who have fretted over neo-Darwinian biology and contemporary astronomy, both of which may appear to discountenance biblical doctrines of creation. Such Christians, though, often suffer the unsettling fate of being labeled as intellectually atavistic fundamentalists, while major Christian academies and mainstream churches persist in being largely untroubled by new sciences and continue to profess an age-old faith in God's creation. Clearly, the centrality to Christian life of belief in creation has been so widely assumed, throughout most of the twentieth century, that it has not been uppermost in prominent theological disputes. Only over the past decade or so have theologians begun to concentrate much more on interpreting faith in God as a sublime Creator. Recently, it is possible that theologians have been somewhat timorous even to raise the Christian subject of God's creation in relation to contemporary sciences.

Since the ecclesiastical condemnation of Galileo and the development of sophisticated modern scientific methods, a widespread social suspicion has arisen, according to which science and theology have been dueling aggressively for centuries. Theology is thought to have lost, leaving the task of explaining the universe to physical sciences.

The theology of Edward Schillebeeckx is noteworthy precisely because of its frequent allusion to the importance of creation. Even though he has never published a sustained monograph on creation, he has frequently underscored its importance and explained his understanding of it. In short, Schillebeeckx has not followed the general trend of neglecting the theology of creation, since he regards belief in creation as entirely viable and even indispensable for Christians today. Indeed, his work is refreshingly intriguing because he has never been daunted by those who imagine that Christian faith in God's creation is unbelievable and unlivable, during an age wherein many imagine that modern science has disproved biblical faith and replaced theology as an intelligent commentator on the world.

THE THEME OF CREATION IN THE WORKS OF SCHILLEBEECKX

Accustomed to ridicule, many theologians in this century have left it to science to explain the universe and the makeup of its human inhabitants, while dwelling instead on issues pertaining to Christian origins, history, and the church. Even twentieth-century studies of Jesus have been resolutely historical and slow to speculate at length on the role of a risen Christ in the cosmic scheme of a divine creation.

No such wariness of the issue of creation is to be found in the writings of Edward Schillebeeckx. Quite the contrary is the case. He has frequently insisted upon the driving force of creation faith in his theological vision. Illustrations abound. In his book *The Eucharist,* he says this: "The dogma of creation and the metaphysical realism that is the consequence of this dogma are at the center of all theological speculation" (147). Much later in his career, Schillebeeckx had not changed his mind. He declared in 1993, during an interview to mark his eightieth birthday: "I regard the creation as the foundation of all theology. . . . There is so much talk of the history of salvation that there is need to reflect anew on the concept of creation. . . . We need to find new words to say what creation is. We know all about evolution, but almost nothing about creation" (*I Am a Happy Theologian,* 47).

Roughly a decade earlier, Schillebeeckx had given another interview to mark his reception of the Erasmus prize from the queen of the Netherlands. In the published version of the exchange, he explained why he was more predisposed to base theology on a theology of creation rather than a treatment of salvation or redemption. He noted that because of his Thomist background, he found himself in disagreement with certain Protestant theologians who treated creation from the vantage point of redemption. He observed that he preferred to see creation itself as the foundation of theology, rather than viewing it in relation to redemption, because the latter option ran the risk of regarding nature and humankind as corrupt when dissociated from redemption (see *God Is New Each Moment,* 68). For Schillebeeckx, Christian belief in creation involves a confidence that nature and humans are good in themselves, quite apart from being viewed in the broad sweep of a history of salvation.

Just as the theme of creation is foundational for Schillebeeckx's understanding of the practice of theology, it is also paramount in his explanation of one of theology's primary tasks—to illustrate in what sense Christians may maintain that they actually know and perceive God with their faith. Otherwise stated, Schillebeeckx's practice of theology has a marked epistemological bent, and the theme of creation stands at the center of his explanations of human cognitive awareness of the reality of God. He once commented: "This problem of the actual nature of our knowledge of God may seem academic, but it is a matter of 'to be or not to be' for religion" (*God and Man,* 169, n. 11). In *God Among Us,* he concludes that "[t]heology is a matter of speaking about the absolute which appears within the relative" (157).

Schillebeeckx's entire published output can be regarded as an attempt, sustained over decades, to explain what it might mean for Christians to say that the absolute, called God, can be perceived through the contingent facticity of human history. The bedrock of his explanation is actually a doctrine of Thomas Aquinas that asserts that God can be spoken of, because creation exhibits the effects, so to speak, of divine activity. Put differently, by what is perceived in a created world, believers can speak of the cause of all things encountered. Thomas's precise text is contained in his *Summa Theologiae* (Ia, q. 1, a. 7, ad 1). Examples of Schillebeeckx's reliance on it can be found in his book *God and Man* (39, 136).

Creation is not only named by Schillebeeckx as the foundation of all Christian theology in general, and his work in particular; it also sustains several of the diverse theological topics he has explored during his career. When he first published a book on Mary, the mother of Jesus, its initial title was *Mary: Christ's Most Beautiful Creation.* The work was subsequently issued in English as *Mary, Mother of the Redemption.* Even so, it still contains the striking observation that Mary is "the maternal mother of the omnipotent creator of the universe" (109).

In his book on the Eucharist, Schillebeeckx observes that creation, since it is the beginning of a covenant of grace, forms the general background to the Eucharistic event. The notion of creation is also indispensable to his general theory of sacraments. His early work, *Christ the Sacrament of the Encounter with God,* begins by observing that the core of religion is a personal communion between God and people (3). The book then observes that human beings reach God through creation: "life in this created world gains a new and deeper meaning when man lives in the world as one who has received this call from God in his innermost being. The world of creation then becomes an actual part of the inner yet still anonymous dialogue with God" (7–8).

The theme of creation is also central to Schillebeeckx's book *Marriage: Human Reality and Saving Mystery,* which he published in Dutch in 1963. Its first chapter treats the account of creation in the ancient scriptures of Israel and expounds Israel's early understanding of marriage: "It was not the sacred rites which surrounded marriage that made it a holy thing. The great rite which sanctified marriage was God's act of creation itself" (15). Yet another illustration of the crucial role that the notion of creation plays in Schillebeeckx's theology can be taken from his mature christology. The three tomes of his christological trilogy, *Jesus, Christ,* and *Church,* present Jesus as the condensation or concentration of creation, by which is meant that everything entailed in Christian belief in a divine creation is encapsulated in the life of Jesus professed as Christ.

Before explaining in more detail precisely what Schillebeeckx means by his constant talk of creation, a word would not be out of place on how he first came to study creation during the early phase of his career. Two stages in his life as a young man influenced his later explanations of creation. The first goes back to the period between 1946 and 1947, when he was studying in Paris. There he made a close study of Jean-Paul Sartre's analysis of human finitude, *Being and Nothingness.* In the following section it will be seen how crucial the concept of finitude is to Schillebeeckx's broad comprehension of creation.

The second stage was a ten-year period in his life, 1947–1957, when he taught dogmatic theology in the Dominican House of Studies in Louvain, Belgium. One of the five different subjects he taught intermittently during those years was the theology of creation. Between 1956 and 1957, he distributed among his students mimeographed copies of his lecture notes on creation. The notes were issued in two volumes. The first ran 366 pages, and the second 330. Copies are housed today in the Schillebeeckx archives in Nijmegen. They bear the collective title of "Theological Reflection on Creation-Faith" *(Theologische bezinning op het scheppingsgeloof).* They provide a massive quarry of information about creation as it is treated in the Bible and subsequent Christian theology. Hence, though Schillebeeckx never published a large book on creation, his lecture notes contain more than enough material for such a project. Indeed, a good deal of their contents has surfaced in his other publications.

Having begun his university career lecturing on creation, Schillebeeckx reexamined the matter intensively before he retired in 1983. His own words explain his tactic:

> I returned to this topic at the end of my university career. For two years I gave courses on creation. I analyzed it in Genesis, I studied it in the Assyrians and Babylonians and in many other accounts. I found the same imagery as in Genesis. I traced a panorama of creation in patristics, in the Middle Ages, above all in St. Thomas. I studied the war between evolutionists and creationists (*I Am a Happy Theologian,* 47).

WHAT IS CREATION?

Having underscored the primacy of creation in Schillebeeckx's thought, the central task of this chapter is to elaborate what he means when he speaks of creation, of God as a Creator, and of Jesus as the concentration of divine creation. While Schillebeeckx's writings are peppered with comments on creation, there are three of his books in particular that contain concise explanations of his general understanding of creation: (1) chapter 16 of *God Among Us,* "I Believe in God, Creator of Heaven and Earth"; (2) chapter 6 of *Interim Report,* "Kingdom of God: Creation and Salvation"; and (3) chapter 5 of *Church: The Human Story of God.*

A scrutiny of these three passages and several other scattered comments in Schillebeeckx's works reveals a view of creation that is both deeply traditional and startlingly innovative. In his elaboration of creation, he is at pains to present what he takes to be an ancient Jewish and Christian faith in creation. In other words, he seeks to unravel the faith of believing communities over time, rather than to offer his own purely original perspective. His writings frequently defer to Irenaeus and Thomas Aquinas when interpreting Christian belief in a divine creation. Even so, especially during the latter stages of his theological career, he has presented a view of creation that differs markedly from anything, for example, that Aquinas would say. Quite unlike the latter, Schillebeeckx concludes that by creating human beings God begins an adventure, as it were, and actually becomes vulnerable or defenseless by so doing.

Schillebeeckx stands much more in line with Aquinas when he refuses to speak of a divine creator as a being who is distinguishable from created beings. For Aquinas, God is not an essence that possesses an existence, but the very act of existence itself. Hence, while God is being, creatures may only be said to possess being by participating in God's sheer act of existence, to use premodern scholastic terminology (see *Summa Theologiae* Ia, q. 44, a. 1). Nothing in Schillebeeckx's theology contradicts such a view. He also agrees with Aquinas in affirming that: (a) humans resemble God as imperfect images of God; (b) creation is not constrained purely to the past, but is a continuous divine preservation of created reality; (c) the created world and the people who populate it are inherently good and not intrinsically evil; (d) creation establishes humans in a genuine autonomy, and does not involve a divinely orchestrated and predestined gainsaying of human freedom.

Quite apart from Schillebeeckx's deference to Aquinas, whenever he turns his attention to elaborating Christian faith in creation he frequently takes care to clarify what *is not* involved in that faith. In particular he insists that creation-faith does not provide an explanation for the origin and inner constitution of the universe. Nor is it, he says, a dualistic metaphysical worldview. It differs, too, from both emanationism and pantheism. In his terms, faith in creation cannot be construed as an explanation, dualism, emanationism, or pantheism. Each of these terms deserves clarification before Schillebeeckx's more positive account of creation can be appreciated.

MISAPPREHENSIONS OF CREATION-FAITH

Creation As an Explanation

Schillebeeckx himself has noted an intellectual war between evolutionists and creationists over belief in creation. One of the more interesting aspects of his work is that he is totally unperturbed by new insights of empirical sciences regarding the makeup of physical reality. This is because he does not regard the Christian doctrine of creation as either a scientific chronology or a cosmology: "Belief in creation does not claim to give an explanation of the origin of the world" (*Church,* 229). He leaves it to sciences such as astronomy, biology, or anthropology to elaborate the physical beginnings of this universe and the people who populate it.

For Schillebeeckx, belief in creation is a belief about God, not about matter. To pit science and theology against one another as rival explanations for the origin and constitution of matter thus becomes a pseudo-problem. Hence, Schillebeeckx's principal step in elucidating belief in creation is to assert that it does not involve a faith that posits God as an explanation for things and events. He concludes that to regard God as an empirical elucidation results in two lamentable consequences. The first is a view that existence, and especially human existence, is fixed and controlled by God as a kind of cosmic puppet show, or, to use Schillebeeckx's own playful terms, "a large-scale Muppet show" (*Church,* 230). If God controls and explains everything, then any attempt by humans to change a divinely preordained arrangement exposes itself as blasphemous, even if unintentionally so.

The second fault of regarding creation-belief as a divinely arranged account of the way things, people, and events happen to be is that God is then misperceived as a powerful guarantor of an established order. God does not become "*Salvator,* Savior, as Christians call him, but *Conservator,* as the Roman Hellenistic religions called him (*Church,* 230). Within Schillebeeckx's theology, the underlying danger of regarding belief in creation as an explanation is that it denies the most basic feature of human existence, namely, finitude or contingency. The same peril stymies views that misconstrue authentic Christian belief in creation as dualism, emanationism, or pantheism. Consequently, to understand Schillebeeckx's account of creation, it is necessary to attend to what he means by finitude or contingency. His view of human contingency will be explained below, after the ensuing comments on dualism, emanationism, and pantheism.

Dualism

Metaphysics has long been concerned with discerning features of reality as distinct from mere appearances of what is real. Dualism is a metaphysical worldview both ancient and contemporary, that posits "the existence of a twofold first and supreme principle, a principle of good and a principle of evil" (*Christ,* 672). In his description of metaphysical dualism in *Christ* (672–75), Schillebeeckx concludes that Jewish, Graeco-Roman, Hindu, Christian, Buddhist, and Islamic religions all reject dualism. Nonetheless, he names a type of Persian religion, Zoroastrianism, together with Manichaeism, as markedly dualistic outlooks.

In Schillebeeckx's view, dualism initially arose as an attempt to explain evil and human suffering. It does not regard human limitation or contingency as the normal state of creation, but as derived "from some fault in it or from a mysterious primal sin" (*God Among Us,* 91). By refusing to accept human finitude as a normal situation, dualism places a more complete human flourishing either in an early, ideal era of existence at the beginning of time, or in a remote, utopian future at the end. In the former situation, subsequent human history is construed as a fall from an original state of well-being. In the latter position, that history becomes a progressively perfecting evolution moving toward an ideal state of affairs. In both instances, once again according to Schillebeeckx, the current contingency of human beings is downgraded and effectively effaced: "In both cases there is a failure to take account of contingency as a characteristic of human beings and the world. Historicity is then reduced either to a genetic development of a pre-programmed plan or to a process which takes place by the logic of development" (*Church,* 230).

Emanationism

Like dualism, emanationism is a belief that human beings and things in the world do not exist in their rightful state. While dualistic worldviews stem primarily from a motivation to account for evil and suffering in the light of goodness, emanationism is impelled by a desire radically to assert that God is utterly transcendent to all things.

Emanationism emphasizes divine transcendence by blurring a distinction between God as Creator and all creatures. It does not regard creatures as independently other than God, but as degraded deity or lesser forms of the divine that have emanated or issued forth from God. Schillebeeckx describes the view of emanationism and its stress on divine transcendence in this way:

> God is so great and so exalted that he is above concerning himself with creatures and thus compromising himself. He entrusts himself to a caretaker, a first governor of a somewhat lower order. In this conception the world and men are degradations of God—degraded deity, because this issuing of things from God is also seen as a necessary process (*Interim Report,* 1–12).

The key feature to note regarding emanationism is that it does not make a clear distinction between God and creatures, but regards the latter as impaired outgrowths of the former. We shall see in a moment why Schillebeeckx finds such an outlook resolutely mistaken.

Pantheism

Schillebeeckx nominates pantheism as a fourth misapprehension of authentic Christian belief in creation. Like dualism and emanationism, this is a theistic metaphysical worldview. In essence it is the belief that God is manifested in all things, or that all things are God. Another type of pantheism asserts that everything apart from God is an illusion. Whatever its form, pantheism contrasts with panentheism, which is the belief that all things exist in God; pantheism also contrasts with deism, the belief that God created the world aboriginally and then prescinded from any subsequent direct involvement with it. Like emanationism, pantheism obscures a clear distinction between creator and creatures, since it includes the latter as being part of the definition of God. For Schillebeeckx, in a pantheistic conception of creation, "God does not seem to be present with sufficient power to be able to bring into existence autonomous and yet non-godly being" (*Interim Report,* 114). Pantheism also obscures divine gratuitousness or serendipity, by regarding all things as necessarily existing in God.

Creation Explained Positively

So much for what belief in creation is not. How, then, does Schillebeeckx state more positively the peculiarity of Christian belief in creation? In the first place, he insists that faith in creation is fundamentally a belief about God. It involves a doctrine about God's identity, and is not predominantly concerned with the origin and constitution of the physical universe: "What is God going to do with his own divine life? Creation is ultimately the meaning that God has wanted to give to his divine life. He wanted, freely, also to be God for others, and expected them, with their finite free will, which was also open to other possibilities, to accept his offer (*Church,* 231–32). It is in this sense that belief in a divine creation does not compete for intellectual credence with either a scientifically established chronology or an empirical cosmology: "Belief in creation does not give us any information about the inner constitution of human beings, the world and society. To seek this out is the task of philosophers and scientists, of human beings" (*Church,* 231).

Asserting that faith in creation is primarily a belief about the meaning of God's life, the second step Schillebeeckx takes to elucidate the peculiarity of that faith, in counterpoint to other metaphysical outlooks, is to observe that creation involves a divine action that simultaneously has two consequences. Creation is an action of God that (1) endows human beings with a finite, non-godly character; and (2) at the same time initiates a history of a human quest for salvation: "God freely creates humanity for salvation and human happiness, but in this same action, in sovereign freedom, he seeks himself to be the deepest meaning, salvation and happiness of human life" (*On Christian Faith,* 18).

Schillebeeckx makes no secret of the situation that his explanation of faith in creation is really a reformulation of the theology of Irenaeus of Lyons, whom he quotes as declaring: "The glory of God is the happiness of living humankind; but the happiness of humankind is the living God" (*For the Sake of the Gospel,* 58). These words of Irenaeus are regarded by Schillebeeckx as "the best definition of what creation means" (*Interim Report,* 116). Schillebeeckx also describes them as Irenaeus's summary of the Christian gospel (*For the Sake of the Gospel,* 58).

Having clarified that creation belief is concerned with God and posits that God acted to bring nondivine reality into existence and, by so doing, launched a history of salvation, Schillebeeckx takes a third step in his explanation, by concluding that the divine action of creation is by no means an exclusively past event: "creation is not a single event somewhere in the beginning, but an ongoing dynamic event. God wills to be the origin, here and now, of the worldliness of the world and the humanity of man. He wills to be with us in and with our finite task in the world" (*Interim Report*, 116).

Finitude and Belief in Creation

All that stated, there is a good deal more at the heart of Schillebeeckx's clarification of faith in creation than his conclusions that creation (a) is essentially concerned with God's life; (b) involves a divine action; and (c) is not tied to the past. The single most significant of all Schillebeeckx's many and diverse comments on creation concerns finitude. To grasp his understanding of creation, it is essential to consider what he means by finitude or contingency. For Schillebeeckx, finitude is the defining characteristic of both human beings and the world. He regards it as par excellence the never-failing source of all religion (*Church*, 233). In effect, the terms *finitude* and *contingency* serve as synonyms in his writings and are freely interchanged.

Schillebeeckx has noted himself that he began to explore the notion of contingency in depth after making a study of Sartre's magisterial work *Being and Nothingness,* when he was studying in Paris in 1946. Published in 1943, *Being and Nothingness* is a long essay in phenomenological ontology. It is driven by a single existential question: What is involved in being a human? Schillebeeckx recently described his reaction to that work: "I have examined the concept of contingency and nothingness *(le néant)* in Sartre which led him not to accept God. Sartre makes a profound analysis of the contingent without accepting God" (*I Am a Happy Theologian,* 47).

Contingency is a technical philosophical term that, for Schillebeeckx, means that "in and of itself, the creature has no reason to exist and cannot itself explain its own existence: it is, and yet it might (in and of itself) equally well not have been; in this sense it is 'accidental.'" (*God and Man,* 164, n. 7). The word *accidental* here is simply a synonym for *contingent.* For Schillebeeckx, religious believers and unbelievers alike are all inescapably finite, yet they experience their finitude differently, in the sense that they interpret it in opposing ways. Believers experience contingency, and, since every experience is simultaneously an interpretative event, they interpret it precisely as a referent to that which is not finite, namely God. In other words, human limitation of itself suggests divine illimitability. For unbelievers, contingency is interpreted otherwise, as a pure constraint, or void (see *I Am a Happy Theologian,* 48; and *On Christian Faith,* 61–62).

Being finite, all human beings can feel as if they exist in a complete vacuum, or as if they are utterly left in the lurch, as it were. Yet Schillebeeckx effectively insists that their very finitude simply highlights that creatures are not gods or replicas of God: "God is God, the sun is the sun, the moon is the moon, and human beings are human beings" (*God Among Us,* 92). However, central to Schillebeeckx's understanding of creation is the conviction that a creature's finitude is neither a flaw nor or a mistake. Creaturely contingency simply implies that a creature is not divine. Schillebeeckx's theology is imbued with a profound anthropological confidence, because he insists that "[h]umanity and the world are not the result of a fall, an apostasy from God, nor are they a failure, much less a testing ground in expectation of better times" (*God Among Us,* 93). They are simply not-God.

Schillebeeckx further teases out his view of creation by explaining what is meant by the Christian doctrine of "creation out of nothing" (*creatio ex nihilo*). He takes this to be a symbolic way of asserting that contingency means that people and their world hang by themselves, so to speak, in a vacuum, suspended over complete nothingness. There is nothing apart or between them and God. Even so, the perception of nothingness, the sense of being in a void, need not breed debilitating anxiety, since the complete difference between God and creatures is a limitation of the latter, not the former: "The boundary between God and us is our boundary, not that of God . . . we recognize the divinity of God in the recognition and acceptance of our limits and those of nature and history" (*Interim Report,* 115). Recognizing a boundary between God and all things finite, Schillebeeckx explains that belief in creation involves faith that the human experience of nothingness and finitude is counterbalanced by "the absolute presence of God in and with the finite" (*Interim Report,* 114).

Creation As an Adventure

Speaking of God's presence with the finite enables Schillebeeckx to make a daring comment about creation that, as indicated above, clearly distinguishes his thought from that of Thomas Aquinas. Schillebeeckx calls creation an adventure in which God becomes defenseless. He accepts that for a human to be created means that he or she exists in the presence of God. However, as far as God is concerned, Schillebeeckx concludes that creation renders God somewhat vulnerable, since it involves a yielding on God's part that makes room for the other:

> By giving creative space to human beings, God makes himself vulnerable. It is an adventure full of risks . . . The creation of human beings is a blank check for which God alone is guarantor. By creating human beings with their own finite and free will, God voluntarily renounces power. That makes him to a high degree dependent on human beings and thus vulnerable (*For the Sake of the Gospel,* 93).

By describing creation as a divine adventure full of risks and played at high stakes (*Church,* 90, 232), Schillebeeckx avoids any suggestion that God has predetermined the course of human history. He maintains that even though God is the Lord of history who initiated the adventure of creation, God does not expect human beings to implement a preordained divine blueprint for shaping the future, but has established humankind as the principle of its own action. Consequently, human beings cannot foist off on God the task of solving their problems and shaping their destiny (see *Interim Report,* 117–18).

Creation, Salvation, and Secularization

The question of human beings and their problematical sufferings surfaces in Schillebeeckx's theology in terms of the theme of human salvation. He concludes that God's creative bringing into existence of all non-godly reality is simultaneously the beginning of a history of salvation. Schillebeeckx frequently notes in his writings that the question of salvation is a great driving force currently: Who or what will redeem humans from everything that debilitates them? He observes that this question, while once the province of religion, has now become uppermost in secularized settings quite apart from religious and theological circles (see *Church,* 231–32).

In speaking of secularization, Schillebeeckx has noted how many people now conclude that religion and the church will disappear, in view of an accelerated process of secularization since the Second World War. He understands a process of secularization as an augmented tendency of human beings to explain themselves and their larger social contexts purely in terms of human reason, and without deference to either God or religion. For Schillebeeckx, however, secularization cannot serve as a satisfactory theory of human salvation. This is so for two reasons. First, the human experience of finitude cannot itself be entirely secularized. For believers, it becomes a source for belief in God: "for the believer, non-divine finitude is precisely the place where the infinite and finite come most closely into contact" (*Church,* 234). In the second instance, just as finitude itself can be evocative of the divine, so too can people's experience of cohumanity. Ethical quests to recognize the equal worth of human beings need not be purely secularized undertakings. Experiences of being humans of equal worth with others can be evocative of God's presence to all that is finite and human.

Schillebeeckx, unconvinced that secularization is a satisfactory account of human salvation, avers that belief in creation has a critical and productive force of its own. In other words, he concludes that Christian creation faith has an inexhaustible potential for expectation and inspiration (see *Church*, 232). In short, if human history is not a puppet show with God pulling the strings, then its follows that the transformation of the world, and the overcoming of human suffering, lies in the first instance in the hands of human beings themselves (see *Interim Report,* 118).

ETHICS AND HUMAN KNOWLEDGE OF THE CREATOR

All of this raises the matter of the ethical dimension of Christian faith creation. It was noted above that the theme of creation is central to Schillebeeckx's religious epistemology: people may know that there is a God by perceiving the effects of God's creative activity in a contingent world. However, during the course of Schillebeeckx's career, he has significantly altered the way he describes human cognitive contact with a divine creator. In his early theology, before the mid-1960s, he explained God's knowability primarily in the context of religion, and designated sacramental experience as the apex of human encounter with God. After 1966, though, he began to speak of God's accessibility in the context of ethics. In his book *Church,* he propounds that God is not accessible apart from a praxis of justice and love.

It is vital to recognize, at this juncture, that a doctrine of creation still undergirds Schillebeeckx's more recent religious epistemology. Writing as recently as 1997 in the journal *Concilium,* he declared: "the act of creation places human beings in their autonomous, albeit finite and mortal, humanity and gives them free responsibility for their ethical action in their world and for the autonomous quest for ethical criteria for their action" ("Documentation: Religion and Violence," 131). In stating as much, Schillebeeckx directly argues against the French atheist Maurice Merleau-Ponty.

The latter charged that references to the divine absolute stymie human autonomy. He insisted, as well, that religions are inherently violent. Schillebeeckx acknowledges that religion is mediated by culture, and that any religion can become allied with a violent culture. He denies, however, that Christianity is intrinsically violent, and asserts that an ethical quest for justice and love among human beings actually mediates divine transcendence to human immanence.

In Schillebeeckx's terms, God is never directly transparent to human beings, but is always mediated through creation. In his mature theology, he nominates human experiences of suffering as the primary facet of creation in which God's transcendence is mediated. This leads him to speak of God's "mediated immediacy" to people. The term *mediated immediacy* is not unique to Schillebeeckx, since it appears in the writings of other authors such as Karl Rahner and John Baillie. As explained in chapter 1 of this book, for Schillebeeckx the term connotes that humans can never enjoy a direct access to God in their history. A mutual relationship may exist between God and people, because God's presence is mediated through creation. However, there is an immediacy only, as it were, from God to humankind. There is no way in human history for people to apprehend God directly. From a human perspective, there is only a mediation of God's presence. The primary form of that mediation is a praxis of justice: "The most obvious, modern way to God is that of welcoming fellow human beings, both interpersonally and by changing structures which enslave them . . . God is accessible above all in the praxis of justice" (*On Christian Faith,* 65–66).

CHRISTOLOGY AS CONCENTRATED CREATION

Even though the cause of human beings to improve their lot rests firstly in their own hands, Schillebeeckx points out that their cause is God's cause as well, since by creating, "God takes the side of all his vulnerable creation" (*Interim Report,* 127). In the story of Jesus, Schillebeeckx sees a supreme expression of God's love for, and presence among, human beings. Thus his suggestion that christology is concentrated creation: belief in creation is linked to belief in the person of Jesus as God's definitive salvation for people (see *Interim Report,* 128; and *God Among Us,* 105).

In his writings on Jesus, Schillebeeckx makes much of the biblical notion of the kingdom of God. He regards it as a biblical expression for the very nature of God, which is "unconditional and liberating sovereign love." (*On Christian Faith,* 19). That love, however, receives a visible expression when human beings are seen to live in liberating relationships that are peaceful and reconciled. Furthermore, for Schillebeeckx, the liberating love of the kingdom of God is also tellingly uncovered in the life and work of Jesus, who, by healing and restoring people to fuller lives, manifested God's salvation in their midst. In Schillebeeckx's words: "The kingdom of God is the presence of God among men and women, affirmed or made welcome, active and encouraging, a presence which is made concrete above all in just and peaceful relations among individuals and peoples" (*For the Sake of the Gospel,* 117).

Christology has the task of interpreting discursively the identity and significance of Jesus Christ. Schillebeeckx's habit of describing christology as concentrated creation attempts to decipher Jesus' peculiarity by linking the second article of ancient Christian creeds, "I believe in Jesus Christ," with the first, "I believe in God the Father Almighty, Creator of heaven and earth." For Schillebeeckx, christology is a way of rendering belief in creation more intelligible, by explaining it in relation to human history in general and the story of Jesus' life in particular. If Christian belief regards creation as the beginning of salvation, then to speak of christology as concentrated creation is to emphasizes that redemption offered by God the Creator is manifested, or condensed, in the man Jesus.

GOD AS PURE POSITIVITY

Schillebeeckx's theology of creation holds in tension a cluster of interrelated topics: the nature of God, the inherent goodness of secularity or contingency, human desires for salvation from evil and suffering, and Jesus' intensified manifestation of God's kingdom. However, of all these topics, the most significant is the notion that Christian belief in creation is a recognition of God's nature: "Belief in creation means that this nature reveals itself (*Interim Report,* 126). To inquire into Schillebeeckx's theology of creation is concurrently to examine his understanding of God.

That understanding now needs to be teased out a little further. Like many other theologians, Schillebeeckx's way of talking about God combines traditional and original components. With Christian tradition, he professes that God is the almighty creator of heaven and earth. In general, however, his understanding of God turns on four ideas, not always espoused in the same way by other theologians: (1) God as pure positivity; (2) divine absolute freedom; (3) God and the future; and (4) God's humanity.

The core of Schillebeeckx's theory of God is the conviction that God is what he calls "pure positivity." While such an expression might sound overly abstract, it is simply a way of asserting that God does not want people to suffer. "[God is] the promoter of all that is good and he opposes all that is evil. He is not a God of life and death, as he would appear to be at certain levels of the Old Testament. If he were, he would be an ambiguous God. No, he is pure positivity. He fights against the beast Leviathan. He opposes evil" (*God Is New Each Moment,* 109).

By asserting that God is pure positivity, Schillebeeckx abjures all forms of theologically dualistic world-pictures in which evil is coupled with goodness as coequal attributes of God's nature. In addition, he employs the term to insist that belief in God is not a projection onto God of human attributes, but actually involves nonprojective elements of reality. The concept of pure positivity serves Schillebeeckx to confirm Jewish and Christian traditions that reject "all names and images of God which injure and enslave human beings instead of liberating them" (*Church,* 75). For Schillebeeckx, "Jesus knows how human rule over fellow men in fact pollutes and enslaves" (*God Among*

Us, 36). The rule of God, however, is utterly positive, a rule of righteousness, love, mercy and freedom.

The second pillar of Schillebeeckx's language about God is the assertion that God is absolute freedom. Once again we are confronted with an abstraction. Nevertheless, the belief that God is unconstrained freedom specifies expectations that human beings can have both for God and for themselves. To regard God as free, without constraint, means that human beings cannot view God as a convenient explanation for the state of their world. God can never be construed as a function for human beings, or as a hypothesis they may use to explain reality. Within such a scheme, God becomes "pure gratuitousness" and "excessive luxury" (*For the Sake of the Gospel,* 69).

Western theistic language, inspired in part by the metaphysics of Parmenides, has often spoken of God's immutability. Schillebeeckx prefers not to conceive of God as unchanging and unchangeable, but as absolutely free. For him, to speak of God's absolute freedom is to assert that God can be constantly surprising or new in people's lives. Thus, rather than describing God as immutable, Schillebeeckx concludes that God is "eternal youth," "new each day," and "a constant source of new possibilities" (*God Is New Each Moment,* 291).

While such language might appear overly innovative and thoroughly unfamiliar, it actually places Schillebeeckx in a Dominican theological tradition traceable to Thomas Aquinas. To view God as absolutely free, eternally youthful, and constantly new is to resonate with Aquinas's teaching that humans can never know the nature of God. Aquinas is renowned for the five arguments he uses in his *Summa Theologiae* to assert that there is a God. It is not always noted that soon after outlining his arguments, he makes an extremely arresting remark. He says that people are able to know *that* God is, but not *what* God is. For Aquinas, human beings do not know the nature of God, but only what God is not (*Summa Theologiae* I, q. 3, introduction). Schillebeeckx's position that God is absolutely free stresses the same point: "God is absolute freedom. And that means that, as long as human history has not been completed, as long as the totality of history has not been given, we cannot know God's being—there is always something more and so there is always openness" (*God Is New Each Moment,* 29).

Speaking of an incomplete human history and the openness of the question of knowing God's being raises the matter of the eschatological aspect of Schillebeeckx's understanding of God. In the late 1960s, Schillebeeckx developed what he called a new understanding of God. His new understanding turned on the idea of God and the future. Inspired by the philosophies of the German Marxist Ernst Bloch and the critical theorist Herbert Marcuse, he concluded that contemporary scientifically advanced cultures are more orientated toward the future than the past. Appropriating a philosophy that accords a primacy to the future, Schillebeeckx concluded that the transcendence of God cannot be tied to the past, since it involves an as-yet-unknown eschatological future. He unfolds his new understanding of God in chapter 6 of his book *God the Future of Man.* There he speaks of God as "the 'One who is to come,' the God who is *our* future . . . the 'wholly Other' . . . and the 'wholly New'" (181).

For Schillebeeckx, God, the One who is to come, is not only pure positivity and absolute freedom, because, as strange as it may seem, God can also be said to be human: "God is more human than any human being" (*God Among Us,* 61). What, though, does it mean to speak of the humanity of God? Are not all boundaries between creatures and creator obliterated by language of God's humanity?

The opening pages of Schillebeeckx's *Church* contain a wonderfully concise statement of the theological goal that drives his work: "This book is about the life of men and women and their bond with God as God has become visible above all in Jesus of Nazareth, confessed as the Christ by the Christian churches—which are increasingly aware that they live in a secular world amidst other religions" (xiii). This text highlights the four building blocks of Schillebeeckx's theology: (1) human beings; (2) their contact with God through faith; (3) God's historical manifestation in Jesus; and (4) the circumstances in which believers attempt to articulate their faith today.

Undergirding each of these building blocks is a concept of humanity. With regards to humans and their attempt to encounter God, Schillebeeckx is keenly aware that their historical situation for doing so is resolutely dehumanized: "people are falling short, going short, and above all being shortchanged" (*Church,* 232); "there is an *excess* of suffering and evil in our history. There is a barbarous excess, for all the explanations and interpretations" (*Christ,* 725). Consequently, Schillebeeckx nominates what he calls a "criterion of humanizing" as the cardinal condition for the credibility and possibility of Christianity.

In other words, Christianity is essentially concerned with liberating people from economically, socially, and politically downtrodden or dehumanized states of existence. Within such a view, the symbols "God" and "Jesus" assume a critical and productive force (see *Interim Report,* 105).

Stated otherwise, these symbols are interlaced not only with each other, but also with dehumanized people. A key assertion in the just-cited text at the opening of the book *Church* is that God has become visible in Jesus. Schillebeeckx is very clear that Christian belief in God is determined by what it concludes about Jesus: "The story of God is told in the story of Jesus" (*God Among Us,* 31). Moreover, "God discloses *his being in the humanity* of Jesus" (*For the Sake of the Gospel,* 47). Subsequently, in Schillebeeckx's terms, Jesus redefines who God is and what humanity can be: "In the man Jesus the revelation of the divine and the disclosure of true, good and really happy humanity coincide in one and the same person" (*On Christian Faith,* 17). In short, to speak of the humanity of God is to conclude that the realization and definition of humanity is to be found, ultimately, in God.

CONCLUSION

To conclude and sum up, Edward Schillebeeckx regards belief in creation as the bedrock of Christian theology. He understands it as a matter concerning the nature of God, rather than the physical origin of the universe. He explains that creation is an (ongoing) action by God that establishes humans in their finitude and launches a history of salvation in which, ultimately and eschatologically, God wishes to be the happiness and redemption of human beings. God is the lover and salvation of freely finite humans. Axial to Schillebeeckx's theory of creation is the notion of finitude. All that is contingent is neither a mistake nor a flaw. To be finite is simply to be nondivine. Even so, finitude itself is suggestive of its opposite, namely God.

While creation is a constant theme in Schillebeeckx's work, he has discussed it with new emphases in his later writings. After the mid-1960s, he spoke of creation much more in connection with impaired humanity, or the suffering of the poor and downtrodden. Since the 1970s, he has spoken more frequently of christology as concentrated creation. Over the past decade, he has made an explicit link between creation and ecology (see *Church,* 235–40). He asserts that God cannot be envisaged merely as a God of human beings: "with inorganic and organic creatures we share in one creation" (*Church,* 236).

Nonetheless, Schillebeeckx's discussions of God and creation remain largely centered on humans in general, and even more particularly on the historical man Jesus. For Schillebeeckx, human beings are God's regents (*Church,* 238) and the very image of God (245). They enjoy a superior place in creation. Even though they are servants of creation and must look after animals (237), they also have "a somatic spiritual awareness, something transcendent, as a result of which they can recall their relationship with God" (238). Schillebeeckx's theology of creation is an expansive elaboration of the nature and possibilities of that relationship.

SUGGESTIONS FOR FURTHER READING

Schillebeeckx's small book *On Christian Faith: The Spiritual, Ethical, and Political Dimensions* (New York: Crossroad, 1987) serves as a highly instructive introduction to his theology in general, and his understanding of God and creation in particular. Each of its four chapters develops an understanding of God. It contains a wonderfully concise explanation of belief in creation (*On Christian Faith,* 17–18). Ideas presented there are developed in greater detail in *God Among Us: The Gospel Proclaimed* (New York: Crossroad, 1983), chapter 6; and *Interim Report on the Books "Jesus" and "Christ"* (New York: Crossroad, 1980), chapter 6. The final chapter of *Church: The Human Story of God* (New York: Crossroad, 1990) unfolds Schillebeeckx's later theology of creation. In *God the Future of Man* (New York: Sheed and Ward, 1968), chapter 6, he elaborates his notion of God in relation to the future and eschatology. *God Is New Each Moment: Edward Schillebeeckx in Conversation with Huub Oosterhuis and Piet Hoogeveen* (New York: Seabury, 1983) is another repository of his reflections on God, along with the third part of *For the Sake of the Gospel* (New York: Crossroad, 1990). For the concept of "mediated immediacy" see *Christ: The Experience of Jesus As Lord* (New York: Crossroad, 1980), 814–17.

4

Experience and Revelation

Mary Catherine Hilkert

WELL BEFORE THE END of the second millennium, Edward Schillebeeckx identified the ultimate question confronting humankind and the cosmos as the religious question of salvation—the promise of final well-being. Human scientific and technological discoveries have provided genuine advances for human life, but often without consideration of the consequences for the rest of creation. Efforts to control and manipulate the future of both humankind and the earth pose serious ethical questions and underscore the realistic possibility of the destruction of both. With their implicitly absolute claims to offer final well-being, science and technology raise the question of whether human creativity, in the end, threatens both the meaning of history and the future of the cosmos. As Schillebeeckx has queried: "Will the 'guardian of creation' (Gn 2:15, 1:28) become its betrayer?" (*On Christian Faith,* 2).

Further, the extent of human injustice and violence, including violence done in the name of religion, mocks the religious claim that reality is finally gracious, that, in the end, all creatures—and creation itself—fall into the hands of the living God. Is it credible, in the twenty-first century, to speak of human history and all of creation as under the guidance of a liberating creator? Can Christians continue to speak of the absolute saving presence of the God Jesus called Abba, and of the liberating power of the Spirit? If the world is indeed "charged with the grandeur of God," as Gerard Manley Hopkins proclaimed (in his "God's Grandeur", *Poems and Prose,* 1953, 27), where are the traces of God's saving presence to be found? Is revelation necessary for human communities to believe that God is active in their midst? If so, how and where does that revelation occur?

Modern theologians from Friedrich Schleiermacher, the "father of liberal Protestantism," to the transcendental Thomist Karl Rahner have argued that God is to be found in the depths of human experience. On the contrary, dialectical theologians who have followed the lead of Karl Barth in facing squarely the realities of evil, suffering, and sin have insisted that the transcendent and hidden God is revealed only in the word of God—in Jesus the Christ, in the scriptures that give witness to him, and in the church's proclamation of the gospel. In his recent writings, Schillebeeckx proposes a third possibility: God is revealed in human experience, but in a dialectical, rather than a direct fashion. The ultimate mystery of compassion at the heart of reality surprises us as reality resists our human plans and expectations, and as efforts on behalf of those who suffer disclose "something extra" in human experience: the absolute presence of the creator God.

Schillebeeckx's conviction that the encounter between God and humanity occurs within, but is not identical with, human experience involves a number of subtle and interrelated moves. The aim of this chapter is to identify these. In his most recent writings, Schillebeeckx first carefully distinguishes the terms *salvation* and *revelation*. Salvation, or the absolute presence of the creator God, cannot be identified with revelation—the experience, recognition, and celebration of the universal presence of God's saving grace. Because revelation occurs in human experience, we next turn to Schillebeeckx's discussion of the relationship between experience and interpretation and the necessary horizon of faith, within which the religious experience of revelation occurs. His own Christian tradition further shapes Schillebeeckx's theology of revelation as he explores the Christian claim that Jesus is the definitive revelation of God. In that context, Schillebeeckx explains that just as Christianity began with an experience of salvation from God in Jesus, the Christian tradition remains a living one only if it is handed on through a living history of discipleship. Finally, if that tradition is to be both living and faithful, it will comprise new moments of revelatory experience, prompted by the spirit of Jesus, that remain at the same time genuine actualizations of the apostolic faith of the community.

Following the movement of Schillebeeckx's thought, from the broad context of God's universal offer of salvation to the specific question of the discernment of fidelity within the Christian tradition, we turn first to his discussion of the history of salvation as the human context for any discussion of revelation.

THE REALITY OF SALVATION AS FOUNDATION FOR REVELATION

Christians and other religious believers usually turn first to the texts, symbols, and practices of their traditions when attempting to locate the presence of God. Schillebeeckx, however, cautions that while religious traditions provide a searchlight for believers, the traces of the living God are to be discovered in the history we have called secular and the world we have considered profane. Salvation cannot be identified with revelation, since God's saving presence is not limited to our awareness of that reality. In contrast to the medieval claim that there was no salvation outside the church, Schillebeeckx asserts, "there is no salvation outside the world" (*Church,* 12). The world, not the church, is the primary locus of God's saving action.

While the history of salvation and that of revelation are not identical, salvation does provide the necessary human framework for any religious claims about reality. If there is no historical evidence that the power of love is stronger than the power of evil, then any religious claims of God's unconditional love for creation or a "God bent toward humanity" will prove mere ideology. But where are the signs of a history of salvation? According to Schillebeeckx, salvation occurs wherever good is furthered and evil resisted. He identifies "fragments of salvation" in human experiences of meaning, joy, and love, in political cooperation for justice and peace, in personal and social reconciliation, and in the majesty and marvelous interdependence to be discovered in creation. But Schillebeeckx notes that positive experiences of beauty, meaning, joy, and harmony have been threatened repeatedly by forces of destruction and hatred, by threats of violence and by the abuse of human power. The forces of evil that have been unleashed in the last century alone include the Holocaust, multiple genocides, nuclear and biological warfare, and ecological devastation. In a broken world and a history of radical suffering and injustice, the claim that "all will be well" (Julian of Norwich, *Showings*) for human beings and all of creation is far from self-evident.

Given that reading of the present moment in history, Schillebeeckx points to a very specific form of pre-religious experience as the most basic experience of salvation accessible to all human beings: negative experiences of contrast. In radically negative situations, human persons spontaneously protest: "No, it can't go on like this, we won't stand for it any longer" (*God the Future of Man,* 136). Although we have no consensus on what constitutes "livable humanity" (the *humanum*), the indignation that arises when the human is violated is already an indication of an ethic that implicitly affirms a fuller future for humanity. The "no" to human evil, according to Schillebeeckx, discloses an "open yes" to a genuinely human future. Situations of injustice, oppression, and evil are not the final word about the character of reality as a whole, precisely because human beings can and do protest, resist, and hope for a different future. A basic trust in reality, that can be described only as an "openness to the unknown and better," is nurtured and sustained by the fragmentary but real experiences of meaning, happiness, and well-being that also constitute some portion of our lives (*Church,* 6).

In recent writings, Schillebeeckx also describes a parallel in "modern ecological experiences of contrast" that move human beings to protest the violation of all of creation, and to implicitly affirm solidarity with all other living creatures and with the earth (*Church,* 239). The fundamental experience of salvation that emerges in the dialectic between positive fragmentary experiences of final well-being and negative contrast experiences that prompt resistance and action are human experiences shared by agnostics and believers alike. At the same time, those human concrete and pre-religious experiences of salvation are the basic reality to which believers point when they speak in the language of faith of the experience of revelation.

Believers name acts of human liberation as God's redemption (or salvation), while nonbelievers do not. Yet the concrete work of liberation is shared and recognized by human persons from a variety of religious traditions, as well as by those who claim none. Further, the most basic shared human experience of all is that of confronting the limits of human finitude. What nonbelievers see as the final limit, believers identify in faith as the absolute saving presence of God that sustains, empowers, and transcends all human action. Is faith, then, merely a matter of a different cognitive interpretation of the same experience?

Schillebeeckx rejects that notion, arguing that the interrelationship of experience and interpretation is far more complex.

EXPERIENCE OCCURS WITHIN A TRADITION OF INTERPRETATION

According to Schillebeeckx, human experience is always interpreted experience. It involves both an event that occurs in nature or history, and a framework for interpreting that event. The very ability to assimilate new perceptions is always related to a previous history, both personal and collective, that has resulted in one's present horizon for understanding. Operating out of a basic preunderstanding, we are selective in our perception of reality. We notice or fail to notice new data. We attribute significance to symbols, actions, and words.

The cumulative history that forms one's interpretive horizon also serves to keep one open to new experiences. Truly experienced persons, Schillebeeckx remarks, are the most open to new dimensions of reality, as they integrate new moments into an expanding sphere of reference. Far from precluding an objective dimension of experience, this expanding horizon, guided by critical reflection on past experience, makes one more open to encounter reality in its givenness. By way of analogy, Schillebeeckx observes that the trained musician hears more dimensions in a symphony than does a person with an untrained ear.

The interplay between perception and thought is constant and subtle. New experience is possible only within an interpretive horizon or a tradition of experience, but that framework, which includes previously developed models and concepts, is constantly corrected, changed, and revised in light of new and unexpected encounters. Frequently reality resists our expectations and forces us to rethink our previous judgments. At times our encounters with reality confirm or verify our expectations, but more often, Schillebeeckx suggests, we learn by way of discovery. Hence he describes new experience as both critical (it calls into question inherited insights and previous frameworks) and productive (it evokes new and unexpected ways of perceiving, interpreting, judging, and acting). The cognitive dimension of experience is crucial here. The initially projected framework and critical reflection are part of the experience itself. Human beings have to make conjectures, form hypotheses, and experiment if reality is to be encountered, but the experience itself calls us to rethink our models, to confirm, revise, or reject our hypotheses.

Eventually, this self-correcting process of learning can result in a fundamental paradigm shift, in which a radically new framework for perceiving reality is necessary if we are to understand adequately the data of new experience. We are familiar with this basic process of conversion in moments of scientific discovery. Einstein's theory of relativity, for example, provided a framework for understanding the universe that could account for evidence inexplicable within the horizon of Newton's laws of nature.

In the *Christ* book, Schillebeeckx argues that new experience carries a claim to authority particularly when it fails to confirm previous expectations: "Truth comes near to us by the alienation and disorientation of what we have already achieved and planned" (*Christ,* 35). Experiences that confirm our previous assumptions may or may not find their source in a reality beyond our projection and hopes. The very refractory character of discontinuous or surprising experiences is the best guarantee of a revelation of reality that surpasses our imagination and control. Our failures remind us that we are finite. We do not define or control reality; rather, reality sustains and guides us.

One of Schillebeeckx's perduring convictions, drawn from his phenomenological background and crucial to his theology of revelation, emerges at this point: experience contains a dimension of "givenness" that comes from beyond the subject. While there is no uninterpreted experience, neither can experience be reduced to the subjective construct, or creation, of the interpreter. Reality remains independent of the perceiver, something we cannot manipulate or change. While reality is encountered only as perceived, fundamental elements of interpretation are given in the experience. Still, these "primary elements of interpretation" cannot be distinguished neatly from the subjective interpretation framework of the experiencing subject.

In a recent clarification of his position on this question, Schillebeeckx remarks: "[T]he offer-from-God . . . provides its own *direction* of interpretation, as the normative basis of our non-arbitrary interpretations of faith" (*Church,* 38). Earlier, Schillebeeckx had used the experience of love—which, he notes, has a close connection with the experience of grace—to illustrate the interpenetration of experience and interpretation. Interpretation based on prior experiences of love is involved in the very act of experiencing a new relationship as "love." Later the experience may be expressed in language taken from literature (e.g., Romeo and Juliet), the scriptures (e.g., the Song of Songs or 1 Cor 13), or from various cultural descriptions of love. Those interpretative expressions of the experience both deepen it and well up from the experience itself.

Three further aspects of Schillebeeckx's understanding of the relationship of experience and interpretation are integral to his contemporary discussion of the explicitly religious experience of revelation, and should be clarified before we turn to that topic: the distortion of experience by ideology, the narrative character of human experience, and its depth dimension.

Experience and Ideology

While the interpretative horizon has the positive side of making new experience possible, it also has the negative effect of making our perceptions of new data selective, limiting our understanding, and biasing our judgment. In various ways in his earlier work, Schillebeeckx consistently noted that human knowledge is necessarily perspectival and limited. In his farewell address at the University of Nijmegen as well as in his recent writings, however, he has focused more attention on the human construction of all models, the concealed elements in our experience, the ideological use of language, and the necessity for some form of "hermeneutics of suspicion," as called for by the "masters of suspicion"—Feuerbach, Marx, Freud, and Nietzsche, among others. Schillebeeckx accepts their basic insight that human consciousness can unconsciously repress and distort its perception and expression of reality. Thus, for experience to exercise a genuine authority—to be competent, rather than to be a distorted form of ideology—it needs to be rationally investigated for the possibility of distortion and critically appropriated. Because experiences are mediated socially, politically, and economically, experience can serve as a competent guide and authority only when it critically takes account of the specific conditions under which it came about.

Narrative Character of Human Experience

Highlighting the complexity of all human experience, Schillebeeckx concludes that there is no such thing as direct experience. Rather, experience takes place in a dialectical process, in an interplay of perception and critical reflection. Genuine revelations of reality that are not merely thought or produced by human beings have a cognitive critical and liberating power that moves individuals and groups to become witnesses to their experience. Referring to the narrative structure of human experience, Schillebeeckx observes that those who have had an authoritative experience (one with the power to disclose reality) spontaneously want to express what has happened. Experience is communicated primarily though word, through the telling of stories. Traditions, formed from collective experience, become the social framework for understanding—the common stories of families, communities, and cultures. Narration opens up the possibility of sharing in a new story, the possibility of a genuinely new experience of one's previous experiences.

Once again, however, new narratives, like new experiences, do not necessarily carry the authority of reality confronting us with new truth. Rather, experienced persons and communities exercise critical reflection and judgment as they incorporate new facets of experience into their "living traditions." This very capacity of discerning judgment or "discerning the spirits" develops as the result of a history of experience that includes critically digested perceptions. Further, while the disclosure of a new experience involves a process of disintegration as an aspect of transformation, the discovery of the new is also, in some sense, a rediscovery. Because we are a part of the reality that reveals itself to us, the alienation that results from the unexpected brings the new element into view as something that is somewhat familiar, even if beyond all previous expectations.

Depth Dimension of Human Experience

Because we learn by discovery, Schillebeeckx maintains that all human experience has a revelatory structure. But all experiences do not disclose the same dimensions of reality. Rather, in the midst of our ordinary daily lives, certain events and experiences provide a point of breakthrough, even cause a kind of "gestalt shift" in the way we live and understand ourselves and life. These are the experiences that constitute a radical conversion, including the possibility of religious conversion. Whether suddenly or gradually, something surprising happens through which, upon reflection, we recognize deeper dimensions of ourselves and of reality. Even a smile or a friendly glance, Schillebeeckx observes, can open a new world for us.

Further, there are radical moments of "limit" or "boundary" in life, experiences of contingency and finitude in which the fundamental question of the meaning of human life as a whole emerges. Unlike Schleiermacher, however, who located revelation in the direct "feeling" (*Gefühl*) of absolute dependence, Schillebeeckx insists that the experience of radical contingency is itself mediated by all kinds of experiences of relative limits in our lives. The boundaries of human experience are reached in encounters that overflow with a "surplus of meaning," but cannot be expressed in ordinary secular language as well as in negative experiences of suffering, injustice, and, ultimately, death.

In depth experiences of meaning and in the struggle with apparent meaninglessness, human beings experience reality as a whole as either fundamentally trustworthy or ultimately absurd. It is precisely here—in the boundary moments of finitude or contingency—that specifically religious experience becomes possible. Using the notion of "disclosure experience," which he first appropriated from Ian Ramsey's work on religious language, Schillebeeckx explains how the horizon of faith makes possible a genuinely new "experience with experiences"—the religious experience of revelation.

THE RELIGIOUS EXPERIENCE OF REVELATION AND THE HORIZON OF FAITH

Schillebeeckx emphasizes that religious experience is not a special feeling or a direct encounter with the divine; rather, it is an experience of the graciousness of reality as a whole, in spite of all the evidence to the contrary. Within the context of radical human finitude, something deeper is disclosed and evoked—the absolute saving presence of God, or, as Schillebeeckx describes it, "[t]he experience of reality as a gift which frees us from the impossible attempt to find a basis in ourselves" (*Christ,* 47). Both positive disclosure experiences and negative contrast experiences form the foundation that grounds the religious claim that there is a mystery of graciousness at the depth of human experience, and of reality as a whole, that believers identity as "the divine," or God.

In recent writings, Schillebeeckx gives priority to experiences of suffering and dark night as mediations of the divine (*Christ,* 816). As human beings respond to evil, injustice, and suffering with hope, endurance, protest, and resistance, something beyond human finitude is disclosed: the absolute saving presence of God, who sustains and empowers that hope and resistance. Schillebeeckx remarks that for contemporary believers, the mystical experience of God as source of all that is, is mediated most often through ethical and political engagement with the poor (*Church,* 72–77).

In the dialectic between positive fragmentary experiences of meaning, joy, and love and negative experiences of contrast that call forth ethical resistance and hope, Schillebeeckx suggests that "we can *experience* something that transcends our experience and proclaims itself in that experience as unexpected grace" (*Christ,* 78; 897, n. 158). Since revelation in the religious sense refers to the manifestation of the divine within the human, the eschatological within the historical, it cannot be discovered in a direct appeal to self-evident experience. Rather, reflection is demanded if we are to recognize the call that summons us beyond the limits we have taken for granted. Describing this "transcendence within immanence," Schillebeeckx explains that revelation occurs within human experience, but that the two are not identical. Rather, revelation involves "the crossing of a boundary within the dimensions of human existence" (*Christ,* 62). In revelatory experience, there is a dimension of givenness "from above" or "from beyond," the specifically transcendent dimension (the *experienced*).

Here Schillebeeckx clearly distinguishes his position, both from the modernist identification of revelation with human experience in its depths, and from the neo-scholastic understanding of revelation in terms of a propositional "deposit of faith" contained in scripture and tradition (largely identified with dogma or official church teaching). Even in his early work contained in the two-volume *Revelation and Theology,* Schillebeeckx distinguished between "revelation-in-reality," or the encounter between God and humanity that occurs in history and definitively in Jesus, and "revelation-in-word," the necessarily limited and historically conditioned conceptual expressions of that mystery.

God's gracious self-offer always transcends human understanding and expression.

In his earlier writings, Schillebeeckx described the encounter between God and humanity as a dialogue in which God's self-offer constituted revelation, and faith was identified with the human response. In recent writings, however, he draws an even closer connection between revelation and faith. The very experience of reality as grounded in a transcendent dimension of graciousness, as well as further claims that the divine is personal or that God has been revealed in Jesus Christ, occurs only in the context of some sort of tradition of faith. Hence Schillebeeckx describes revelation as "an action of God as *experienced* by believers and *interpreted* in religious language and therefore expressed in human terms, in the dimension of our utterly human history" (*Christ,* 78, emphasis in original).

While revelation as God's initiative in the divine-human encounter always grounds the human response of faith, the offer is completed and recognized only in the response. Revelation is not an objective "given" that historically precedes a later subjective "response"; rather, revelation occurs only within the horizon of faith. Based on the convictions that there is no uninterpreted experience and that revelation occurs within human experience, Schillebeeckx remarks that the believer and the nonbeliever experience reality differently. Faith is not merely an interpretation that can be applied retrospectively to one's previously neutral (uninterpreted) experiences. Rather, faith is the horizon within which the believer perceives reality and experiences human life. Hence Schillebeeckx concludes that "the religious person experiences grace [and] does not just interpret it" (*Christ,* 54).

Borrowing a term from the philosopher Ludwig Wittgenstein, Schillebeeckx describes faith as an alternative "language game" through which secular human history is interpreted (and thus experienced) according to the "grammar of hope." Religious language points to the disclosure of God's creative presence precisely as mediated within human experience, or what he frequently refers to as mediated immediacy (see chapters 1, 3, 6, and 7). The believer, speaking at the limits of experience as described in profane or scientific language, dares to utter a further word. Especially in Western cultures, where science and technology propose the dominant values, a large part of reality falls outside the horizon of possible human experience. Expressions of protest emerge in the aesthetic, the contemplative, the playful, the spontaneous, and, ultimately, the religious. One of the important functions of the language of faith is simply to keep open the question and possibility of transcendence in a radically secular world.

The alternative vision of faith, and thus the experience of God's self-offer, can be expressed only metaphorically and symbolically, since faith claims to speak about a depth dimension of reality that is unavailable to conceptual and rational thought. Only the evocative language of faith can render open and comprehensible to others the substance and meaning of the disclosure experiences that occur at the limits of human experience. As witnesses tell the story of their experiences of grace, a social frame of reference is created and transmitted. The story of faith becomes an invitation to others to share the experience of human life in light of faith. Just as all experience occurs only in the context of a specific framework of interpretation, religious experience occurs only in the context of specific religious traditions. Each offers a unique framework (search pattern) within which believers experience human history in relation to the divine.

CHRISTIAN EXPERIENCE: JESUS AS DEFINITIVE REVELATION OF GOD

Central to the Christian tradition of faith is the claim that in the life, death, and resurrection of Jesus, God has been definitively disclosed to be "God of the living" and "God bent toward humanity." As Schillebeeckx frequently repeats, Christianity began with an experience—of salvation coming from God in Jesus. Standing within the interpretive framework of Israel's dream of the coming reign of God, the disciples experienced something that both fulfilled and reoriented their expectations. In the preaching and in the liberating lifestyle, death, and resurrection of Jesus, his followers experienced the saving presence of God in their midst in a radically new way.

In their expression of the Easter event ("I have seen the Lord") as well as in later metaphors they used for the experience of salvation (e.g., redemption, justification, forgiveness of sins), or in their later naming of Jesus with titles such as Christ, Lord, or Son of God, the earliest Christian communities spoke in language drawn from their social-cultural milieu and religious traditions. But limited human expressions always "break up under the pressure of what Jesus really was, said, and did" (*Interim Report,* 26). Resistant reality, now recognized, named, and experienced as the presence of God in Jesus, continued to break open limited human expectations and expressions.

The faith of later generations of Christian believers remains dependent on the historical mediation of the expressed experiences of faith of earlier generations of believers. Even the original expressions of faith cannot communicate the fullness of the mystery encountered. Nevertheless, the "source experience" of faith of the apostolic community is essential to the faith of all believers in the tradition, since it was the first generation of believers who encountered Jesus historically, and who experienced in his life and in the new disclosure of the Easter event definitive salvation coming from God. The apostolic experience of salvation became a message, the *kerygma,* that extended to others the possibility of living the Christian life.

Hence, according to Schillebeeckx, the question of whether faith derives from experience or "comes from hearing" (Rom 10:14) poses a false dilemma. The Christian message began as an experience. But the experience of salvation that took place in the concrete history and resurrection of Jesus is available to later generations only if the disciples of Jesus continue to hand on the Christian story in a living tradition that "in words and actions bridges the gulf between us and what happened then" (*Interim Report,* 7).

HANDING ON A LIVING TRADITION OF FAITH

This notion of living tradition is central to Schillebeeckx's understanding of revelation. Tradition is constituted precisely by a history of vital experience. In Schillebeeckx's words: "What was experience for others yesterday is tradition for us today, and what is experience for us today will in turn be tradition for others tomorrow" (*Interim Report,* 50). In continuity with Yves Congar's distinction between "Tradition" and "traditions," Schillebeeckx had noted already in his early writings on revelation and tradition that the "deposit of faith" entrusted to the church and handed on from apostolic times refers to the "mystery of Christ," not only to formulations about or teachings of Jesus.

Fundamentally, the living Christian tradition is constituted by the Holy Spirit, active in and through communities of Christian discipleship.

No one creates the Christian story anew, or discovers Jesus in an unmediated fashion. Rather, contemporary believers encounter the testimony of earlier witnesses of faith in the ongoing movement that Jesus initiated and the Spirit sustains. However, any tradition continues to exist as a vital reality only insofar as it is able to address and incorporate new cultures and historical situations. The "culture shock" that results when earlier expressions of the gospel no longer convey the critical and productive force of the Christian faith is, according to Schillebeeckx, a necessary "life shock." This shock calls forth new expressions of the gospel, so that it might become a universal historical message of salvation.

The transmission of the Christian tradition in every age and culture requires far more than the repetition of the kerygma or doctrinal formulations. A living tradition of faith, Schillebeeckx insists, demands a true "updating" that puts the gospel message into operation in the present day, in face of "completely new experiences which are themselves foreign to the Bible" (*Jesus,* 753). Schillebeeckx's consistent interest in hermeneutics (see chapters 1 and 2) has been prompted by the danger that culturally antiquated formulations of the Christian faith, rather than the demands of the gospel, will become the stumbling block to contemporary believers.

Even the biblical texts that mediate salvation in Jesus as experienced by the earliest Christian communities—and thus provide the "inescapable and historically reliable point of departure for the Christian tradition"—remain nonetheless the culturally and historically conditioned expressions of a movement that has continued in the Spirit of the risen Jesus, and that must be reexpressed uniquely in every cultural context (*Jesus,* 44). Similarly, the later doctrinal formulations of the Christian faith, while essential to a living tradition that is mediated through history, cannot be identified with the deeper mystery to which they point: the experience of revelation. The gospels' claim to universal significance becomes credible only if the proclamation of faith can be reinterpreted and reactualized in every new cultural situation.

The claim that at the depth of reality is the God who is "bent upon humanity" and who "wants a future for all creation" cannot be reinterpreted and transmitted in a purely theoretical fashion. It must be proved true in the discipleship of communities of believers who strive to make the promise of salvation a concrete reality in the contemporary world. The hope that at the heart of reality lies the God whose true name is compassion is beyond human comprehension for two reasons: because it is an eschatological promise within the confines of human history, and because the absurdity of evil is utterly unintelligible and resistant to all theorizing. In the face of radical evil, theoretical expressions of faith break down in their ability to transmit the mystery of revelation in history. The "scarlet counterthreads" of suffering in the fabric of human history stand in irreconcilable contrast to any claims of universal theoretical meaning to history.

The Christian belief that the meaning of universal history is to be found in the life story of Jesus becomes a living tradition only when that story is retold in the lives of his followers. Contemporary believers can preach God's fierce opposition to suffering only if they preach as Jesus did: in person and action as well as in word. Remembrance in the biblical sense *(anamnesis)* is a living remembrance through action in the present. Without some experience of the truth of the gospel as mediated in history, the claim to speak the "word of God" is not only a metaphor, it is sheer illusion.

In fact, Schillebeeckx remarks that ethical action carries "the greatest density of revelation," since it makes the promise of salvation present in history in real, though fragmentary, ways. At the same time, praxis without proclamation loses the orientation and critical force of the gospel. Thus Schillebeeckx also highlights the practical and critical effect in narratives. Stories forged in experience have the power to touch and transform the human experience of others. Specifically in the context of suffering, narrative has the further power of retrieving the history of those whose lives have been forgotten, the invisible characters in the human story who have been dismissed as insignificant. Narrative and praxis are integrally related, because remembrance of past suffering carries an implicit ethical demand—it becomes a stimulus for liberating action. At a new moment in the tradition, new responses to the gospel imperative are demanded; "new memories" of Jesus are discovered.

Because of the sustaining and empowering presence of the Holy Spirit within the Christian community, there is a continual interaction between remembering and later experience. Recalling the Johannine promise that "the Spirit will bring all things to remembrance" (Jn 14:26, 15:26, 16:13–14), Schillebeeckx maintains that the "new memories" of the Christian community are not less authentic expressions of revelation simply because they are new. Rather, precisely because Christian revelation occurs as interpreted experience within human history, the contemporary reactualization of the tradition in praxis and narrative participates not only in the transmission of tradition, but also in its ongoing creation.

MUTUALLY CRITICAL CORRELATION OF APOSTOLIC AND CONTEMPORARY EXPERIENCES OF FAITH

While new expressions of the Christian tradition must be forged in every unique historical situation, it is precisely because of their claim to reactualize the gospel of Jesus that the contemporary proclamation and praxis of the church must be held in a mutually critical correlation with the rest of the tradition, most particularly with the originating moment in the "phenomenon of Jesus." New inculturations of the Christian tradition make a claim to being "new moments in the tradition." At the same time, authentic contemporary inculturations of the Christian tradition must be at once "creative" and "true to Jesus" (*Jesus,* 753). Hence Schillebeeckx maintains that the New Testament has an irreplaceable and unique role in the Christian tradition, since it mediates contact with the apostolic faith experience, the primary response to Jesus as God's self-offer in history. Thus it gives "the most direct, uniquely practical and historically reliable access to the original event, the Christian movement that took its impetus from Jesus of Nazareth" (*Jesus,* 58).

The apostolic faith is mediated in history, however, only if Christian experience continues to be a viable option in later generations and in other cultures. There is no abstract Christian faith; there is only the faith as inculturated and made concretely available in communities of Christian believers. Thus the Christian tradition, like all human experience, is mediated necessarily through social and political structures.

Reflecting on the insights of critical theorists (see chapters 1 and 2), Schillebeeckx recognized the danger here: the necessary historical mediation of the gospel in human structures and language may distort the very tradition it is attempting to transmit. Human history is a "flesh and blood affair," Schillebeeckx reminds us; it includes sin as well as grace, unconscious as well as conscious elements of interpretation. False concepts and repressive structures that benefit a dominant group emerge in the power struggles of history, including that of the church. Unless a critical perspective on the Christian tradition is maintained, untruths or nonsense can be consciously or unconsciously legitimated by those in power to preserve their own interests.

While Schillebeeckx's recent work emphasizes more of the discontinuous breaks or "ruptures" that occur in the process of handing on a living tradition, he nevertheless remains convinced that the living tradition of faith will transcend every ideological formulation and will break through all repressive processes and structures, since the Holy Spirit is the ultimate subject and guarantor of the Christian tradition. Further, a necessary critical perspective on the Christian tradition emerges ultimately, according to Schillebeeckx, from the liberating and critical character of the gospel itself. The prophetic Spirit of God is at times the author of those breaks, since the Spirit destroys idols, including human frameworks of interpretation that limit or destroy the revelation of the mystery of God.

Discovering the authority of revelation located in human experience is a complex phenomenon that requires critical reflection and discernment. The authority of revelation cannot be identified solely with the apostolic expression of faith, much less with any particular later mediation of the Christian tradition, including contemporary inculturations. Rather, locating the authority of revelation in human experience requires a mutually critical correlation of tradition and new experience.

The story of Jesus made available to us through the New Testament does not simply confirm contemporary human experience. Every epoch and culture has its own unique sensitivities, but also its biases and limitations. Hence, every age and culture can disclose unique aspects of revelation, but each culture also has its own possibilities for distortion of the tradition. The apostolic experiences of faith, as expressed in the New Testament, critique our limited and sinful perspectives on the basis of the memory of Jesus and the vision of the reign of God he proclaimed and enfleshed.

The critical questions that confront present inculturations of the Christian faith (e.g., experiments in liturgy or ministry) that claim to be creative yet faithful actualizations of the gospel in a new time are these:

To what extent is the historical identity of Christianity made present in a new way, and to what extent is it compromised or distorted in a new praxis or expression of the tradition?

Schillebeeckx notes, however, that the apostolic and traditional formulations of revelation must be critiqued from the perspective of contemporary experience. Recognizing that some may consider it blasphemous to assert that the "word of God" can be criticized by human experience, Schillebeeckx hastens to specify that it is human words about the word of God that are in need of reevaluation. Again, the complex structure of experiences of revelation becomes apparent. Revelation never occurs as pure "word of God"; it occurs in "utterly human history," as interpreted in the context of a specific tradition of faith and as expressed in culturally limited language. Differing cultural vantage points offer the possibility of identifying the limitations of other inculturations of the gospel.

The ultimate theological reason for the necessity of critique of the Christian tradition from the perspective of a "new moment in the tradition" is that God's revelation in Jesus can never be absolutely identified with the historical church, or with its specific cultural and potentially ideological manifestations. Rather, the power of God revealed in the resurrection of Jesus always can open up new possibilities and create a future that exceeds both past memories and present expectations and limits.

While the Holy Spirit may indeed be "doing a new thing" at a new moment in history, Schillebeeckx still cautions that the Holy Spirit is the Spirit of Jesus. The Christian tradition has its norm in its fidelity to Jesus. Hence, new moments in the tradition must also establish their fidelity to "the great Christian tradition." Discovering the living God in the history of human experience requires a careful process of "discernment of spirits," as contemporary communities of believers, in fidelity to Jesus and the apostolic tradition, strive to share the Christian experience of revelation with others by "writing a fifth gospel with their lives."

SUGGESTIONS FOR FURTHER READING

For Schillebeeckx's most recent discussion of the relationships between salvation and revelation, revelation and experience, and experience and interpretation, see the first chapter of *Church: The Human Story of God* (New York: Crossroad, 1990). A more popular treatment of some of the key issues can be found in *On Christian Faith: The Spiritual, Ethical, and Political Dimensions* (New York: Crossroad, 1987), chapters 1 and 4. The most extended treatment (in English) of the relationship between revelation and experience is to be found in *Christ: The Experience of Jesus As Lord* (New York: Crossroad, 1980), 29–79; however, some issues discussed there are clarified or revised in the opening chapter of *Church*. Briefer versions of key aspects of the material in *Christ* are located in *Interim Report on the Books "Jesus" and "Christ"* (New York: Crossroad, 1980), 3–19, 50–63; and in "Can Christology Be an Experiment?" (*Proceedings of the Catholic Theological Society of America* 35 [1980]: 1–14). For a concrete example of the importance of mutually critical correlation in the process of preserving a living tradition, see Schillebeeckx's homily "I Still Have Much to Say to You (John 16.12–15)," in *For the Sake of the Gospel* (New York: Crossroad, 1990), 169–74. Two untranslated sources that develop the need for ideology critique in the process of transmission of a living tradition include "Erfahrung und Glaube," in *Christlicher Glaube in moderner Gesellschaft,* Teilband vol. 25 (Freiburg: Herder, 1980); and Schillebeeckx's farewell address at Nijmegen, *Theologisch geloofsverstaan anno 1983* (Baarn: Nelissen, 1983). Two other valuable essays related to the topic of the transmission of a tradition of faith are "The Crisis in the Language of Faith As a Hermeneutical Problem" (1973); and "The Role of History in What Is Called the New Paradigm" (1989), both reprinted in *The Language of Faith: Essays on Jesus, Theology, and the Church* (Maryknoll, N.Y.: Orbis, 1995). For the early roots of Schillebeeckx's theology of revelation, see *Revelation and Theology* (New York: Sheed and Ward, 1967, 1968), vols. 1 and 2. Parts 1 and 2 of *The Schillebeeckx Reader* (Robert J. Schreiter, ed., New York: Crossroad, 1984) provide an excellent introduction to the development of his theology of revelation.

5

The Story of Jesus As the Story of God

John P. Galvin

In an influential programmatic essay, "Current Problems in Christology," originally published in 1954, the German Jesuit theologian Karl Rahner lamented the failure of contemporary Catholic theologians to address new central christological issues. Literature abounded in other areas, Rahner noted, such as the theology of grace and even Mariology, and debates raged concerning such topics as the extent of Christ's human knowledge and the precise nature of the hypostatic union. But a general presumption prevailed among Catholic theologians that the decisive, foundational issues of christology had long since been resolved. In the fourth and fifth centuries, ecumenical councils at Nicaea, Ephesus, and Chalcedon had settled matters concerning the person of Christ by teaching that Jesus Christ was truly God and truly human, one person (divine) in two natures (divine and human). In the Middle Ages, St. Anselm of Canterbury developed the account of Christ's work that soon became standard in Western thought: in his death on the cross, Christ had freely offered himself to God as infinite satisfaction for human sin. The task of christology was to repeat and defend these established teachings, not to reexamine their bases or expand the field of inquiry to include broader questions.

In Rahner's judgment, this widespread presumption was wrong. Without denying the validity of the conciliar formula or the value of the traditional theory of satisfaction, he argued that a host of other problems urgently required attention, foremost among them issues arising from recent biblical studies and from the pastoral need to rearticulate central convictions of Christian faith with a view to the specific concerns of modernity. The formulations of the past were a beginning as well as an end: starting points as well as conclusions. The task of christology was not simply one of conserving the received tradition; it included as well an obligation to retrieve from the past the memory of forgotten truths, and a duty to address creatively new questions and problems.

While the accuracy of Rahner's diagnosis was widely acknowledged, the christological program he envisioned was not pursued immediately. In the following years, the energies of most theologians were absorbed by issues concerning the church and the sacraments—the major themes on the agenda of the Second Vatican Council (1962–65). Since the early 1970s, however, it has become increasingly clear that confronting the challenges that Christianity faces in the modern world necessitates fundamental reexamination of central aspects of the church's faith; as a result, christology (together with the doctrine of God) has occupied central stage in the theological discussion of recent decades. Rahner himself summarized much of his thought on christology in an important section of *Foundations of Christian Faith* (New York: Seabury, 1978). Hans Küng devoted over half of *On Being a Christian* (Garden City, N.Y.: Doubleday, 1976) to a presentation of christological themes, and Walter Kasper published a comprehensive textbook on christology, *Jesus the Christ* (New York: Paulist, 1976). In addition to these major books, numerous studies have examined individual christological questions or provided introductory accounts of modern christology on a more popular level.

Among these works, Edward Schillebeeckx's massive christological project clearly holds a prominent place. Schillebeeckx has addressed christology from a distinctive perspective that sheds fresh light on the topics he examines. In addition, more than any other contemporary systematic theologian, he has elaborated his christological thought in detailed engagement with the writings of recent biblical scholars. As we shall see, the result is an intriguing—and provocative—retelling of the story of Jesus as a story of God.

THE PROBLEM OF EVIL AND THE OPTION FOR NARRATIVE

Schillebeeckx's christology begins with a problem, not a formula or a theory. His quest for a suitable starting point common to all human life and, therefore, accessible to all leads him to concentrate on the universal experience of evil, the bitter awareness that the history of the human race is one of suffering. Without disparaging the significance of other concerns, Schillebeeckx remains convinced that the problem of evil, concretized most disturbingly in the suffering of the innocent, is both the primary issue that has preoccupied religions and philosophies of the past and present, and the most urgent challenge faced by Christianity today.

Needed in response to the presence of evil is not an explanation of its existence or a theory about its origin or purpose. As Karl Marx noted in his famous eleventh thesis on Feuerbach, the point is not to interpret the world differently, but to change it. In themselves, neither explanations nor theories offer helpful solutions. On the contrary, they can easily prove counterproductive, as they may suggest that evil is inevitable—ineradicably rooted in the order of things—and thus promote an attitude of resignation and passivity. For these reasons, Schillebeeckx maintains, the problem of evil is not amenable to theoretical argument or resolution.

Rather than theory, the proper reaction to evil is concrete opposition to its reign: "the only adequate response is via a practical exercise of resistance to evil, not a theory about it" (*Jesus,* 620). But this resistance, in turn, is in need of support and direction; otherwise, in the face of intractable and deep-seated problems, it will surely prove ineffective and short-lived. Here widespread human practice offers a sure guide: "People do not *argue* against suffering, but tell a story" (*Christ,* 698). At the root of such stories lie contrast experiences, in which we grasp the tension between the general sway of injustice and the fleeting achievement of meaning and reconciliation. Unlike theories, which tend to domesticate problems and thus to perpetuate them, the telling and retelling of stories preserves dangerous memories, awakens liberating hopes, and provides a framework for expressing specific anticipations of a better future in parables and symbols—the only suitable vehicles of communication in a world where evil still abounds. In view of the per vasive problem of suffering, discourse is necessary, and the appropriate primary form for discourse is that of a narrative with practical intent.

But the selection of a story cannot be arbitrary, and the right one is hard to find. In the judgment of Christians, the story to be told in the face of evil is christological. To tell this story today, in view of contemporary perceptions of concerns to be addressed and of modern standards for proper historical narrative, is a particularly demanding task. Yet it is this project that Schillebeeckx has undertaken, for his understanding of the problems that theology must confront both necessitates a pursuit of christological issues and dictates his choice of christological method. As a result, his christology does not concentrate on a christological formula, not even the hallowed formula of the Council of Chalcedon that Christ is one person in two natures, truly divine and truly human. Nor does it develop a soteriological theory—not even the traditional theory of Christ's atoning sacrifice. Fully aware of how hard it is to tell a story well, yet firmly oriented on the narrative form of the gospels, Schillebeeckx instead attempts to retell the life story of Jesus as a liberating story of God.

NARRATIVE AND EXEGESIS

"It began with an encounter" (*Christ,* 19). As Schillebeeckx recognizes, "the starting point of the Christian movement was an indissoluble whole consisting on the one hand of the offer of salvation through Jesus and on the other of the Christian response in faith" (*Christ,* 66). While discussion of Jesus requires particular attention to the first aspect of this composite—"those features of the 'historical Jesus' which may have led to the New Testament confession of him" (*Christ,* 22)—our historical access to Jesus remains mediated through the prism of the responses he evoked from others. To reach the Jesus of history, it is necessary to retrace one's way through the gospels, which are composed from the perspectives of their early Christian authors yet enshrine earlier historical material. This, in turn, demands careful consideration of the issues raised by modern historical-critical scrutiny of the New Testament.

Thus, to accomplish his goal of retelling the story of Jesus, Schillebeeckx found it necessary to immerse himself thoroughly in exegetical literature. Though not a professional exegete, he has attained sufficient mastery of the literature and methods of exegesis to enable him to pass well-informed judgments on biblical questions. While his perspective remains that of a systematic theologian, his presentation of Jesus bears witness to the depth of his exegetical studies and provides a valuable summary of New Testament research at the time of the publication of his major works.

In pursuing these issues, Schillebeeckx proposes five criteria helpful for distinguishing what may actually be ascribed to the historical Jesus, from subsequent amplifications by the early church: the presence of material that diverges from the theological tendencies of the work in which it appears; the existence of material that cannot plausibly be attributed to sources other than Jesus; the presence of the same material in diverse traditions; consistency in content between a given detail and the overall picture of Jesus; and, finally, the standard of Jesus' execution—Jesus' life must be such that it accounts for his rejection and death. Application of these criteria, in wide-ranging dialogue with modern biblical scholarship, allows him to provide an unusually rich and detailed account of Jesus' public life.

JESUS' PUBLIC LIFE

Schillebeeckx presents Jesus'life as a sustained and varied offer of definitive salvation from God, in a context marked by intense suffering and correspondingly heightened longings. Jesus' joyful gospel of God's graciousness is expressed in both his preaching and his conduct, clearly distinguished from John the Baptist's somber message of divine judgment, despite the two prophets' common stress on hope and ethical commitment.

Jesus' preaching was addressed to all Israel and concentrated on the theme of God's kingdom, of God's benevolent rule. What Jesus meant by the term "kingdom of God" emerges from his ministry as a whole, not from direct explanation on his part. His open-ended parables interrupt the courses of events, forcing his listeners to think further and revealing through their effects what God is like. His enunciation of the beatitudes (a core of which derives from Jesus himself) shows him as the bearer of good tidings to the poor. Throughout his preaching, Jesus indicates as a present reality God's radical "no" to all forms of evil, for the kingdom of which Jesus announces the imminent arrival is, in fact, at hand in and through Jesus himself.

The same liberating message is embodied in Jesus' prophetic life, for his company was experienced as the presence of God's saving rule. His activity as healer and exorcist, thought difficult to document in detail, evoked an incipient faith in the sense of a turning of people toward him. Table fellowship with him, and even more the common life of his chosen disciples, communicated a sense of well-being and freedom in his presence. In sum, Jesus not only used parables to speak about God; he was himself, in an even deeper sense, a parable in person: God's own parable of mercy and liberation.

Yet Schillebeeckx's probing of Jesus'life does not rest content with a summary of what Jesus said and did. In his judgment, it is necessary, even on purely historical grounds, to inquire into the unifying source of Jesus' message and conduct. Anything less would mark a failure to recognize the extent to which the mystery of Jesus' person is indirectly accessible to us in and through his behavior, a blindness to the fact that while Jesus never placed himself beside God's kingdom as a second topic in his preaching, still "his person is never entirely separable from his message and ministry" (*Jesus,* 258). The inseparability of Jesus' message from his person is a central factor in Schillebeeckx's christology.

In his analysis, Schillebeeckx locates the foundation of Jesus' public activity in his consciousness of deep intimacy with God, who benevolently opposes evil and refuses to allow it to have the last word. Jesus' message and manner of life reflect a confident hope that cannot have been grounded in the calamitous history of the world. Their only possible source lies in an intuitive grasp, on Jesus'part, of the sharp contrast between the evil he observed and his personal experience of God.

To capsulize this abiding awareness at the heart of Jesus' ministry, Schillebeeckx has coined the term "Abba experience." Originating from *abba,* the Aramaic word for "father," the term is based on Jesus' frequent reference to God as Father in the gospels, and especially on its appearance (in Greek transliteration) in three New Testament texts (Mk 14:36 ["Abba, Father, all things are possible to you; remove this cup from me; yet not what I will, but what you will"]; Rom 8:15 [in the Spirit "we cry 'Abba! Father!'"]; Gal 4:6 ["God has sent the Spirit of his Son into our hearts, crying, 'Abba! Father!'"]).

Despite his choice of this terminology, Schillebeeckx's insistence that a conviction of intimacy with God lies at the source of Jesus' public activity rests on an overall consideration of Jesus' life and message, not on an exegesis of the passages in which the word *father* appears. Schillebeeckx's choice of language simply reflects, in terminology rooted in the New Testament, the loving proximity and trust that characterize Jesus' relationship with God.

As Schillebeeckx recognizes clearly, these considerations in themselves do not establish the validity of Jesus' claim. Historical investigations alone cannot determine whether his Abba experience was well founded or illusory. But they do show that, in this case, the message and the messenger are inseparable. For this reason, any effort to assess the truth of what Jesus proclaimed will ultimately find it necessary to weigh the consequences Jesus faced for having advanced his gospel.

THE CRUCIFIXION

The stark fact of Jesus' crucifixion inevitably raises questions for any theologian, and it does so with particular urgency for Schillebeeckx, who accents so strongly the salvific impact of Jesus' presence. His narrative treatment of the subject includes an examination of Jesus' approach to death and an analysis of early Christian interpretations of the crucifixion; in addition, he offers his own reflections on the theological meaning of the cross. Each of these three aspects deserves separate consideration.

Jesus' Approach to Death

Aware that texts in the gospels are often formulated from the perspective of the early church, modern treatments of Jesus' approach to death understandably hesitate to rely on biblical passages in which Jesus discusses in advance his own death. While a few scholars, such as Rudolf Bultmann, doubt that we are able at all to determine how Jesus faced death, Schillebeeckx follows the more moderate consensus that Jesus, long aware of potential danger from many hostile forces, gradually achieved certitude of impending violence. His steadfast adherence to his mission under these adverse circumstances implies on his part acceptance of death as a consequence of continued fidelity to his ministry. The early church was, thus, justified in its unanimous attestation "that Jesus went to the cross freely and deliberately" (*Jesus,* 302).

In arguing this position, Schillebeeckx stresses that a decisive break in the public evaluation of Jesus occurred well before his death, at the point where mounting opposition to his message coalesced into the personal rejection that eventually culminated in his crucifixion. Aware of this reaction and conscious as well of the tension between his approaching execution and his message of God's kingdom, Jesus must have pondered the meaning of the death he was to undergo. In view of this situation, it is possible and legitimate to ask if Jesus not only accepted his death freely, but also provided for his disciples an advance interpretation of its significance.

In addressing this issue, Schillebeeckx proceeds quite cautiously. On the one hand, he appeals to a critically reliable text in the Last Supper tradition ("Truly I say to you, I shall not drink again of the fruit of the vine until that day when I drink it new in the kingdom of God," Mk 14:25) to argue that even face to face with death, Jesus confidently retained unbroken assurance of eventual salvation and vindication. On the other hand, holding that we have no certainly authentic passage in which Jesus ascribes salvific value to his death, Schillebeeckx suggests that Jesus left his death as a final prophetic sign for others to interpret on the basis of his life. In any case, Jesus' fidelity, in life and death, to his gospel of salvation far surpasses in importance any reconciliation of his message and his fate on the level of theory.

Early Christian Interpretations of the Crucifixion

Continuing his narrative presentation to include the reflections of the early church, Schillebeeckx draws on the work of numerous exegetes to outline three major early Christian interpretations of the crucifixion: Jesus'death was seen as that of the eschatological prophet-martyr; as the death of the righteous sufferer; and as a redemptive, atoning death. These interpretations, which antedate the writing of the New Testament, may well have developed simultaneously in different Christian communities.

One line of thought readily accessible to early Christians accented Jesus' prophetic life and drew on the Old Testament theme that true prophets are often rejected and meet violent ends. As the parable of the vineyard (Mk 12:1–12) and other texts imply, this perspective serves to indicate that Jesus' claims are not undermined by the crucifixion. Related in substance to this conception, but drawing on different Old Testament background, is a second approach that appeals to the psalms and the wisdom literature. Especially evident in the passion narratives of the synoptic gospels, this perspective identifies Jesus as the righteous sufferer, persecuted precisely because of his justice but eventually vindicated by God. While these two models could rest content with the insistence that Jesus' salvific significance is not destroyed by his shameful end, a third category of interpretation attributes redemptive, atoning value to the crucifixion itself. This theme, which makes considerable use of the Servant Songs of Isaiah 40–55, is reflected in the New Testament accounts of the Last Supper and in much Pauline material.

In addition to classifying early Christian interpretations of Jesus' death into these three basic categories, Schillebeeckx also maintains that some New Testament sources reflect the existence of early Christian communities that were not particularly troubled by Jesus' death and that, therefore, developed their christology with little or no attention to that subject. While this judgment, largely based on an argument from silence, is open to question, it is clear that the early church's reaction to the crucifixion was not uniform, but included diverse strands of thought.

In addition to considering the treatment of Jesus'death in the formative years of Christianity, Schillebeeckx also examines in detail the thought of the New Testament authors themselves, with careful attention to their further development of the original themes. He remains convinced, however, that "New Testament Christianity can only be a model indirectly, and not directly" for later Christians (*Christ,* 561). While committed to whatever is entailed by Jesus himself, Christians are free to articulate their faith in new and different ways; they are not bound to use categories standard in the past, even those anchored in biblical tradition.

The Interpretation of the Crucifixion in Schillebeeckx's Theology

Unlike theological conceptions that envision death as the final, climactic event of human freedom, Schillebeeckx's own theological interpretation of the crucifixion stresses the passive character of death and its negative dimension. "In Jesus' death, in and of itself, i.e. in terms of what human beings did to him, there is only negativity" (*Church,* 127). Such negativity is all the more evident in an unjust and violent execution like that of Jesus. God, the great opponent of human suffering, cannot have willed Jesus' passion and death in any direct sense. The immediate agents of the crucifixion were Jesus' enemies, who brutally removed him from our midst, and no theology can legitimately permit the memory of this evil to be blunted in subsequent glorification.

In keeping with these principles, Schillebeeckx insists that "first of all, we have to say that we are not redeemed *thanks to* the death of Jesus but despite it" (*Christ,* 729). Although he immediately qualifies this comment by noting that the expression "despite the death" does not say enough, he judges that we lack categories suitable for filling this unfathomable "does not say enough" with meaningful content. While speaking at times of the value inherent in Jesus' death, Schillebeeckx's usual procedure is to locate salvific meaning elsewhere, either in Jesus' free acceptance of death (as distinct from death itself) or in divine conferral of value on Jesus' death through the resurrection.

Thus, on the whole, Schillebeeckx is more favorable to portrayals of the crucifixion as the death of a prophet-martyr and of the righteous sufferer than he is to interpretations of Jesus' death in the categories of atonement and redemption. The first two approaches, while largely bypassed in the history of theology, tend far more than the third to link Jesus' death to his public life, thus lending themselves to use in narrative presentations and thwarting impulses to isolate the crucifixion and interpret its meaning in purely theoretical fashion. Development of their content corresponds well to basic interests of Schillebeeckx's thought, especially since retrieval of neglected aspects of the Christian tradition is an important element in his overall theological program.

THE RESURRECTION

The resurrection inevitably poses problems for any effort to compose a narrative christology. Even the gospels do not attempt to provide a narrative of the resurrection, though they do, of course, affirm it in their stories about the finding of the empty tomb and the appearances of the risen Lord. Schillebeeckx's christology offers reflections on both the nature of the resurrection and the revelation of the risen Christ to his followers. To grasp accurately his position on these important issues, it is essential to remain alert to the distinction between the resurrection and its revelation.

The Nature of the Resurrection

Schillebeeckx's treatment of the resurrection is marked strongly by his insistence on the negative character of death—of death in general, and of Jesus' crucifixion in particular. For this reason, he rules out any conception of the resurrection as "the other side of death," a position common in the work of many modern theologians. Instead, Schillebeeckx sees Jesus' resurrection as a divine correcting victory over the negativity of his crucifixion, a new and different event after death that confers upon Jesus' death a new meaning. The resurrection is real and affects Jesus personally; without it, the historical Jesus would be merely a tragic failure. Nevertheless, the resurrection is meta-empirical and meta-historical. For this reason, it cannot appropriately be cited as apologetic proof, as one statement of faith can never serve as legitimization for another. Nor can the resurrection be narrated directly, a characteristic reflected in the gospels' refraining from attempting such narratives (and, one might add, a possible indication of the limits of narrative as a comprehensive vehicle of Christian theology).

The Revelation of the Risen Jesus

But if the resurrection itself is meta-empirical and meta-historical, on what grounds do Christians come to profess that Jesus is risen from the dead? Since the gospels' references to predictions of the resurrection by the historical Jesus are suspect of being products of the early church's christological reflection, Schillebeeckx's analyses of the revelation of the resurrection—one of the most controversial aspects of his theology—

concentrate on New Testament traditions about the empty grave and the appearances of the risen Lord. Schillebeeckx's initial reconstruction has undergone some modification, largely in response to criticism of his work. Throughout, however, his position is characterized by the conviction—not shared by all theologians—that "there is not such a big difference between the way we are able, after Jesus'death, to come to faith in the crucified-and-risen One and the way in which the disciples of Jesus arrived at the same faith" (*Jesus,* 346).

In studying the empty grave stories, Schillebeeckx notes the discrepancies in the various accounts and concentrates on their function in the different gospels as articulations of the church's faith in Jesus' resurrection. Originally he judged that the historical basis of these accounts could no longer be ascertained, since the tradition may originate from a later practice in Jerusalem of conducting Easter services at the site of Jesus' tomb. In response to widespread criticism of this hypothesis, Schillebeeckx later concluded that the grave may have been found empty, but still insisted that this was not a factor in the public origin of Christian faith, for no visit to the tomb could, as such, provide sufficient basis for belief in Jesus' resurrection. Thus Schillebeeckx, like most contemporary exegetes and theologians, now concentrates chiefly on the New Testament tradition about appearances of the risen Jesus.

Schillebeeckx's analysis of the appearance tradition rests on his conviction that since the disciples had somehow let Jesus down at the time of his arrest, some sort of conversion must lie between this failure and their later faith. In an unusual methodical procedure, he attempts to understand the gospel accounts of Jesus' appearances by examining the three New Testament narratives of Paul's experience on the road to Damascus (Acts 9; 22; 26). From a study of these texts, Schillebeeckx concludes that the story of this event underwent gradual transformation, from an account of Paul's conversion (Acts 9) through a transitional version (Acts 22) to a report of Paul's mission (Acts 26). The gospel narratives of Jesus' appearances to the disciples parallel the final form of the tradition about Paul, inasmuch as they too accent the theme of mission.

In view of all these considerations, Schillebeeckx hypothesizes that the appearance narratives found in the gospels may be the end product of a tradition that, in its early stages, reflected the idea of conversion. He proposes that intimate personal religious experiences of a renewed divine offer of forgiveness of sin, through Jesus, led to the disciples reassembling at the initiative of Peter. This conversion experience—which is not identical to the resurrection itself—is at the root of the ancient listing of appearances in 1 Corinthians 15:3–8. The later gospel appearance narratives are not historical reports, but theological elaborations of specific aspects of the church's faith in Jesus' resurrection.

Schillebeeckx's initial writing on the appearance tradition, like his study of the empty grave, has been subjected to considerable criticism, and he has modified his position in response to some objections. His later treatments of the issue refrain from stressing the theme of conversion experiences and consider the historical genesis of belief in the resurrection to be an open question, provided only that its divine source is recognized and that supranaturalistic conceptions of the origin and growth of the disciples' faith are excluded.

In any case, the story of Jesus does not end with resurrection appearances. In addition to weighing those features of Jesus that constituted an offer of salvation from God, christology must also attend to Christians' expression of what they have experienced in encounters with Jesus, and how they have responded to him in faith. While seeing a "grain of truth" in Rudolf Bultmann's "denial of a smooth continuity between the Jesus of history and the Christ of the church's faith" (*Church,* 106), Schillebeeckx nonetheless insists that "there is no gap between Jesus' self-understanding and the Christ proclaimed by the Church" (*Jesus,* 312).

EARLY CHRISTIAN INTERPRETATIONS OF JESUS

In examining the history of Christian thought about Jesus, Schillebeeckx is especially attentive to the seminal period (roughly two decades) between Jesus'death and the writing of Paul's Epistles, the oldest books of the New Testament. In view of the limitations of the available sources, we can only seek to reconstruct the thought of this first Christian generation by extrapolating from the traces preserved in later texts. While acknowledging the inevitably tentative nature of such research, Schillebeeckx adapts some analyses of Helmut Koester to offer a plausible summary of the diverse assessments that Jesus evoked from the earliest Christians.

Following Koester, Schillebeeckx distinguishes four creedal tendencies in early Christianity. A "parousia christology" concentrated on Jesus'future role as son of man and coming judge, while a second type, sometimes termed a "divine man christology," presented Jesus chiefly as a worker of miracles. "Wisdom christology" remembered Jesus as teacher and collected his sayings; in some subspecies, it identified him as wisdom incarnate. (The christological doctrine of the early ecumenical councils is a further development of this model, which has, thus, proven quite influential on Christian thinking.) Lastly, an "Easter christology," reflected strongly in the Pauline writings, directed attention toward Jesus' death and resurrection. Each of these trajectories of early Christian thought captured a real facet of Jesus' life and, for that reason, should be recognized as fundamentally legitimate.

Nonetheless, none of the four early strands of interpretation of Jesus was fully comprehensive, and none, in Schillebeeckx's judgment, is able to account for the merger of the four trajectories in the canonical books of the New Testament. For this reason, diverging from Koester, Schillebeeckx posits the existence of a more basic category, one that preceded the differentiation of the four trajectories and laid the foundations for their later unification. Sifting through the evidence in the New Testament, he weighs three models available in the Jewish tradition that could have been adopted for this purpose: eschatological prophet, messianic son of David, and son of man.

While all three of these titles were eventually applied to Jesus, Schillebeeckx judges that eschatological prophet was the original basic category. Son of man suggests an otherworldly figure, and messiah requires extensive reinterpretation to avoid inappropriate nationalistic connotations. Eschatological prophet—not simply a preacher with an apocalyptic message, but the long-awaited prophet, like Moses (see Dt 18:15–18), who speaks with God face to face and bears God's final word—is suitable for conveying Jesus' location in the prophetic tradition, and his superiority over all other prophets. Rich in theological implications, this initial identification of Jesus captures well the facts of his life; in due course, it also gave rise to the other titles and to the later christological trajectories.

Schillebeeckx's treatment of later New Testament elaborations of its basic theme of definitive salvation from God in Jesus will be considered in the following chapter, on his soteriology and theology of grace.

Their value, and the value of postbiblical products of further christological reflection, are largely to be measured by how adequately they reflect a full and comprehensive picture of Jesus. For the final norm and criterion of any interpretation of Jesus of Nazareth is Jesus of Nazareth himself (see *Jesus,* 43).

CONCLUSION

To a greater extent than any other contemporary systematic theologian, Edward Schillebeeckx has developed his christological position in detailed confrontation with the texts of the New Testament, and with the issues raised and examined in modern biblical scholarship. His work also reflects keen awareness of recent philosophical currents, and of the contemporary problems that Christian faith is required to address. For these reasons, Schillebeeckx's writings on christology offer instructive access to modern reflection on Jesus; they are especially valuable for indicating concretely where the chief disputed questions lie. At the same time, they provide a rich resource for deepened personal meditation on Jesus of Nazareth, as foundation and object of Christian faith. Here, Schillebeeckx's insistence on the inseparability of Jesus' message from his person and on the interconnection of Jesus' public life and death is particularly important.

Nevertheless, as is only to be expected in a project of this scope, serious questions may still be raised about various aspects of Schillebeeckx's thought. Is he correct in his emphasis on the category of the eschatological prophet for understanding the historical Jesus and reconstructing the development of christology in the early church? Does his assessment of the crucifixion in primarily negative terms do full justice to the importance of Jesus' death, and to the fact that Jesus' manner of life brought him to this end? Does his treatment of the resurrection as a divine correcting triumph over death's negativity unintentionally devalue the significance of this life? Is his reconstruction of the origin of Christian faith in Jesus' resurrection historically plausible and convincing? More generally, does his preference for narrative over theory imply some false dilemmas, and does his concentration on the problem of evil impede access to certain other dimensions of a full presentation of Jesus?

Whatever the answer to these questions may be, Schillebeeckx's narrative christology remains a major contribution to contemporary theology, and a rewarding source for modern Christians to use in their efforts to reflect anew on the central object of their faith.

SUGGESTIONS FOR FURTHER READING

The chief sources for Schillebeeckx's christology are, of course, his massive volumes *Jesus: An Experiment in Christology* (New York: Seabury, 1979) and *Christ: The Experience of Jesus As Lord* (New York: Crossroad, 1980). Schillebeeckx has responded to various critics of these works in *Interim Report on the Books "Jesus" and "Christ"* (New York: Crossroad, 1980). In addition, documentation has been published of his extensive correspondence and conversation with the Congregation for the Doctrine of the Faith, with regard to his christology, in *The Schillebeeckx Case (Ted Schoof, ed., New York: Paulist, 1984)*. These later works have helped clarify some aspects of his thought.

Yet these volumes, however important, are not fully suitable for readers seeking an introduction to Schillebeeckx's christology. Some shorter texts are of more value for this purpose. While *The Church with a Human Face: A New and Expanded Theology of Ministry* (New York: Crossroad, 1985) is chiefly concerned with issues concerning ministry, the christological section of its opening chapter (pages 15–34) offers a succinct and readily accessible summary of Schillebeeckx's thought on Jesus. A similar christological summary, with explicit reflections on the universal significance of Jesus Christ, may be found in *Church: The Human Story of God* (New York: Crossroad, 1990), 102–86.

Finally, three chapters (pages 33–44, 103–15, 180–87) in *God Among Us: The Gospel Proclaimed* (New York: Crossroad, 1983), a collection of Schillebeeckx's sermons, lectures, and essays on spiritual topics, are equally useful in this regard. Taken together, "Jesus the Prophet," "I Believe in the Man Jesus: The Christ, the Only Beloved Son, Our Lord," and "How Shall We Sing the Lord's Song in a Strange Land? (Ps 137:4)" provide a reliable guide to Schillebeeckx's chief christological themes. Here his positions are clearly articulated on the nature of soteriology, the necessity of narrative theology, the identification of Jesus as the eschatological prophet, the theological significance of Jesus' public life, and the principles needed to interpret the crucifixion and understand the resurrection. These shorter pieces are recommended as the best avenues of approach to Schillebeeckx's retelling of the story of Jesus as a story of God.

6

Salvation: Living Communion with God

Janet M. O'Meara

AT THE BEGINNING of the twenty-first century, we have become increasingly aware that the concrete realities of our human existence as a history of ongoing suffering and oppression now seriously threaten the very survival of humankind, as well as that of the natural environment. Science and technology, once trusted to bring us total emancipation, are now a source of disillusionment and grave anxiety. The precariousness of the situation presses the question of salvation as a secular as well as a religious concern. These times challenge the Christian claim that God's definitive and universal salvation has been given to us in Jesus the Christ. What bearing does Christian faith in Jesus as universal redeemer have on the realities of the contemporary world? What is the universal and salvific relevance of the Christian gospel of salvation in the context of the crucial issues that confront us today on a global scale?

It was with the intention of addressing these questions that Edward Schillebeeckx initiated a process of investigation and critical reflection that resulted in the monumental trilogy *Jesus, Christ,* and *Church.* The structure of Schillebeeckx's soteriological project consists of three distinct but interrelated movements: the christology of *Jesus,* an analysis of New Testament understandings of salvation, and basic moves toward a contemporary soteriology. Schillebeeckx's investigation is motivated by the hope of providing a new focus for traditional Western christology, a perspective he feels is much needed in light of the critical question whether it is still possible to experience Christian salvation. He sees the challenge to be that of creating new traditions in and through which the good news of God's salvation in Jesus becomes activated and actualized in today's world.

In his christology Schillebeeckx seeks to discover, in the image of Jesus reconstructed by historical criticism, what is unique and particular about Jesus of Nazareth that led from pre-Easter discipleship to the New Testament confession of Jesus as definitive salvation from God. Schillebeeckx contends that only after a critically reconstructed picture of Jesus' message, way of life, and consequent execution is it possible to discover how the whole of this could have been experienced as his "salvation" at that time. In a further step, it can be asked how people today might experience the "final good" in this Jesus event.

In the introduction to *Christ,* Schillebeeckx clarifies the immediate connection between the first two moments of his emerging soteriology. Whereas in *Jesus,* Schillebeeckx's concern was with those aspects of the "historical Jesus" that may have led to the New Testament confession of him, in *Christ* his attention shifts to the New Testament elaboration of the ongoing experience of Jesus as salvation from God. In other words, the focus of *Christ* is the continuation of the process of identifying Jesus of Nazareth that began with an initial encounter between Jesus and some first-century Jews, who "followed after" him during his ministry and then later knew him to be alive and present beyond death in the community of believers.

Through this encounter with Jesus, the first community of disciples found renewed meaning and purpose in their lives. The experience of renewed life in Jesus, the crucified-and-risen One, led the disciples to further reflection. They began to analyze their experience and to consider its various aspects in terms of available socioreligious models. Familiar things were viewed from a new focal point. "On the basis of their common experience they arrived at what we might call a Christian theory of grace, the beginnings of what in Christian tradition is called a 'theology of grace': soteriology, a thematic account of the meaning of Christian redemption and Christian salvation" (*Christ,* 19–20). The experience of salvation from God in and through Jesus found written expression in the corpus of writings that form the New Testament. In these documents, the meaning of grace points to a Christian oneness of experience that found great variety in expression according to the historical socioreligious circumstances of the New Testament communities.

Schillebeeckx understands this basic experience to be the constant unitive factor of Christian faith. By "oneness of experience," he means a communal-ecclesial encounter "which obliges people to define the ultimate meaning and purport of their lives by reference to Jesus of Nazareth." In more traditional terms, this means a common experience "which causes people to interpret Jesus' life as the definitive or eschatological activity of God in history for the salvation or deliverance of men and women. The constant unitive factor . . . is that particular groups of people find final salvation imparted by God in Jesus of Nazareth" (*Jesus,* 56; see *Christ,* 463).

In part 2 of *Christ,* Schillebeeckx explores the question of how the New Testament communities expressed the one basic experience of salvation from God in Jesus according to the horizons of their concrete historical experiences and understandings. The purpose of this inquiry is to discover a normative orientation and inspiration for a contemporary soteriology. In part 3, he concludes his investigation with a synthetic description of the four structural elements he contends must be present in any contemporary theology of grace that is both faithful to the gospel and relevant to the present.

At the time he wrote *Jesus* (1974) and *Christ* (1977), Schillebeeckx's soteriological investigation was motivated by the hope of providing a new focus for traditional Western christology, in light of the critical question whether it was still possible to experience Christian salvation in the ambiguities and paradoxes of the late twentieth century. The changes that occurred not only in the world but also, and especially, within the Roman Catholic church during the 1980s caused Schillebeeckx to shift somewhat the perspective of *Church* (1989) from his original plan to complete the trilogy with an ecclesiology. Although disheartened that the Second Vatican Council's vision of the church had not been given institutional form, Schillebeeckx found great encouragement in "an unprecedented and authentic flourishing of the gospel" in grassroots movements among the laity (*Church,* xiv). Thus while still an ecclesiology, as originally intended—albeit "in a minor key" (xix)—the focus of *Church* is a "church of men and women bound to God which . . . has a critical presence in solidarity with men and women 'in the world,' with their problems, great and small, and their 'secular,' authentically human and inhuman history" (xiv).

With *Church,* Schillebeeckx's emerging soteriology completes the "turn to the world" that he decidedly took in *Christ,* making more evident and developing more fully the identification between salvation and God's absolute presence in creation that undergirds his entire soteriological project. God's universal salvific intention for creation is realized whenever and wherever evil is resisted and good is furthered. In the first chapter of *Church,* Schillebeeckx establishes a clear distinction between salvation and revelation. Religions and churches are not salvation, but rather contexts in which and through which people become explicitly aware of God's saving activity in the whole of creation. Christians find God above all in Jesus Christ, in whose life, death, and resurrection is disclosed the being of God as human salvation (see chapter 5). But questions of Christ's uniqueness and universality emerge with new significance in *Church,* with Schillebeeckx's understanding of the universality of salvation in and through the liberating praxis of men and women. Addressing these questions in chapter 3 of *Church,* Schillebeeckx concludes that Jesus is universal, but not absolute, savior. Moreover, the uniqueness of Christianity is found in the ways that the followers of Jesus continue to actualize the history and memory of Jesus' praxis of the kingdom, that is, the very being of God as salvation of men and women.

Although Schillebeeckx identifies salvation with God's absolute presence in creation, he develops his emerging soteriology almost exclusively in relation to human history, and thus emphasizes the political relevance of the Christian gospel, that is, justice and peace. Nevertheless, in *Church,* especially the final section, he begins to address the cosmic dimensions of redemption and liberation.

NEW TESTAMENT UNDERSTANDINGS OF GRACE

From his analysis of New Testament scholarship, Schillebeeckx derives a descriptive theological synthesis in which grace emerges as a new way of life, given by God in Jesus the Christ. In the New Testament, grace means the sovereign, free, and unconditional love of God, manifested in history as a merciful and compassionate concern for human beings, especially for those who experience the greatest need. It is asserted throughout the New Testament that the historical appearing of Jesus is the grace of God. Although the entire earthly life of Jesus is the proffer of God's salvation, Jesus' self-giving to the point of death—that is, his suffering and death on the cross—is the all-embracing sign of grace in the New Testament. Without the resurrection, however, the earthly life and dying of Jesus remain open and problematic. Thus in the New Testament, "the death and resurrection of Jesus are the determinative climax of the grace of God in Jesus the Christ" (*Christ,* 467). Only then does Jesus become the source of God's saving grace. Only the risen Jesus imparts eschatological salvation: the gift of the Spirit.

In the resurrection, the community of the followers of Jesus is empowered to proclaim in human history the good news of God's salvation in Jesus the Christ. By grace, the Christian is given a new identity in Christ that is a new mode of existence. As existence in grace, Christian life is patterned after God's unconditional love as manifested in Jesus' person, message, and praxis of the kingdom even unto death. This way of life is a new alternative for human living that is made possible through a share in the relationship that binds Jesus to the Father through the Spirit. Thus, the New Testament understanding of grace has both a mystical and an ethical dimension.

As a way of life, Christian existence in grace is given concrete form in specific sociohistorical circumstances. Schillebeeckx sees the New Testament churches as graced communities sent forth as a critical and creative consciousness to actualize the righteousness of God in human history. In this way, the New Testament indirectly provides a model for "the building up of Christian communities in the world and for the forming of a better society" (*Christ,* 560). The particular form that grace takes is something that must be continually decided anew, according to the sociocultural conditions of historical existence. Therefore, it is necessary to complement a theological analysis of grace with an analysis of historical circumstances.

On the basis of his investigation of New Testament understandings of grace, Schillebeeckx makes several observations that he judges as pertinent to a contemporary appropriation of the Christian experience of salvation. First, a given tradition of grace undergoes continual development and reinterpretation as it is lived out historically. Second, since it is historically situated, an experience of grace takes place within already existing sociocultural and religious patterns of experience and interpretation. While being sympathetic to these patterns of interpretation, Christianity must maintain a critical function in regard to the structures and models that it assimilates into its experience. Third, the New Testament theology of grace comprises distinct, alternative, and complementary traditions, namely the synoptic, Pauline, and Johannine traditions. From this fact, Schillebeeckx concludes that in new historical situations, it is not only permissible but necessary to develop new traditions that are faithful to the one basic experience of salvation from God in Jesus. Thus "every community throughout the world has to write its own history of the living Jesus. . . . The account of the life of Christians in the world in which they live is a fifth gospel; it also belongs at the heart of Christology" (*Christ,* 18, 425).

Before taking up the question of a contemporary experience of Christian salvation, Schillebeeckx proposes four structural elements that must be taken into account in any current soteriology that is both rooted in the apostolic tradition and relevant to the present historical situation. The first of these is God and the divine history with human beings: God has self-revealed as a sovereignly free God of unconditional love, whose "cause" is the furthering of human well-being and happiness. "As Creator, God is the author of good and the antagonist of evil . . . the guarantor that human life has a positive and significant meaning" (*Christ,* 638). God's glory lies in the happiness and salvation of humankind.

Second, the nucleus of God's history with human beings is found in Jesus the Christ. The person of Jesus, in his life and above all in his death, in unbroken communion with God reveals the meaning and purpose of human existence, which has its source and fulfillment in the God of Jesus who is unconditional love.

Third, human history can be seen as discipleship: the gift of the Spirit, as the bond between Jesus and Christian communities, is both a share in Jesus' relationship with God and a mandate to continue the history of Jesus in the world. "Therefore we can only speak of the history of Jesus in terms of the story of the Christian community which follows Jesus" (*Christ,* 642).

Fourth, human history will have an eschatological consummation: definitive salvation belongs to the absolute freedom of God, who will bring the good begun in human history to its final consummation in a way that transcends all expectations. The way that the New Testament gives specific form to these four dimensions of the experience of grace provides a normative orientation for future generations of Christians. In fidelity to the apostolic tradition, the present generation must articulate its own theology of grace.

THE PRESENT SITUATION

The demands and responsibilities that confronted the first generations of Christians were of a different kind than those faced by Christians today. Hence, a conscious fidelity to the apostolic norm of the gospel necessitates a critical understanding of the urgent demands and responsibilities of people today, to whom the same good news is directed. At the beginning of the third millennium, it has become increasingly evident that science and technology, once regarded "as the historical liberators of humankind," now pose the greatest threat to survival. If used to further the well-being of people and the environment, science and technology can be in genuine service of human liberation.

> But in reality the sciences function as the instrument of human power, of rule over nature, power over society, power over human beings, both female and male. Science is the key to the military might of nations; science is the secret of their economic and social prosperity, in fact often to the detriment of others. Faith in verifiable knowledge and technical know-how as the only instrument for overcoming human disaster is a dominant factor in our present-day cultural world, regardless of whether we look to the north or the south, the west or the east (*Church,* 2–3).

The problem does not lie with science and technology per se, but with the nonscientific and absolute claims that human beings accord them.

In the process of secularization that began in the Enlightenment, science proclaimed that religion had become obsolete. As a consequence, ethics was separated from religion. Now, ironically, it is science and technology that press the religious and ethical questions. The potential for self-destruction that lays in the absolute and value-free claims of science raises a question: is a finite being "ever to be understood and liberated on its own terms? Does not the relationship to 'the transcendent' (he? she? it?) which men and women experience and live out belong with the unfathomable ground of our human creativity and therefore with the deepest and ultimate inspiration of all humanism?" (*Church,* 4) Indeed, in the current situation it is the responsibility of theology to safeguard belief and hope in a transcendent, liberating power that loves human beings and that will overcome evil. Moreover, a theology that is relevant to our times will be one that relates religion to the world and "is concerned for humankind and its humanity in its social and historical context" (4). Given the precariousness of the present situation, this concern carries an ethical mandate.

The risk of detaching the human person from ethics is a danger today, in the demand for a value-free ethics that rejects not only religion but also modern secularized standards based on a human foundation. As Schillebeeckx observes, value-free ethics are "setting our very humanity at risk" (*Christ,* 658). In his assessment, the situation of estrangement between ethics and religion means that Christianity must accord ethics a certain priority over religion. This is not at all to deny the reciprocal relationship between the two (see *Church,* 30–33, 91–99). Ethics are essentially concerned with the basic questions: what the human being is; how, therefore, people should live; and for what kind of humanity must we finally decide. These basic ethical questions are intrinsically connected with worldviews and religious options. In other words, the question of the final significance of human existence is implied in every question of ethical immediacy.

The concrete historical reality, however, is humankind in need. The fact is that the vast majority of the world's population suffers at the hands of the privileged few. Thus:

> [T]he specific starting point for ethics is . . . our indignation at human beings in concrete history who are everywhere injured: at the disorder both in the human heart and in society and its institutions. The actual threat and attack on the *humanum* . . . is a specifically ethical challenge and an ethical imperative, embedded in very specific negative experiences of contrast, of human misfortune and unhappiness, here and now (*Church,* 29).

The ethical imperative is not an abstract norm, but "an event which presents a challenge: our concrete history itself" (*Christ,* 659). In specific terms, this means that the "ethically good" is that which realizes the good and overcomes evil with respect to the actual situation. Put another way, "what is ethically good will emerge only from a praxis of liberation and reconciliation" (*Christ,* 659).

Furthermore, because of the vast expansion of scientific technology, the consequences of human activity no longer simply pertain to individuals and small groups. Regardless of the cultural and ethical traditions particular to them, all nations are facing the worldwide ethical problem. What is at stake is the future of humankind. On a global level, humankind is faced with the critical charge of deciding the future of the world and of humanity, while also determining humanity's meaning. What is needed is an ethics of worldwide responsibility that can guarantee not only human survival, but also meaningful human survival. This challenge, however, poses the further question of what is a meaningful humanity. Is there a universally valid view on this question?

The human person is a "being caught up in history." Human "nature is itself a history, a historical event, and is not simply given" (*Christ,* 732). That is to say, humanity is a future reality that can only be achieved in the course of human history. The dilemma of our history as one of suffering makes the task of realizing the *humanum* both pressing and perplexing. In matter of fact, the question of how to achieve a livable humanity has arisen from concrete conditions of alienation and woundedness of various kinds. "Salvation and humanity, being saved, integrity in a truly human and free way is in fact the theme of the whole of human history" (*Christ,* 732). Thus, people have become conscious of the fact that history is the place where salvation or human wholeness is decided or rejected; and the decision is an explicitly conscious one.

Given that the *humanum* is a future reality, Schillebeeckx contends that in directing the task of achieving a livable humanity, people have at their disposal no more than a set of anthropological constants. These constants present constitutive conditions that must always be presupposed in any human action, if humanity is to be livable. Schillebeeckx identifies six such constants, which he sees "as a kind of system of coordinates, the focal point of which is personal identity within social culture" (*Christ,* 733). In delineating these constitutive aspects of humanity, Schillebeeckx's expressed concern is "the creative establishment of specific norms for a better assessment of human worth and thus for human salvation" (*Christ,* 734).

The first anthropological constant is the relationship of human beings to their corporeality and, via this, to nature and the ecological environment. A balance must be maintained between the value of technology and that of aesthetic and enjoyable converse with nature. The second constant is the human being's essential relatedness to others. The structure of personal identity includes the element of being together, through which one shares oneself with others and is confirmed in existence and personhood.

The third essential dimension of humanity is the relationship of the person to social and institutional structures. As a dimension of personal identity, social structures deeply influence human inwardness and personhood. Although structures and institutions develop into an objective form of society, they do not exist independently of human reason and the human will to preserve them. In situations when they enslave and debase human beings rather than liberate and protect them, there exists an ethical demand to change such structures.

Schillebeeckx identifies the fourth anthropological constant as the conditioning of people by time and space. The abiding dialectical tension between nature and history means that there are forms of suffering and threats to human life and well-being that cannot be removed by technology and social intervention. Because of its historicity, human existence involves a task of understanding one's own situation and unmasking critically the meaninglessness that human beings bring about in their history. This means "that the presumption of adopting a standpoint outside historical action and thought is a danger to true humanity" (*Christ,* 739).

The fifth anthropological constant is the essential relationship between theory and practice. As a historical process of changing meanings, human culture needs permanence. A mutual relationship of theory and practice is the only responsible guarantee of a permanent culture that is increasingly worthy of the humanum.

The sixth dimension of humanity is religious and "parareligious" consciousness. This constant finds expression in a variety of different utopian conceptions of life that seek to give meaning and context to human existence in the world. In most utopias, the human person is understood as the active subject of history, without being the all-controlling principle that is responsible for the whole of history and its final outcome. This principle is called fate by some, evolution by others, and humankind by yet others. For the religious person, this is the living God. A utopian view "is always a form of faith, in the sense of a 'utopia' which cannot be scientifically demonstrated, or at least can never be completely rationalized" (*Christ,* 741). Schillebeeckx asserts that in this way "faith" is an anthropological constant throughout human history, a constant without which humane and livable human life and action become impossible.

Because human culture is an irreducible synthesis of the six anthropological constants, the synthesis itself is a constant. This synthesis constitutes the reality that heals human beings and brings them salvation. The six constants mutually influence one another. They delineate the basic form of human existence and hold one another in balance. Undervaluation of one of these dimensions threatens the whole, thereby damaging human society and culture. The anthropological constants, however, do no more than present constitutive conditions for a livable humanity. Specific norms must be worked out on the basis of these values: the task of creating such norms is an imperative that confronts human beings here and now. Moreover, there will always be pluralism in the area of specific norms, even though the same basic values are recognized. Learning to live with pluralism is one of the tasks of a livable modern humanity. Nevertheless, if ethical norms are to be viable, they must be capable of being tested in valid intersubjective discussion. This holds even if the basic inspiration comes from a religious belief.

CHRISTIAN SALVATION

The problem of the relationship between the ethics of human liberation and the grace of redemption is of central concern for a contemporary mediation of Christian salvation. There is ample evidence that a widespread pluralism exists in respect to this question. The relevance of the Christian gospel for a social and political world order is neither clear nor self-evident. In a first move toward offering a solution to the problem, Schillebeeckx affirms the dialectical relationship between interior and social freedom, as well as between religious traditions and the sociohistorical circumstances in which they originate and develop.

True liberation or salvation is overcoming all personal and social forms of alienation. It is the "being-in-wholeness" of the person and history. To the extent that history liberates men and women for true humanity, it is "God's saving history, and is so independently of our awareness of this gracious structure of salvation, but not without the occurrence of intentional human liberation" (*Church,* 10). Moreover, if people are to grasp what Christians mean by salvation, they must have some experience of human liberation. It is only in a history in which people are liberated for true humanity that God can self-reveal as salvation of and for men and women.

> [W]here human good is furthered and evil is challenged in the human interest, then through this historical practice the being of God—God as salvation for men and women, the ground for universal hope—is also established and men and women also appropriate God's salvation—in and through acts of love. Human history, the social life of human beings, is the place where the cause of salvation or disaster is decided on (*Church,* 12–13).

The decisive factor is whether we stand in solidarity with the suffering humanum or are on the side of the oppressors. Schillebeeckx therefore raises the question "whether the freedom of the children of God is not pointed towards a social liberation as an integral ingredient of eschatological salvation from God. In other words, the question whether Christian freedom or redemption is not directed towards political and social liberation as a condition of its own possibility" (*Christ,* 745).

It is characteristic of the structure of the development of Christian faith that Christians uncover latent dimensions in their tradition as a result of stimuli introduced by sociocultural circumstances. Although the gospel of Jesus is an inclusive message of freedom and love for all people, the consequences of this "good news" are only gradually revealed in the ongoing development of human consciousness. It is quite possible, then, that at a particular historical moment, an emancipatory process of liberation can become a necessary demand of historically situated Christian love. Nevertheless, because it is precisely in their service to God that religions are also a service to human beings and the world, it is necessary that Christians investigate the particular religious and critical force of their solidarity with emancipation movements. At issue here is whether believers and nonbelievers simply do the same thing under different names, or whether the Christian gospel gives a service to the world that is specifically religious.

Whereas religion must draw on an experience of God in order to be of service to the world, Western scientific technology has created sociocultural conditions in which belief in God is no longer simply taken for granted. On the one hand, a highly scientific and technological experience in Western societies has made faith more difficult than in the past. On the other hand, the enormity and extent of innocent human suffering in the past century have challenged belief in the presence of a divine omnipotence in human history. If men and women can nowhere experience God's presence and saving power at work, belief in God "is sheer ideology, a loose statement the meaning of which cannot be verified in any way" (*Church,* 88).

But Schillebeeckx posits the experience of creatureliness as the foundation of all religious awareness. By this he means "an experience of ourselves, others and the world in which we feel as a norm something which transcends at least our arbitrary control of ourselves" (*Christ,* 811). It is an experience of givenness that is the root of all religion, as a mediated immediate relationship with God. "Mediated immediacy" concerns the unique relationship between finite beings and the infinite God who is absolute origin. Whereas the term *immediacy* refers to the divine manner of the real presence of the creator to the creature, *mediated* describes the mode in which people encounter the divine presence. God is directly and creatively present in the creature. In this case, mediation does not destroy immediacy but produces it. All that is not God derives the totality of its existence and activity from the creator, who, as absolute freedom, transcends all things through interiority. This means that the living God is the depth dimension of all reality. The fundamental medium of the creator is creation. The relationship between the infinite creator and the finite creature are mediated through an encounter with the world, human history, and human beings.

The structure of the presence of God as mediated immediacy implies that the human response to God has a similar structure of mediation. In other words, although religion cannot be reduced to cohumanity and sociopolitical concerns, it cannot do without this mediation. God's saving power never breaks in from outside human history. Rather, God's grace is present in the structure of historical human experience and praxis. Because of the constitutive relationship between personal identity and the social structures that provide freedom, sociopolitical improvements form an integral part of what is experienced as the grace of God. "Here the divine reality proves itself to be a reality, as the one who wills good and opposes evil, the liberator from alienation" (*Christ,* 814). It follows that wherever human liberation is possible, it remains a universal human task in the name of God. "We cannot shift on to God what is our task in the world, because of the unsurpassable boundary (on our side) between the finite and the infinite" (*Church,* 231).

In creating human beings with finite free will, God entrusts creation and human history to human beings. In so doing, "God voluntarily renounces power," and "in this world becomes 'defenceless' and vulnerable . . . sin in the world of creation in fact renders the Creator defenceless in the extreme." Although the human choice to break communion with God and to refuse human solidarity "puts limits on God's power," God remains "present in redemption and forgiveness. . . . In other words, this limit is not God's limit but our limit: the limit of finitude and above all our free sinfulness. But God is also present to save beyond this limit, if necessary as the final judge" (*Church,* 90–91; see also 120, 125–26, 128). A final healing of the division in human existence in the world can only be the consequence of an absolute freedom and creative love that embraces the whole of reality.

Consequently, all hope for the future based on human creativity must be taken up into a hope founded on God's own saving creativity. "For believers, this surplus of hope over and above what is constantly realized in history is grounded in what they call God's creation-for-his-saving-purposes," that is, God's absolute presence in all of creation (*Church,* 99). A critical religious consciousness recognizes the manifestation of God's saving nearness in any action that promotes human well-being, while, at the same time, it opposes a complete identification of human salvation with any given or anticipated sociopolitical form. All human liberation stands under the divine proviso. The history of redemption can neither be identified with nor detached from the history of emancipation. Christian salvation is a historical mediation of God's saving immediacy. As such, it includes both mystical-contemplative and sociopolitical dimensions.

Schillebeeckx calls the fundamental awareness of God's mediated-but-nevertheless-real immediacy the mystical aspect of belief in God. This mystical depth in which the immediacy of God is the essential element can be experienced in both positive and negative ways. There are positive disclosure experiences of the givenness and goodness of life, in which there occurs a change in perception from the mediating to the mediated, that is, God's presence. Schillebeeckx understands "explicit prayer" as a person's effort to see this immediacy. Immediacy can also be experienced as a "dark night," that is, as "a nothingness of fullness":

God's presence as a pure experience of faith, communicated in the mediation of extreme negativity. Faith is certainly more than a theoretical conviction when it persists even when "every empirical foundation and every guarantee have been removed and one weeps over the fiasco of one's life" (*Christ,* 815).

The mediation of God's presence in negative experience is particularly relevant to contemporary circumstances and awareness. Human beings have created and perpetuated a history that is dark with suffering and oppression. Moreover, the reality of the history of human suffering continues in spite of the progress of emancipation and in spite of God's redemptive action in Jesus. The fact that both redemption and emancipation are found within conditions of suffering gives an inner tension to any understanding of redemption and any attempt at self-liberation.

Human suffering, however, also has a productive and critical epistemological value. As an experience of contrast, suffering includes characteristics of both contemplative and practical forms of knowledge. On the one hand, although in the form of negative experience, suffering comes upon one in a way that is similar to the passive structure of positive contemplative experiences. On the other hand, under the aspect of critical negativity, the reality of suffering resists the passivity of the contemplative dimension in a way that leads to a possible action that will overcome both suffering and its causes. As an experience of contrast, suffering indirectly implies an awareness of the possible positive significance of the humanum. It follows that action to overcome suffering is possible only through an implicit anticipation of a potential universal significance to come. Thus, the particular productive and critical epistemological value of the experience of contrast in suffering is a knowledge that looks for and opens up the future. Schillebeeckx concludes that in the present historical circumstances, contemplation and action can only be connected through the history of suffering and the ethical awareness that comes to birth in it.

The particular story of Jesus of Nazareth is part of the history of accumulated human suffering. Jesus' message of the unconditional love of God and corresponding praxis of solidarity with socioreligious outcasts met in his day with violent opposition and rejection. "Like God, Jesus identifies himself par excellence with the outcast and rejected men and women, the unholy, so that he too himself finally becomes the one who is rejected and outcast." Because of the continuity between Jesus' praxis of the kingdom and his death, "the saving significance of Jesus finds its climax in the crucifixion and does not lie in the crucifixion taken in isolation" (*Church,* 124). Jesus' suffering and death in solidarity with the rejected and broken of the world give unconditional validity to his message and praxis: God is irrevocably present as salvation for men and women, even in situations of extreme negativity. The notion of God's saving immediacy in the mediation of extreme negativity is central to Schillebeeckx's understanding of the saving significance of the death of Jesus. The redemptive force of this death does not lie with suffering and the negativity of failure as such, but with unbroken communion and solidarity to the point of death.

In the radical alienation of suffering and death, Jesus lives out the meaning of God's rule as sovereignly free but in total solidarity with people. "This means that God determines in absolute freedom, down the ages, who and how he wills to be in his deepest being, namely a God of men and women, an ally in our suffering and our absurdity, and also an ally in the good that we do" (*Church,* 126).

As the correction of the negativity of death, Schillebeeckx understands the resurrection as an event that is both new and different from Jesus' suffering and death. Yet this does not mean that he views the resurrection as an extrinsic addition. He cautions against detaching the significance of the resurrection from the career of Jesus, which includes his death. In the sense that God's saving power was already at work in Jesus' proclamation and praxis of the kingdom in which his death shares, his career is a historical anticipation of his resurrection. As Schillebeeckx reminds us, "we cannot detach the defencelessness of Jesus on the cross from the free power and the positivity which revealed itself in his actual career of solidarity with oppressed men and women on the basis of an absolute trust in God." On the cross God is absolutely present with Jesus, but this presence is "without the misuse of power" (*Church,* 127–28). God expresses the divine power over evil in the defenselessness of the suffering death of Jesus, to give human beings the space to be themselves in solidarity with victims of injustice. God and Jesus are not thwarted by suffering and death.

The surmounting of death in the resurrection is God's definitive acceptance, validation, and final fulfillment of the earthly life of Jesus. It is precisely in this way that the cross of Jesus acquires a productive and critical force in the dimension of human history. In spite of the disruption caused by the fatal rejection of Jesus' person and message, there is continuity between the hidden dimension of what took place on the cross and its manifestation in the resurrection, namely, the living and unbroken communion between Jesus and God. In the death and resurrection of Jesus, the human rejection of God's offer of salvation and the persistence of this offer extended in the risen Jesus meet each other. "Through the resurrection, God actually breaks that rejection of definitive salvation" (*Jesus,* 641). God's living presence is an "undeserved abundance" of meaning stronger and more penetrating than the abundance of nonmeaning that is the ultimate enemy: death. Schillebeeckx describes God's triumph over death as the "eternally new event" of God's divinity, which brings earthly life to fulfillment.

The living God who is the future of human history is in the risen Jesus, the presence of the future. In this way, Christian faith finds in Jesus the promise and the possibility that human history can be realized as a history of salvation. The promise of the eschatological future, anticipated in Jesus' career unto death on the cross, "is confirmed by his resurrection from the dead by God as in fact a praxis of the kingdom of God: salvation for all men and women" (*Church,* 176). For Schillebeeckx, Jesus has universal significance precisely because he reveals the true identity of the one God and in and through the disclosure of true humanity. In his career and praxis, Jesus of Nazareth "points essentially to God and to the coming of the kingdom of God for which he himself gave his life. . . . For Jesus, God's cause—the kingdom of God as salvation for men and women—is more important than his own life" (*Church,* 121).

Likewise, "the risen Jesus of Nazareth continues to point to God beyond himself. . . . God is absolute, but no single religion is absolute" (*Church,* 166). As definitive revelation of the one God who is redeemer of all, Jesus has unique and universal, but not absolute, significance. The "distinctive and unique feature of Christianity is that it finds the life and being of God" manifested in the historical, and thus limited, particularity of Jesus of Nazareth. Jesus is "indeed a 'unique' but nevertheless 'contingent'. . . manifestation of the gift of salvation from God for all men and women" (*Church,* 165).

The saving significance of Jesus becomes effective in history through his followers. Jesus was convinced of an essential connection between his proclamation and praxis and the coming of the kingdom of God as salvation for men and women. Likewise, "the consequent faith conviction of his followers that the mission of Jesus has a definitive, eschatological and universal significance . . . necessitates a continuation of Jesus' earthly mission by his disciples beyond the limited time of his earthly life. . . . The fact is that becoming a disciple of Jesus is an essential element of his message . . . the 'church' is essentially discipleship of Jesus" (*Church,* 155).

The abiding presence of the Spirit of the risen Jesus puts the community of disciples into contact with Jesus' praxis of the kingdom. *Pneuma* and *anamnesis:* the living memory of Jesus' career, handed on in the living tradition of the church, and the abiding presence of the Spirit in the church community. As the living *memoria passionis Christi,* Christians must "go the way of Jesus," that is, reject oppressive powers in a praxis of solidarity with the poor and oppressed of the world, even to the extent that this commitment includes the *via crucis,* the way of the cross. It is only in this way that redemption through Jesus has concrete universal significance, that the uniqueness and distinctiveness of Christianity has meaning and intelligibility. The universality of the Christian gospel is a task to be realized in specific historical situations.

Schillebeeckx sees the present situation of structural world poverty as the current context in which the challenge of the Christian gospel assumes a specific social dimension. To the extent that the church opts for the poor, it has a universal significance that includes both the poor and the rich, in that the gospel's predilection for the poor and oppressed is at the same time a judgment on oppressive power structures and, thus, a call to conversion. A praxis of liberating the humanum for good and true humanity through the creation of a just world order is an essential part of the universality of Christian faith, "and this is par excellence a non-discriminatory universality" (*Church,* 170).

Given the ambiguity of human history as a mixture of sense and nonsense, belief in a universal meaning of history only validates itself in a course of action that tries to overcome suffering, on the strength of the religious conviction that things can be otherwise. The thematization of universal meaning can be achieved meaningfully only with a practical-critical intention that, through historical commitment, attempts to remove meaninglessness from human history step by step. That is to say, the Christian gospel will be critically productive, credible, and capable of offering hope to the world only if it is a consistent praxis that gives concrete form to a living communion with God.

The current environmental crisis, which is fundamentally related to unbridled economic gain, has raised the question whether the Christian understanding of the kingdom of God includes the material milieu. With inorganic and organic creatures, human beings share in " one creation." While there is "something in human beings that cannot be reduced to nature," they and nature are interrelated. In contrast to the rest of creation, "human beings have a somatic spiritual awareness, something transcendent, as a result of which they can recall their relationship with God" (*Church,* 238). Consequently, they have been entrusted with creation as a task to be achieved. On the basis of the environmental crisis, human stewardship is subject to ethical values and norms. "In and through human action it must become clear that God wills salvation through humankind for all . . . creation" (*Church,* 245).

Definitive salvation transcends present experience. Although everything is decided in human history, the last word is not with history but with the living God, whose absolute presence supports finitude. The possible despair that can be caused by the contingency and woundedness of existence is taken up and transcended by the inexhaustible abundance of God. Divine possibilities cannot be limited to earthly expectations and achievements. Nevertheless, partial salvation is realized whenever and wherever the goodness of creation is confirmed and furthered. In this way, human love supported by absolute love becomes the sacrament and promise of God's redemptive love offered to the whole of God's creation. "The challenging call from God is thus: 'Come, my dear people, you are not alone'" (*Church,* 246).

SUGGESTIONS FOR FURTHER READING

Schillebeeckx's investigation of the New Testament theology of the experience of grace is found in part 2 of *Christ: The Experience of Jesus As Lord* (New York: Crossroad, 1980). This lengthy study is followed in part 3 by a concluding synthesis in which Schillebeeckx proposes four structural elements that he sees as indispensable for a contemporary theology of grace. Pertinent passages from this material are found in part 4 of *The Schillebeeckx Reader* (Robert J. Schreiter, ed. New York:

Crossroad, 1984). While he directly addresses the question of a contemporary soteriology in part 4 of *Christ* and in *Church: The Human Story of God* (New York: Crossroad, 1990), especially chapters 1, 2, 3, and the epilogue, Schillebeeckx anticipates issues pertinent to this undertaking in part 4 of *Jesus:An Experiment in Christology* (New York: Seabury, 1979). Significant selections from *Jesus, Christ,* and *Interim Report on the Books "Jesus" and "Christ"* (New York: Crossroad, 1980) are found in part 3 of *The Schillebeeckx Reader.* A number of homilies in *God Among Us: The Gospel Proclaimed* (New York: Crossroad, 1983) highlight aspects of Schillebeeckx's developing soteriology. See in particular "I Believe in Eternal Life," "Belief in a New Heaven and a New Earth," and "Belief in Jesus As Salvation for the Outcast." God's salvation in Jesus is discussed in connection with creation and the biblical notion of the kingdom in "Kingdom of God: Creation and Salvation," in *Interim Report.* See also "I Believe in God, Creator of Heaven and Earth" and "I Believe in the Man Jesus: The Christ, the Only Beloved Son, Our Lord," in *God Among Us.* Another book that examines issues and questions pertinent to a contemporary praxis of salvation is *On Christian Faith:The Spiritual, Ethical, and Political Dimensions* (New York: Crossroad, 1987). See especially "Who or What Brings Salvation to Men and Women? The World and God," and "Jesus As the Question of Men and Women to God: Mysticism, Ethics and Politics."

For Schillebeeckx's recent discussion of Jesus as universal, but not absolute, savior, see *Church,* chapter 3; and "The Religious and the Human Ecumene," in Marc H. Ellis and Otto Maduro, eds., *The Future of Liberation Theology: Essays in Honor of Gustavo Gutierrez* (Maryknoll: Orbis, 1989), 177–88 (also in *The Language of Faith: Essays on Jesus, Theology, and the Church,* Maryknoll, N.Y.: Orbis, 1995, 249–64).

7

Spirituality

Donald J. Goergen

FOR EDWARD SCHILLEBEECKX, spirituality is not just one aspect of human life that can be singled out for particular attention. Rather, he says, for Christians spirituality is the whole of human life interpreted from the perspective of authentic Christian praxis. Although all of Schillebeeckx's works can be construed as a theology of Christian praxis, some of them focus more specifically on Christian praxis or on the conventional theme of the spiritual life.

Schillebeeckx has been influenced by the Dominican tradition in spirituality, of which he himself is both an exponent and also "a new moment." He has written on Dominic, Albert the Great, Thomas Aquinas, and others. He has acknowledged the influence of modern Dominicans, particularly Marie-Dominique Chenu, who probably more than anyone else was Schillebeeckx's inspiration. Chenu guided his doctoral dissertation on the sacraments, and it was Chenu who introduced the phrase "signs of the times" into modern Catholic theology. A key to understanding Schillebeeckx's spirituality is the foundational idea of *présence au monde.* The term originated with the Dominican Henri Lacordaire. It was developed by Chenu, had its influence at the Second Vatican Council, and has been consciously acknowledged by Schillebeeckx as influential in his own hermeneutical project. *Présence au monde* is the grace of understanding deeply one's own times and the capacity to respond accordingly.

For Schillebeeckx, a definitive, final exposition of Christian spirituality cannot be given, since we ourselves are part of the Christian story, and it has not thus come to a close. The present provides a new moment in the history of Christian spirituality. A theology of Christian spirituality must begin with the story of Jesus, and brings that story up to date with one's own times. Any particular Christian spirituality is valid only as a specific modality of "following after Jesus," and only insofar as it has a living relationship to the present. Schillebeeckx's theology can be seen as a bridge between an interpreted historical past and the situation in the world and church today.

Foundational to Schillebeeckx's studies of Jesus, to his reflections on ministry and preaching, to his understanding of church and hermeneutics are, as Lacordaire put it, the twofold *présence à Dieu* and *présence au monde.* This framework for understanding the spiritual life goes back to Dominic himself, who instructed his own followers to speak only to God or about God. Schillebeeckx indicates his interiorization of this in one of his homilies: "Religious life should be a *pointer to God.* . . . [I]t is towards that *speaking to* and *about* God that the Dominican life is directed" (*For the Sake of the Gospel,* 23).

In Schillebeeckx's theology, Christian spirituality is a particular way of being human. It cannot be imposed from the outside, or enforced. It never means living "only for God," with little concern for others or our history. Following Jesus can never be a mere repetition of some earlier form of Christian spirituality. Rather, it is Christian creativity in a historical context. Spirituality is always a new adventure, with Abraham and Sarah as models: "They set out on a journey, not knowing where they were going" (Heb 11:8).

There are two indissoluble elements in Christian praxis: interiority and exteriority, and they belong together; either becomes false if broken away from the other. Spirituality can never be reduced to the inner life and a circle of friends. Such a false spirituality becomes asocial, apolitical, ahistorical, and noncontextual. Christian spirituality is concerned with what it means to be human and, thus, with the whole social, political, economic, and ecological context in which human life is shaped.

Christians are aware that authentic mystical forces will be set free for humanity and greater justice only through an active participation in history. But just as Christian spirituality is not purely mystical inwardness, neither is it simply and only political and social involvement. This "new" spirituality, both contextual and political, is a reflection of Jesus himself, who identified himself with God's concern and identified God's concern with humanity. Spirituality is about God's concern for human beings.

THE EXPERIENCE OF GOD AS ABBA

For Schillebeeckx, the center of Jesus' spirituality lies in his experience of God, the "Abba experience." With a few exceptions, Abba does not occur as a way of addressing God in prayer in the Judaism of Jesus'time. Yet this seems to have been Jesus' habitual way of praying (Mk 14:36). Jesus' way of addressing God in prayer was unconventional, intimate, familial, and indicative of a religious experience of deep intimacy with God that was unique. Jesus' was an experience of God as caring and as offering a future to humanity, a God who chose to be identified with the cause of humankind, a God who gave people hope. On the basis of his experience of intimacy with God, "Jesus could bring people the message of a hope which is not to be derived from our world history" (*God Among Us*, 88).

Although Jesus' own personal experience of God was unique, his relationship with God was something he envisioned for his disciples. Jesus wanted those who followed after him to have the same relationship with God. The distinction in the fourth gospel between "my Father and your Father" (Jn 20:17) manifests postresurrection Christian theology. Schillebeeckx maintains a distinction between Jesus' experience of God and his disciples' experiences, but not between Jesus' intimate relationship with God and that into which he invited his disciples.

The Abba experience for Christians is, then,one of God as personal. God challenges and talks with human beings, and is even confrontational. In his own spiritual life, Schillebeeckx acknowledges speaking personally to God as to a friend. "If you don't talk to God first, you can't talk about him" (*God Is New Each Moment*, 125). This latter insight reflects not only Schillebeeckx's Jesus research, but also his own appropriation of Dominic's aforementioned exhortation to "speak only to God or about God."

At the foundation of spirituality, for Schillebeeckx, is Jesus, who is a "parable of God and paradigm of humanity" (*Jesus*, 626). Through Jesus, we come to know both God and the human being. Thus, the secret and source of our own life and ministry must be our own experience of God as one who cares for us and for humankind, our own continuing intimacy with God in prayer, our own solidarity with God and experience of God as love.

Grace permeates Schillebeeckx's writings, from his early reflection on Christ as the primordial sacrament in *Christ The Sacrament of the Encounter with God* (1963), through the second volume of his project in christology, *Christ* (1980), to the later works on ministry, *Ministry* (1981) and *The Church with a Human Face* (1985). All his writings on christology, the church, sacraments, ministry, and spirituality are an unfolding of a theology of grace, of God as the one who saves, and of Jesus Christ as the one through whom salvation is revealed.

Grace in the New Testament means the benevolent, free, merciful, and sovereign love of God for humanity, God's bending toward the human, and God's presence to humankind. God is always the one who loves humanity. The whole of the New Testament affirms that Jesus of Nazareth is the supreme sign of this grace and love. Jesus' life and love, to the point of death, reveal God as being in solidarity with people, especially with those who suffer and are victims of injustice. "God's name is 'solidarity with my people.' God's own honor lies in the happiness and salvation of humanity" (*Christ*, 639). God is revealed as a God of human beings.

Our relationship with God, grace, renews and recreates us at the deepest level of our self-identity. Grace is a new possibility for human life, a new mode of human existence. It is a new way of life offered us by God, a call to live community with God and others. This understanding of grace undergirds two typical ways in which Schillebeeckx speaks about God: as concerned for humanity, and as new each moment. The chief concern of God is for humankind. God loves us, and our concerns are God's concerns. Already in 1972, Schillebeeckx spoke about God in this way: "In the life of Jesus it became manifest that his God was a God who is concerned for human beings" (*God Among Us*, 132).

This way of speaking about God is so prominent in Schillebeeckx's writings that it is hard to think of any insight more central. God's rule is centered on the well-being of humankind (see *Jesus*, 237, 239, 240, 241, 652). The connecting link between God and humanity is Jesus. Jesus' cause is God's cause (Jesus' Abba experience), and God's cause is the cause of humanity (the proclamation of the reign of God). "For Jesus, his mystical Abba experience is the source of his prophetic activity" (*Church*, 181).

This emphasis keeps recurring in Schillebeeckx's essays and homilies. In 1978, he described God's glory as "the happiness and the well-being of humankind in the world" (*God Among Us*, 94). In 1979 he wrote, "I am quite clear that to take the part of those in trouble means to follow God himself, God as he has shown his deepest sympathy with human beings in Jesus" (*God Among Us*, 114). This way of speaking continues throughout his writings in the eighties (see *God Among Us*, 174, 197, 82). In 1989, in *Church: The Human Story of God*, the third volume of his trilogy, Schillebeeckx even emphasized a theme that had been emerging among other theologians of the "defenselessness" and "vulnerability" of God, of God's power as a power of love (90). In the late 1980s and since, however, Schillebeeckx has also emphasized that "God is not just a God of human beings" (236, see also 234–46), for there is a unity to all of God's creation. God is a God of creation, a graced creation, and there is more to creation than humanity alone. There is a cosmic dimension to God's reign. God, creation, and humankind all stand together at the center of the Christian life, whose stories are interwoven and inseparable.

In addition to the God whose cause is the cause of human beings, Schillebeeckx's God is a constant source of "new possibilities." On both counts God is the source of hope. New possibilities play a central role in Schillebeeckx's spirituality. The birth of a child is the beginning of a new possibility in our history. This is the basis for belief in eternal life as well: there is no end to the possibilities with which God can surprise us. The future of history remains open. God is always caring and ever new.

The gospel itself can only be handed on through new experiences of it. Schillebeeckx's understanding of tradition is that it is "a living gospel," always new, receptive to those new moments that keep it ever alive, those moments of our own contemporary experience that are something of "a fifth gospel." Tradition calls for new experiences, if it is to be handed on as a living reality (see chapter 4).

> *Becoming* a Christian . . . means having one's own life story inscribed in the family story of the Christian community so that as a result one's own life story takes on a new, "converted," orientation and at the same time continues the thread of the Christian story in its own way. Insofar as it is truly Christian, action of this kind makes our own life part of a living gospel, a "fifth" gospel (*God Among Us*, 127).

"In the end we have here the convergence of two stories, the story of the gospel tradition of faith and the story of our personal and social life which in the best instances has itself as it were become 'gospel': a fifth or umpteenth gospel" (*Church*, 34). Our own new experiences of God are part of the living tradition of the gospel that draws us into following after Jesus and the praxis of the reign of God. God as "ever new," "a living gospel," experiencing God and the gospel, our stories being part of the Christian story, hope from the future—all of these are repeated themes in Schillebeeckx's writings.

FOLLOWING AFTER JESUS

Schillebeeckx's spirituality comprises not only the experience of intimacy with God, but also a "following after Jesus." Jesus, whose very own spirituality is thoroughly Jewish, becomes himself the cornerstone of a spirituality for those who follow him—both before his resurrection and throughout the centuries since. Following after Jesus consists in what Schillebeeckx frequently refers to as "the praxis of the reign of God." Indeed, one can say that spirituality for Schillebeeckx is praxis, and specifically orthopraxis, which Schillebeeckx defines as action in accord with the reign of God, or action on behalf of humankind. Orthopraxis, rooted in one's experience of God, is a following of the praxis of Jesus.

Orthopraxis implies an essential relationship between theory and practice. We cannot have one without the other. Schillebeeckx was already insisting upon this in the late 1960s. The basic problem of theology is not that of the relationship between the past (scripture and tradition) and the present, but rather that of the relationship between theory and practice. How theory manifests itself in praxis is a critical test of the theory. Theology stands under the critical primacy of praxis. The preoccupation with orthopraxis raises the question of how to bridge the gulf between theory and practice. The earthly Jesus'argument with religious authorities was not over a lack of orthodoxy, but over an attitude in which theory and practice had drifted apart, and they had lost sight of God's solidarity with the people. Jesus' refusal to sanction an orthodoxy separated from orthopraxis was the foundation of his critique of Sabbath observance, the Law, and the Temple.

If Christian life or following after Jesus comes down to the praxis of the reign of God, in what does such praxis consist? Only a theology of Jesus reveals this; hence Schillebeeckx's extensive Jesus research. The praxis of the reign of God is manifest in Jesus' proclamation of God's forgiveness and love, in Jesus' healings, in Jesus' table fellowship with outcasts and sinners, in Jesus' approach to the Law, and in his enigmatic parables.

Jesus not only told parables, he was a parable, one of God in solidarity with people. Jesus' sharing table with the disreputable is symbolic or parabolic action—the praxis of a God whose cause is humanity. Jesus did not oppose Torah or Law; rather, he interpreted the Law in a way that centered on human well-being. He insisted that the two great commandments of love of God and love of neighbor were inseparable; they took priority over and relativized cultic and ritual regulations (*Jesus*, 253–54). As there must be an integral link between theology and practice, so there is an integral link between one's human experience of God and the praxis of the reign of God.

Another fact about Jesus is that he attracted to himself disciples and companions—those who went after him—and that he sent some of them forth to proclaim and practice the coming of God. The praxis of Jesus became that of his disciples, of the post-Easter communities that came together in his name, and eventually of the church. This orthopraxis of Jesus is the criterion by means of which a community or church can name itself Christian. The praxis of the reign of God is constitutive of the nature of the church. "The living community is the only real reliquary of Jesus" (*Christ*, 641), for it is in the living community where the praxis of God is continued.

Schillebeeckx's theology is very clearly grounded in human experience, both of God and of suffering, of a "no" to the world as it is and an "open yes" to hope. We have already reflected upon the experience of God. This is God as "pure positivity," who promotes all that is good and opposes all that is evil (see chapter 3). As human beings, however, we also have the experience of suffering, even an excess of suffering and evil, "a barbarous excess which resists all explanation and interpretation" (*God Among Us*, 149). Theology reflects on our human experience of God, and the purely positive existence that God wills for humanity as a contrast to this history of human suffering.

What are we to make of this contrast between the negativity in our world and the positivity of God? Jesus' own experience of the radical contrast had a constructive moment to it, for the negative contrast experience offers a moment of critical awareness. The experience of contrast is at the basis of Jesus' prophetic self-awareness. "Jesus' interpretation of suffering is connected with his deep personal relationship with God, the heart of his life. God and suffering are diametrically opposed; when God appears, evil and suffering have to yield" (*Christ*, 695). "One positive element in this fundamental experience of contrast is invincible human indignation at injustice and innocent suffering" (*For the Sake of the Gospel*, 47). The experience of contrast yields a critique of the history of suffering and holds forth hope for the future.

The prophet, the theologian, the Christian, all who follow after Jesus must have a "critical memory" of this history of human suffering. Although the excess of suffering is an incomprehensible mystery for all, it becomes especially problematic for the person who believes in God. The history of religion and the history of Christian theology have struggled with this memory. One can recall Israel's struggle with suffering and Israel's protest against it, the Hindu insight that each religion is a point of reference pointing to the truth, the Buddhist starting point with the fact of suffering, and even the Enlightenment effort to confront suffering rationally as a problem. Yet in humankind's history, there has never been a successful rational theory to account for all suffering (which is either trivialized or reduced to a particular form).

Since the powers of human explanation fail when they come up against the history and reality of human suffering, the only meaningful response to this is resistance. Thus we come back to orthopraxis. In practice, the people of God must refuse to allow evil the right to exist, for God is the author of good and the opponent of evil. For the person of faith, then, the critical memory of human suffering is a contrast experience that results in hope. The God of Jesus wants humanity's salvation and a victory over suffering. Christianity, however, does not attempt to explain suffering. Followers of Jesus "do not *argue* against suffering, but tell a *story*" (*Christ*, 698), and that story is the story of Jesus: the life, suffering, death, and resurrection of Jesus. Jesus bore witness to a certainty he felt regarding the salvation given by God, that the "making whole" of human life is possible. Faith in Jesus makes it possible to affirm both evil and suffering, and also salvation or a final good in a way that allows us to give the last word to well-being and goodness, "because the Father is greater than all our suffering and grief and greater than our inability to experience the deepest reality as in the end a trustworthy gift" (*Jesus*, 625).

Given the awareness of the history of human suffering, those who follow Jesus necessarily involve themselves in the struggle for justice. Christian spirituality seeks a radical integration of the themes of eschatological salvation and human liberation—one theme not to be neglected at the expense of the other, for God's very own foremost concern is humankind.

POLITICAL HOLINESS

Christian love and holiness are, therefore, necessarily a "political love" and a "political holiness." In the struggle against injustice, the believer is not only responding to the prior grace and experience of God, but also continues to experience the God of Jesus. This political form of love of neighbor is an urgent form of contemporary holiness.

Christianity does not explain suffering. It neither condones injustice nor rationalizes the existing social order. Although Christian history gave rise to a "mysticism of suffering" that emphasized one's personal suffering and in which the cross became a symbol for the legitimization of social abuses, political holiness recognizes Jesus' definition of holiness, which was grounded in his understanding of God. Christian holiness does not legitimate but opposes injustice, because our very understanding of God is at stake.

For Schillebeeckx, in Christian life there is both a political and a mystical dimension. This integral relationship between mysticism and politics, neither of which can be discounted, is rooted in Jesus, who is both parable of God and paradigm of humanity. Both mysticism and politics have the same source: the experience of contrast between God and history, the story of a suffering humanity.

For the follower of Jesus, the spiritual life cannot be reduced to "personal holiness" alone. Nor can social and political life be reduced to their social and political components alone. For Schillebeeckx, "mysticism" is an intense form of the experience of God. "Politics" is an intense form of social engagement, not restricted to professional politicians. Politics without prayer or mysticism becomes barbaric; mysticism without political love becomes sentimental interiority. Christian involvement in the world is a religious praxis, rooted in a particular interpretation of the world, drawing upon the experience of the holy. "Christian politics" is both specifically religious and practically effective, making impossible an idealization of any particular form of the world and, at the same time, forbidding escapism from the world.

Moses, a political leader who brought his people liberation, was a mystic "who spoke to God face to face." For Jesus, the mystical experience of God was the heart and soul of his mission on behalf of the poor. True mysticism has its own intrinsic value, which cannot be located only in its social or political consequences, although it always does have such consequences. Mysticism can become either a flight into inwardness without social awareness or a prophetic mysticism. "Bourgeois religion" attempts to separate religion and politics, salvation and liberation, whereas authentic Christian salvation implies wholeness. True mystics are prophetic, and true prophets are mystical.

Christian life and spirituality are intimately tied up with one's concept of salvation, one of Schillebeeckx's enduring concerns. "Salvation means being whole" (*Christ*, 717), and salvation becomes less than whole if one emphasizes only one dimension of the human—whether this be the sociopolitical or the personal. Social liberation is an integral ingredient of the eschatological salvation offered by God. "Personal salvation" is only partial. Likewise, if sociopolitical liberation claims to be total, it becomes a new form of servitude. Human liberation and Christian redemption are not alternatives, but are both constitutive elements of Christian hope.

The process of liberation, even without being specifically Christian, can be a form of Christian love. In political questions, faith ought not play too large or too small a role. Christian faith is politically relevant, yet it does not absolutize any political system. The gospel moves Christians toward political action, yet does not of itself present us directly with a specific program.

The mystical dimension of faith itself can take the form of political love. There can be no dualism between interiority and exteriority, between love of God and love of neighbor; nor can one be subordinated to the other. "Love of humanity as a disinterested commitment for fellow human beings is at the same time the hallmark of the truth of love towards God" (*On Christian Faith*, 70). Mysticism is possible not only in silence and in contemplation, but also in prophetic struggle. At the same time, the active mystic still needs moments of explicit praise and Eucharist.

The dangerous memory of the life and execution and resurrection of Jesus is the basis not only for liturgical action, but also for political action. Christian faith is not neutral with respect to social and political problems, yet it promotes the autonomy of political reason. It does not give a blueprint for the economic, social, and political order; these pertain to the art of government, the lessons of history, and the social sciences. At the same time, this does not imply that Christian faith and the gospel have nothing to do with the social order. Christian faith has political relevance precisely because Christian salvation implies human liberation. Churches must at all times challenge injustice. Yet social responsibility does not mean that churches take the government of the world into their own hands, or that they ally themselves with one particular political or economic system. The gospel provides the basis for a critique of the world, and this includes the social and political structures of the world. Not to criticize actual injustice in a concrete social order is to make a secret compromise with injustice—to which the God of Jesus says a final "no."

THE SPIRIT, THE CHURCH, AND THE WORLD

Christology was clearly at the center of Schillebeeckx's writings, with the publication of his *Jesus* and *Christ*, but christological concerns had undergirded his theology even prior to the Second Vatican Council. In 1959, he published the Dutch edition of *Christ the Sacrament of the Encounter with God*, which brought into a new focus the profound connections between christology, ecclesiology, the sacraments, and human life. His early theology spoke of a sacrament as an ecclesial act. Jesus Christ is the primordial sacrament of grace. What we ordinarily think of as sacraments are ecclesial acts, in which the Christian encounters God as present.

These ecclesial concerns continued to be significant as Schillebeeckx took up problematic areas such as lay preaching, liturgy, and ministry, all with an eye toward a deeper understanding of the human. His christology, ecclesiology, and spirituality all move with that foundational concern—the desire to specify theologically what it means to be human.

The risen Jesus bestows God's own Spirit, through which the believer enters into a relationship with God and, following after Jesus, into radical service to the world. The world is as much of a concern to Schillebeeckx as the church, if not even more so. His ecclesial questions relate the church directly to the world. Salvation takes place "in the world," in human history: "outside the world, no salvation" (*Church,* 5). Schillebeeckx's developing theology has become a theology of creation. Yet the church is of importance, not because the religions and the churches are salvation, but because they are sacraments of the salvation that God brings about in the world. As Schillebeeckx explains: "Churches are the places where salvation from God is thematized or put into words, confessed explicitly, proclaimed prophetically and celebrated liturgically" (*Church,* 13).

Being church is ministering to and in the world, but God's salvation is available wherever good is promoted and evil resisted. The church and world cannot be defined in opposition to each other. What is present "outside the church," wherever people give their consent to God's offer of grace, even though they do not do this reflectively or thematically, is audibly expressed and visibly perceptible in the church. "The church must therefore be the sphere where, following Jesus, the praxis of the kingdom of God becomes visible, so that it is clear to everyone through this praxis that despite everything there is ground for hope" (*God Among Us,* 120). The church follows after Jesus in the world, where such following is a visible sign of hope.

The church is vitally concerned with both mysticism and human liberation. Mysticism, liturgy, and worship without an essential concern for liberation constitute pseudomysticism, and, likewise, a church that promotes human liberation but has no mysticism is only half itself. In the church, as in the praxis of Jesus, God and the world come together in such a way that God is seen, experienced, proclaimed, and praised as one whose cause is the cause of humankind. The church is a community of "people of God" gathered around "the God of people," as revealed in Jesus Christ (*On Christian Faith,* 47). God reveals God's very own self as being for the sake of our salvation—which cannot be separated from our awareness of the history of human suffering. God, Jesus

Christ, and the church are all postured toward the human and have a human face: Abba, Son, and Spirit. God is a God who loves humanity.

God's universal love for human beings, revealed in the story of Jesus Christ and continuing to be proclaimed through the power of the Spirit, pushes the human (the *humanum*) to center stage in Schillebeeckx's continually developing theology. Salvation is always that of human beings. God's salvation does not turn our gaze away from us, our world, and our experience. Our God is a God who loves us. An ongoing theological concern for Schillebeeckx is: "In what does salvation consist?" Salvation can never be severed from its relationship to the human. God's very own choice has been for an authentic humanism, a religious humanism, even a "humanism of the rejected." Christian salvation comprises both God's redemptive acts and the historical human struggle for liberation. Salvation, however, cannot identify itself with either one to the exclusion of the other. God is always and absolutely for humanity.

Christian salvation is meant as salvation from God, but for human beings. Thus Christian salvation and spirituality are concerned with human beings becoming human. Salvation or spirituality cannot be related solely to a personal holiness alone, or to political or ecological appeals alone, or to an eschatological hope alone, or to a nonhistorical or mystical perspective alone, to the exclusion of the other aspects of the human. Christian salvation, for Schillebeeckx, is not simply a matter of "saving souls." It must be experienced by concrete human beings as saving. Salvation refers to human wholeness, human well-being in all its dimensions. It implies the solidarity of Christians with the processes of human liberation, even when the church has nothing in particular to gain from the liberation movement. Defining the content of full human liberation remains impossible. It is that toward which we strive. In the end, it involves the presence of the living God in the lives of the people, and the presence of the people to their history, the world, and all of creation.

Christian spirituality is, thus, concerned with what it means to be human. In the end, it is a theology of the human. Jesus is paradigmatic of the human, and Jesus discloses that being human, or being whole, involves both an experience of God as intimate and the praxis of the reign of God. Authentic Christian praxis is both mystical and political. Political love, or the political shape that love of neighbor necessarily takes in our world today, constitutes a particular understanding of holiness—an image of God as a God of people, a God whose concern is humanity. To be holy is to be concerned with human beings. Holiness never legitimates an escape from the world, but rather necessitates a *présence au monde* and its struggles for human liberation.

The human, which is God's innermost concern, is not definitively definable and is only fragmentarily found. It is best expressed in symbolic language, or metaphorical speech. Three great metaphors from the New Testament suggest the complete *humanum* (*God Among Us,* 161–62). First is the definitive salvation, or radical liberation, of all men and women for a sisterly and brotherly community or society that is no longer dominated by master-servant relationships: the metaphor of the reign of God. Second is the complete salvation and happiness of the individual person within this society: the metaphor of the resurrection of the flesh. Third is the perfection of the ecological environment necessary for human life: the biblical idea of the new heaven and the new earth.

In *Church: The Human Story of God,* Schillebeeckx adds a fourth, the real significance of Jesus ultimately becoming transparent to all in the midst of so many world religions: the metaphor of the parousia, or second coming of Jesus (133–34). These four metaphorical visions of the eschatological future are the source within Christian spirituality of Christians' power and joy (134).

Again we are reminded that spirituality is not just one aspect of human life that can be singled out. It is the whole of human life, and the making of human life whole. It is following the praxis of Jesus, the praxis of the reign of God, an orthopraxis both deeply mystical and necessarily political. It is an intimate involvement with a God who loves people and all of creation.

SUGGESTIONS FOR FURTHER READING

The most complete collection of Schillebeeckx's homilies, essays, and lectures in the area of spirituality is found in *God Among Us: The Gospel Proclaimed* (New York: Crossroad, 1983). To explore further the aspects of Schillebeeckx's approach to spirituality highlighted in this chapter, see especially "Jesus the Prophet," 33–44; "You Are the Light of the

World (Lk 2:19–32)," 85–90; "I Believe in the Man Jesus: The Christ, the Only Beloved Son, Our Lord," 103–15; "Liberation from Panic (Easter Faith)," 122–27; "Introverted or Turned Towards the World?" 164–74; "How Shall We Sing the Lord's Song in a Strange Land? (Ps 137:4)," 180–87; and especially "Dominican Spirituality," in which his own experience as a Dominican is the basis for his reflections, 232–48.

Later homilies and spiritual writings have been collected in *For the Sake of the Gospel* (New York: Crossroad, 1990). See especially the reflections on Christmas, 45–49; Pentecost, 70–75; John XXIII, 130–40; and the 8 May Movement in the Netherlands, 151–64, the latter in particular exemplifying the increasingly prophetic character of Schillebeeckx's preaching.

For the fuller christological foundations of Schillebeeckx's spirituality, see *Jesus: An Experiment in Christology* (New York: Seabury, 1979), especially 229–71. Schillebeeckx's discussion of God's opposition to human suffering can be found in *Christ: The Experience of Jesus As Lord* (New York: Crossroad, 1980), 670–743. His understanding of "political holiness" and the relationship between mysticism and politics, as well as liturgy and social justice, can be traced in *Christ,* 762–821; *On Christian Faith: The Spiritual, Ethical, and Political Dimensions* (New York: Crossroad, 1987), 47–84; and *Church: The Human Story of God* (New York: Crossroad, 1990), 66–99, 179–86.

Parts 5 and 6 of *The Schillebeeckx Reader* (Robert J. Schreiter, ed. New York: Crossroad, 1984) contain significant excerpts from his writings on the relationship of church and world and spirituality, some portions of which cannot be found elsewhere in English translation. An easily read introduction to Schillebeeckx, which offers rich insight into his own spirituality, is his conversation recorded in *God Is New Each Moment: Edward Schillebeeckx in Conversation with Huub Oosterhuis and Piet Hoogeveen* (New York: Seabury, 1983). Schillebeeckx's most recent articulation of Dominican spirituality is to be found in the text of his unpublished lecture, "Dominicaanse spiritualiteit," delivered at the Dominicaans Mariaconvent in Berg en Dal, 19 March 2000.

8

Church and Sacraments

Susan A. Ross

"THE WORLD and the human history in which God wills to bring about salvation for men and women are the basis for the whole reality of salvation.... There is no salvation, not even any religious salvation, outside the human world" (*On Christian Faith,* 8). This quotation, striking in its emphasis on the concrete context of human religious life, aptly introduces Edward Schillebeeckx's theology of church and sacraments, for it sums up his understanding of the relation between the sacred and the secular. More than anywhere else, it is precisely in those institutions and practices that symbolize the sacred in the world—the church and the sacraments—that this concrete emphasis is needed. And while his theology has changed in content and style over the fifty-plus years of his publications, Schillebeeckx's concern for the concrete and historical life of the church has been constant.

Schillebeeckx first became known to American audiences through the publication of his book *Christ the Sacrament of the Encounter with God,* in 1963. In that work, Schillebeeckx wrote how our life with God is rooted in our life in the world: "Life itself in the world then belongs to the very content of God's inner word to us. . . . Life itself becomes a truly supernatural and external revelation" (8). More than twenty-five years later, he wrote, "there is no situation in which God cannot come near to us and in which we would not be able to find him" (*Church,* 11). In his more recent writings, especially since the late 1970s, Schillebeeckx has become more acutely conscious of the immensity of human suffering in the world, and of the ways in which church structures themselves have become oppressive. His work on the church has, consequently, become more critical. And his writing on the sacraments has become, in the words of one scholar, "fragmentary and suggestive" as he has become far less indebted to the traditional metaphysical categories of sacramental theology and more concerned with the life situations of people in the world (Daniel P. Thompson, "Theological Dissent and Critical Communities in the Catholic Church: A Constructive Interpretation of the Theology of Edward Schillebeeckx," Ph.D. diss., University of Chicago, 1998, 171).

Schillebeeckx's book *Church* is his most recent, and most thorough, presentation of his ecclesiology; he is currently at work on a new book on the sacraments, which is not yet complete. This essay will draw on *Church* and some of the brief writings on the sacraments that Schillebeeckx has made so far available, as well as on some of his writings on the church and the sacraments over the course of his career. Schillebeeckx's theology of church and sacraments, I suggest, has not so much changed as it has intensified over the years, with certain themes in ecclesiology and sacraments receiving greater emphasis in his later writings, and other themes receding nearly completely. What marks the difference between the earlier and the later works is an ever more vivid concern with the structures of human existence and with the massive suffering that human beings experience in their lives.

CONCRETENESS, HISTORICITY, AND SUFFERING

The church and the sacraments are located in the world, where, as Schillebeeckx has emphasized throughout his career, God is revealed. In his earlier writings, he stressed the concreteness of this revelation: that is, how God's presence is found in the particularities of human life—in embodiment, relationships, social structures. God's presence is also historical, in that the particularities of time, place, and social location are also relevant. This is especially significant when it comes to understanding the life of Jesus (see *Jesus*). Although there are issues that concern human existence over time (Schillebeeckx calls these "anthropological constants [that] point to *permanent* human impulses and orientations" [*Christ*, 733]), these issues are always situated within a context, and they have different implications at different times and places.

In his more recent writings, Schillebeeckx has come to see revelation within the context not so much of human history "in general," but of human history as the "history of suffering" (*Church*, chapter 1). His theology of revelation, then, has taken on greater specificity—again, not so much simply as God's presence among human beings, but as "salvation and liberation" from the suffering of the world. The modern world in particular, which has seen so many scientific and technological advances, and which has proclaimed the "end of all historical religions" (*Church,* 3), has been the place not of liberation and salvation, but too often of dehumanizing forces, of ecological disasters, of oppressive social institutions. Religions bear responsibility as well for this suffering, and "they must acknowledge that they have often hidden, spat upon, and even mutilated the face of God's humanity and his care for all creatures, down to the least of them" (*Church,* 4).

But the history of humanity is one not only of suffering, but also of resistance to that suffering. This resistance Schillebeeckx calls the "experience of radical contrast . . . a 'no' to the world as it is" (*Church,* 5). Throughout human history one can identify experiences in which the evils of the world are resisted, if only in fragmentary ways. For Christians, the ultimate symbol of this resistance can be found in the human face of Jesus, who at the same time is "confessed as Christ and Son of God" (Church, 6). Thus there is a two-level structure to Schillebeeckx's understanding of revelation: the first is the human, where liberation is "achieved and experienced"; the second is the religious, where believers come to see this same liberation as the work of God through human beings.

It is in this context that Schillebeeckx situates his ecclesiology. Salvation, he declares, takes place in human history, which provides the place, and the forms, in which salvation is experienced. So one cannot isolate "salvation" from "history": the two are inextricably interlinked. Moreover, "salvation" is experienced historically as human liberation, not in some otherworldly way that draws human beings out of the world.

Sacramentality is, in the Christian tradition, centered in the person of Jesus. God's ultimate self-revelation is found in the completely human life of Jesus of Nazareth, for whom "God's lordship is not just an idea or theory, but first and foremost an experience of reality" (*Jesus,* 142). But God's revelation in Jesus, Schillebeeckx is concerned to point out, is not the "only living way to God" (*Church,* 9). As a human being, Jesus is a historical and contingent individual person "who cannot in any way represent the full riches of God" (9). In this statement,

Schillebeeckx aims to take very seriously the historical figure of Jesus of Nazareth, and to insist that while God is revealed in this human being, God is also concealed. The sacramental character of God's revelation in Jesus means that revelation is ambiguous and fragmentary.

Jesus' own understanding of salvation, of liberation from suffering, was spoken in the language of the kingdom of God: "For Jesus the kingdom is to be found where human life becomes 'whole,' where 'salvation' is realized for men and women, where righteousness and love begin to prevail, and enslaving conditions come to an end" (*The Church with a Human Face,* 20). For Schillebeeckx, "salvation" is thus a concrete and historical reality and is, therefore, sacramental. Rooted in the scriptures, expressed in the life and teachings of Jesus of Nazareth, salvation means God's presence in our struggles against suffering—the "barbarous excess" (*Christ,* 725) of suffering, injustice, and misery in human life.

Schillebeeckx identifies "the process of liberation in human history as the medium and material of divine revelation" (*Christ,* 6). This is to say that what is truly revelatory is human liberation—not a concept or an idea, but a lived reality—and the history of liberation is a truly human history, accessible to believers and unbelievers alike. Thus, examples from the Jewish and Christian biblical tradition show the Exodus event and the human life of Jesus as examples of secular historical events becoming the basis for faith. Not only have concreteness and historicity remained the base point for Schillebeeckx's understanding of God's relation with humanity, but in the last twenty years, that base point has become more specific: it is the concreteness and historicity of the liberation of human beings from suffering.

THE CHURCH AS SACRAMENT

Schillebeeckx's interest in the sacramental nature of the church has been a constant throughout his career. In *Christ the Sacrament of the Encounter with God,* he emphasized the importance of the "community of the faithful" as well as that of the more often emphasized (especially in preconciliar years) hierarchical church. It was during the years of the Second Vatican Council (1962–65) that Schillebeeckx came to a more nuanced understanding of the church as community. This concern has only intensified over the years, as he has devoted more time to studying the historical roots of the church and relating this history to the present. It is also a concern that has brought him into conflict with the hierarchical authorities of the church.

The church's sacramental character—as "sign of salvation"—means that its basis for existence is not itself or its own perpetuation: it "is not concerned with winning as many souls as possible for itself" (*Church,* 184). Rather, the church's mission is "to bear symbolic witness to the kingdom of God through word and sacrament" (157). It is "an ambiguous historical phenomenon" (158) that both reveals and conceals the work of salvation in the world. The church, then, is not identical with salvation, but is rather a "sacrament," a sign, "of the salvation that God brings about in the world he has created" (13). Put another way, "Church and religion are the grateful welcome to what is, as it were, the anonymous, concealed, and modest coming of God into the world" (14).

But because the church is a sign, it is an ambiguous reality, subject to all the limitations that signs possess: the tendency to literalize or become identified with the reality they make present, or to become distanced from that same reality. Thus the church can become "sectarian, clerical and apolitical" (*Church,* 13), resulting in its becoming "incredible and a stumbling block to belief in God" (60). This is particularly a problem in the contemporary world, where the church's maintenance of a rigid, hierarchical structure in the face of struggles for democracy raises serious questions for human beings concerned about liberation in the world.

Like those who "turn their backs on the church" (*Church,* 60), Schillebeeckx is well aware of abuses within it and the problems that accompany both "institutionalization of belief" and the "domestication" of the power of religious experience (59). Like any human institution, the church is subject to problems. Among these, Schillebeeckx would include clericalism, an exaggerated emphasis on hierarchy, and the perpetuation of unjust structures. Historical-critical issues complicate the church's claim to originate in Jesus Christ. Still, Schillebeeckx maintains that the church is a necessary institution; some measure of institutionalization or domestication is necessary, he argues, for belief in God. Without the kinds of specifications found in ecclesial institutions, human religious experience "hangs in a vacuum" and can take on some strange forms, as the twentieth and twenty-first centuries have certainly witnessed.

As sacrament, the church is both "communion" and "institution." As communion, it is the gathering of those men and women who seek the liberation of suffering humanity through their coming together to struggle against injustice, to lament and to celebrate, to remember the life, death, and resurrection of Jesus Christ. As institution, the church is a complex reality that has existed for nearly two thousand years, with a centralized hierarchical structure of bishops, priests, religious, and lay people. Schillebeeckx emphasizes that these two dimensions "call forth the other and need the other" (*Church,* 158). Yet he does not mince words in his critical comments on the tendencies that a large and complex institution can harbor: "But the communal and institutional church . . . does stand over against a bureaucratic and centralist management if it allows a cramping church policy, built on criteria which are not those of the gospel, with arbitrary and injurious attitudes towards men and women" (158).

These comments are very much in line with the development over the years of Schillebeeckx's understanding of sacramentality. In his earlier works, he emphasized a more personalist approach to the sacramental dimension of the church, which, up to this time, had been dependent on the rather abstract language of canon law and Scholastic metaphysics. In addition, he has always avoided a triumphalist or mechanical sense in which God's grace is automatically guaranteed by the church's designation as sacrament, or by the sacraments themselves. His more recent approach to sacramentality has been marked by a strong sense of ambiguity and tension, made more acute by his increasing focus on human suffering. Moreover, the personalist emphasis, while not absent, is tempered by his turn to critical theory, which is suspicious of the structures of the modern world.

Thus the church's sacramentality lies not so much in its visible structures, which it shares with other human institutions, but rather in its way of living out the message of the gospel. However, while the church is a place of action, it is not simply an organization of activists. Its action is ultimately grounded in its relationship with God. Schillebeeckx writes that the churches' praxis is "the realization of the story that they tell, above all in the liturgy" (*Church,* 14).

Schillebeeckx's awareness of the global context of contemporary ecclesiology has also intensified over the years. He notes the importance of Vatican II statements on the possibility of other religious traditions providing ways to God, and he affirms that other religions can be and are "ways of salvation." The universality of the Christian tradition remains—that is to say, Christianity mediates a truth applicable and relevant to all cultures—but its claims to absoluteness and exclusivity do not. Moreover, in the present day, the drive to universalist conceptions of truth has given way to an appreciation for the multiplicity and diversity of religious traditions.

In *Church,* Schillebeeckx discusses various recent approaches to the problem of Christian exclusivity and absoluteness, including Karl Rahner's idea of "anonymous Christianity" and Paul Knitter's rejection of Christianity's claim to universality. Schillebeeckx's own approach to this issue revolves around the question of how "Christianity can maintain its own identity and uniqueness and, at the same time, attach a positive value to the difference of religions in a non-discriminatory sense" (*Church,* 165). The answer to this question must begin with Jesus of Nazareth and his teaching and mission on behalf of the kingdom of God.

Schillebeeckx acknowledges that there is "more religious truth in all the religions together than in one particular religion" (*Church,* 166), and he sees religious multiplicity as a "wealth, not an evil" (167). But while no one religion has a monopoly on the truth, Christianity's own uniqueness lies in its claim that through the life, death, and resurrection of Jesus, humans encounter God and God's saving action in the world, through human action on behalf of the suffering. Jesus, Schillebeeckx emphasizes, was a unique but contingent historical person, and this accounts for both the uniqueness and the limitations of Christianity. The church itself, as a historical institution, and its mission "should therefore be given second place" to the primary message that it is God "who brings about salvation in human history," though Schillebeeckx qualifies this by noting that this "second place" is not "an insignificant one" (*Church,* 183). This statement is completely in line with Schillebeeckx's claim that the church is a sacrament of salvation, not salvation itself.

THE DEVELOPMENT OF THE CHURCH

One of the questions most frequently posed with regard to the church in the modern world is how, with its complex organization and belief structure, it has evolved from the simple communities of the New Testament. Some have argued that Jesus never intended to "found" a church, or that the institutional church itself is a far cry from what Jesus intended by his announcement of the coming kingdom of God. Schillebeeckx acknowledges that "it is quite clear that Jesus did not have the intention of founding a new religious community," and notes that the earliest Christians thought of themselves as part of the Jewish community (*Church,* 15).

But Schillebeeckx's constant concern for the significance of history leads him to the conclusion that the institutionalization of the church is inevitable and, indeed, necessary if the message of Jesus is to have any relevance beyond his own lifetime. In one of the most provocative sections of *The Church with a Human Face,* Schillebeeckx says, "One can say that the communities of God which came into being on the basis of the resurrection of Jesus are what is meant *at the deepest* level in the New Testament by 'the appearances of Jesus'" (34). Christian communities are themselves the places where Jesus' message of salvation and liberation remain living. And this message was then and remains today the standard by which the church is judged.

The early church attempted to live out its understanding of the message of salvation by discerning where, in its own tradition and culture, one could best live out Jesus' message. In the earliest years of the church's existence, for example, one understanding of it was as a pneumatic, Spirit-filled church. This Christian community understood itself to live in "the fullness of time" and consequently saw the world outside its boundaries as soon to pass away. Members of the community saw themselves as inspired by the Spirit and freed from the distinctions of the "world" (such as race, gender, or civil status). But this spirit-filled, egalitarian sense of church eventually gave way to a self-understanding that emphasized a greater sense of order and authority.

Over time, the structures of church order established by its leaders became more and more centralized, as Schillebeeckx carefully shows in his books on ministry. The development of church order (of leadership and the roles of bishops, priests, and laity) grew in accordance with the way the church saw itself at that time, attempting to live out the message of salvation within particular cultural contexts. Eventually, these various structures of order, themselves "adaptations of a religion to its cultural environment" (*The Church with a Human Face,* 69) became identified with the religion itself. Schillebeeckx notes how the post-Constantinian church began the trend, which continued through the Middle Ages and into the Counter-Reformation era, toward the establishment of a strongly hierarchical framework. Today, Schillebeeckx observes how the church has accentuated its own hierarchical structure, through both the doctrine of infallibility and its resistance to democratic forms of governance, especially within the church. In recent years, and particularly in *Church,* Schillebeeckx points out how the church has taken on a strongly antimodern perspective, seen especially in Vatican I, and has, to his regret, rejected the positive results of the Enlightenment, including some bourgeois values and democratic forms of governance.

In the present, the church finds itself in a situation where ecumenical dialogue has come to a "standstill," and where polarization exists not only among the Christian churches but especially within the Roman Catholic church. Infallibility has come to represent not so much the church's confidence in the continuing work of the Holy Spirit in the whole church, but more of a "mysticism of infallibility" that applies only to the person of the pope (*Church,* 199). Rather than the office of the papacy being understood as a way of providing a center for unity, it has come to be the top of the pyramid of authority. The other bishops and the community of faith, Schillebeeckx charges, have been "robbed" of their legitimate authority and authenticity (*Church,* 199). Thus Schillebeeckx strongly challenges the church's claim that its organization is a "divinely willed hierarchical structure" (188). Indeed, in one of the most strongly worded statements he has made on the subject, Schillebeeckx asserts: "To claim that the church cannot be democratic because it is hierarchical is thus simply false reasoning and a magical and ideological use of the word 'hierarchy.'"(220). Rather, he maintains, the church should "follow the non-authoritarian, vulnerable, even helpless, rule of God" (221).

THE CHURCH AS CRITICAL COMMUNITY

As we have already seen in previous chapters (especially chapter 2), the philosophical and sociological movement of "critical theory" has had a powerful influence on Schillebeeckx. In his consideration of the church, critical theory plays an important role. Insofar as the church is a social and historical reality, it is open to criticism on both historical and theological grounds. Therefore, Schillebeeckx sees the role of the theologian as continually reminding the church to be conscious of its own interests: the community of believers in the service of the message of Jesus. This means that new situations can and do give rise to new expressions of the ongoing faith of the church. These new expressions, however, inevitably collide with the human reality of the church. Further, the established order of the church—a historical reality—can, as we have seen, become rigid and resistant to change. Indeed, over the course of church history, this rigidity can, and in fact has, "become fixed as an ideology and itself hinders the original purpose of the church" (*Ministry,* 79).

For Schillebeeckx, this is where the importance of "critical communities" in the church emerges. These communities are critical not only of unjust structures in society, but also of those within the church itself. Based in the local community, these groups strive to live out the message of the kingdom of God by confronting injustice wherever it is found, and by developing new forms of community that respond to the needs of the present day.

This understanding of the church as "critical community" has arisen out of a deep sense of humanity's (and therefore the church's) historicity. It also comes from a new understanding of Jesus. Schillebeeckx's years of study of biblical material (which resulted in the two massive volumes *Jesus* and *Christ*) have had a deep impact on his own ecclesiology. He himself has become more critical of the church's tendency to isolate itself within its hierarchical structures. Consequently, Schillebeeckx has come to place great importance on the ways that present-day Christians are responding to the need for salvation in their own lives and communities.

Some of these ways result in practices that are regarded as "illegal" by the hierarchical church, insofar as they violate official church law.

The continuation of ministerial practice by married priests and leadership of the Eucharist by the nonordained are examples of new ways of living out commitment to the message of Jesus, ways that speak from a new and different theology of church, ministry, and Eucharist. This theology comes out of critical reflection on experience, and an openness to new experiences to discern how God is working in human life today. For Schillebeeckx, these new experiences have a real authority, as they reveal our liberation from oppressive structures even within the church.

Schillebeeckx is especially sensitive to the current "shortage" of priests, despite the men and women who are willing to work in church ministries and yet are unable or unwilling to accept the present conditions for ordination. He has become particularly sensitive to the experiences of women, who find themselves excluded from exercising ministry and from leadership roles, because of a theology that relies on a "historically conditioned cultural pattern" (*Ministry,* 97) and lacks adequate theological substantiation in the present.

In *Church,* Schillebeeckx pays particular attention to the ways in which Vatican II proposed a new vision of the church as People of God, yet at the same time failed to give this new vision any "institutional and canonical protection" (*Church,* 207). Consequently, attempts on the part of laity or theologians to bring about a more democratic structure are frequently met with resistance; conflict comes to be seen as the "fruit of sin" (208), and ideological appeals to the church as "mystery" are made by the hierarchy so as to prevent dissent from official views (210). Schillebeeckx argues vehemently for a more democratic structure, and appeals to the church's own sacramentality as the basis for such a vision: "The church community as mystery cannot be found behind or above concrete, visible reality. The church community is to be found *in* this reality which can be demonstrated here and now." (*Church,* 213).

Schillebeeckx's own critical concerns have brought him into conflict with the official teaching office of the church. Between 1976 and 1979, his work in christology was the subject of an investigation by the magisterium, and this prompted Schillebeeckx to rethink his understanding of the magisterium's role in the life of the church. While acknowledging the tensions that often exist between the pastoral and the academic, Schillebeeckx argues that academic theology is absolutely necessary for a full and coherent presentation of the church's mission. Relying on his Dominican forebear Thomas Aquinas, Schillebeeckx envisions a truly authoritative role for theologians, while urging the church to "make room" for the activity of the Holy Spirit in the work of theologians and among the faithful (*Church,* 227).

FROM SACRAMENTS AS ENCOUNTER WITH GOD TO SACRAMENTS AS DRAMA

For Schillebeeckx, *sacrament* was the central concern of his theology in the 1950s and 1960s. His first work published outside the Netherlands—his two-volume work on marriage and his writings on Eucharistic presence—were and remain major contributions to Christian theology and the contemporary discussions on sacramental changes in the liturgical life of the church. As his attention became more and more oriented to the interpretation of human experience in the present, critical theory, and biblical exegesis, sacraments became less explicitly the focus of Schillebeeckx's work. Now, late in his life, he has returned to the sacraments, but in a way tempered by his concerns for human suffering and his awareness of the secular context of the lives of most Christians.

Schillebeeckx's early work was concerned with the ways that church and sacraments, in the pre-Vatican II church, had come to be seen as isolated from the world in which people lived. At the time, sacraments were most often described in abstract categories, and were seen as more closely related to canon law than to pastoral concerns. As a response to this distorted way of thinking, Schillebeeckx emphasized the rootedness of sacraments within the experiences of our common human life.

But the secularization of the 1960s gave way to another problematic way of seeing sacramental life: as a vague and implicit awareness of God's presence in secular life, as if our experience of God had been "brought down to the level of a pleasant little chat consisting of 'good morning' and 'have a nice weekend'" (*God the Future of Man,* 113). What was missing in this interpretation was an explicit awareness and an expression of God's transforming love within human life. Otherwise the sacraments are only a "trivial commonplace."

In *Christ,* the second volume of Schillebeeckx's christological trilogy, sacraments are described as "anticipatory signs": "They are symbols of protest serving to unmask the life that is not yet reconciled in the specific dimensions of our history" (*Christ,* 836). Influenced by liberation theology and critical theory, Schillebeeckx came to see sacraments and the church's liturgy as symbols that make present and keep alive in our midst the hope for salvation that is not yet accomplished. This hope cannot be relegated to political action alone, although that is not at all irrelevant to the sacraments. The human need for symbolic expression—indeed, the realization that our embodiedness is itself a symbol of our transcendence—must be met in an understanding of self and existence as graced, and in the concrete implications of this graced existence. The entire sacramental life of the church is, thus, a recognition of God's saving presence among suffering humanity. Each individual sacrament provides a focused way of encountering God's liberating action in human life.

In the brief fragments that have emerged from his forthcoming work on the sacraments, Schillebeeckx shares some of the concerns of postmodern assessments of the world. In brief, the postmodern perspective is critical of the Enlightenment's optimistic picture of the world, which trusts in human progress and rationality, and which presents a universalized understanding of human history and personhood. Postmodern views see the self as more fragmentary. Highly aware of the devastation that modernity has wrought on human beings and on the ecosystem, postmodernists are less confident in the power of rationality. Given the massive suffering that human beings have experienced in the modern world, and given greater awareness and sensitivity to historical and cultural differences, postmodern thinkers, including theologians, are far less likely than their predecessors to develop systems in which everything is integrally related. They are more prone to focus on those partial and fragmentary ways in which human beings experience the presence of God.

In the short pieces so far available from his new work on sacraments, Schillebeeckx appears to continue his lifelong emphasis on the broadening of the nature of sacramentality. With the secularization of contemporary society continuing at an accelerated rate, one cannot say—if one ever really could—that we encounter God's saving grace only in church or through the church's sacraments. Salvation is present wherever God's saving grace is present. But this does not mean that the sacraments are therefore unnecessary, or purely extrinsic to salvation. Rather, the sacraments are the places where we acknowledge and celebrate the grace that is already available to us in the world, and where we lament the poverty and injustice that persist nevertheless.

Given Schillebeeckx's deeply sacramental way of seeing human life in the world—that is, that God makes Godself available to human beings in and through the concrete and historical dimensions of their lives—it is not at all surprising that he poses the difficult questions of sacramental celebration alongside human suffering and evil. "What is the relation between, on the one hand, sharing our bread with the poor and sociopolitical action for them, and, on the other hand, the breaking of the bread in the Lord's Supper and the Eucharist?" ("Verzet, engagement en viering," 2; trans. by R. J. Schreiter).

Indeed, Schillebeeckx asks: "Can we celebrate? Even: Dare we celebrate? And above all, what can we celebrate?" ("Verzet, engagement en viering," 2). Thus, the traditional celebrations that Christians have inherited from their tradition must be subject to a rigorous and critical analysis of the ways that they enhance, or detract from, a committed Christian life in the world. In his book, Schillebeeckx promises, there will be less emphasis on triumphalistic celebration and more on the stark juxtaposition of joy and lament, of celebration as well as irritation. What will receive greater attention is the ongoing narrative of human history, "interrupted" by another narrative—that of the story of Jesus. This Schillebeeckx terms the drama of the sacraments, relying on the terms of the early fathers of the church.

Such a sacramental theology, it is safe to surmise, will not be bound to the metaphysical categories of traditional sacramental theology, nor will it be entirely dependent upon the hierarchical structures of the church, which stake their validity on legal concepts. Schillebeeckx's ecclesiology has been highly critical of these categories. Yet his ecclesiology, while critical, is nevertheless still respectful of the tradition, of the need for structure, and is all too aware of human sinfulness.

Schillebeeckx has not addressed the individual sacraments in his recent writings, preferring, rather, to discuss the broader questions of the concept of sacramentality, the role of symbols, and the purpose of sacraments in the world today. He remains deeply committed, however, to the principle of sacramentality, to the need for celebration as well as lament, and to the need for some sort of institutional context in which Christians come together. All of the sacraments direct our attention to the concrete and historical message of salvation. While the sacraments and the liturgy dramatize, represent, and challenge us with the message of God's alliance with us in Jesus, they are completed only in our entire lives, when we are involved in "liberating action in our world" (*Christ,* 836).

As sacrament, the church is found wherever we commit ourselves to making Jesus' message of the kingdom of God a reality in our lives. The sacraments are our inspiration and celebration of this commitment, and even an "irritation" to the world and to the church itself. In church and sacrament, we keep alive what is not fully realized yet: "For as long as salvation and peace are still not actual realities, hope for them must be attested and above all nourished and kept alive" (*Christ,* 836).

SUGGESTIONS FOR FURTHER READING

Schillebeeckx's interest in sacraments is especially prominent in his writings in the 1950s and 1960s. *Christ the Sacrament of the Encounter with God* (New York: Sheed and Ward, 1963) remains a very important work, because of his reworking of the traditional categories of Thomas Aquinas in personalist, existential terms. *The Eucharist* (New York: Sheed and Ward, 1968) and *Marriage: Human Reality and Saving Mystery* (New York: Sheed and Ward, 1965) show Schillebeeckx's thought on particular sacraments and his interest in and concern for the ongoing history of the sacramental tradition. His book of essays *World and Church* (New York: Sheed and Ward, 1971) shows his transition from the Scholastic language of church and sacrament to a more humanistic perspective. His subsequent works on ministry—*Ministry: Leadership in the Community of Jesus Christ* (New York: Crossroad, 1981) and *The Church with a Human Face:A New and Expanded Theology of Ministry* (New York: Crossroad, 1985)—show how church structures evolved over time and transformed the understanding of ministry and office. *Church: The Human Story of God* (New York: Crossroad, 1990), the completion of the trilogy begun with *Jesus: An Experiment in Christology* (New York: Seabury, 1979) and *Christ: The Experience of Jesus As Lord* (New York: Crossroad, 1980), contains the fullest statement of his ecclesiology.

In the last section of *Christ,* Schillebeeckx reflects on the meaning of sacraments as "anticipatory symbols," and also includes as an epilogue a creed and a eucharistic prayer that eloquently convey in liturgical language the depth of his sacramental concerns. His readers eagerly anticipate the completion of his new book on the sacraments, provisionally titled in Dutch, *Jezus' visioen en zijn weg van het rijk Gods: Zinen contrastervaringen tot ritueel gelouterd*. Earlier indications of the main lines of this project are available in "Verzet, engagement en viering," in *Nieuwsbrief Stichting Edward Schillebeeckx* 5 (October 1992): 1–3 (unpublished translation by Robert J. Schreiter, "Resistance, Engagement, and Celebration"); and in "Naar een herontdekking van de christelijke sacramenten: Ritualisering van religieuze momenten in het alledaagse leven" ("Toward a Rediscovery of the Christian Sacraments"), in *Tijdschrift voor Theologie* 40 (2000): 164–87.

For secondary literature, Daniel P. Thompson's 1998 University of Chicago Ph.D. dissertation, "Theological Dissent and Critical Communities in the Catholic Church: A Constructive Interpretation of the Theology of Edward Schillebeeckx," is a superb critical study.

9

Ministry: Leadership in the Community of Jesus Christ

Mary E. Hines

IT IS WIDELY AGREED that there is a crisis in ministry today. There are too few priests; communities are being deprived of the Eucharist for long periods of time; the permanence of the priestly vocation, as well as the universal requirement of celibacy, are questioned. On the other hand, the laity—women and men, married and single—are offering themselves in increasing numbers for pastoral service in the church, including the service of leadership. Many Catholics, women in particular, question the restriction of Eucharistic presidency to celibate men. Some Christian communities experiment with alternative ministerial practices that depart from existing church order. Is this crisis a dangerous assault on tradition? Or is it a significant opportunity for the church's understanding of ministry to expand and adapt to meet today's needs? Schillebeeckx's work on the understanding of office in the church struggles with these difficult questions. How can the church today remain faithful to its authentic tradition while responding to today's pressing pastoral needs?

The primary focus of this chapter will be the fullest expression of Schillebeeckx's thinking on office, *The Church with a Human Face.* This work expands and clarifies *Ministry: Leadership in the Community of Jesus Christ,* his earlier book on the subject. The new work was prompted, at least in part, by a desire to respond to certain criticisms brought to bear against *Ministry,* by both some theologians and the magisterium. In *The Church with a Human Face,* Schillebeeckx responds to these critiques by clarifying his methodological presuppositions more carefully, organizing the theological material more tightly, and nuancing the historical section. Thus, this book provides a good synthesis of his most developed thought on the topic. In some of his more recent work, Schillebeeckx expands and, in some cases, articulates his positions more strongly, calling in particular for a more democratic church order as an appropriate response to today's social and ecclesial realities. The chapter will conclude with a consideration of these questions.

A possible point of confusion for English readers needs to be clarified before proceeding. Although the term *ministry,* used in the English translations of Schillebeeckx's works, conveys in present usage a wide variety of services in the Christian community, the Dutch term that it translates *(ambt)* refers more narrowly to the service of leadership. The main focus in these works is office in the church, or the evolution of and present concerns about the ordained ministry, although Schillebeeckx does touch on some aspects of the wider discussion.

His work on ministry is an excellent example of the distinctive methodology that he has developed over the course of his long theological career. He begins with the present-day praxis of ministry in the church. He finds there negative experiences, leading to the crisis described above. "The dominant conceptions about the practice and the theology of ministry seem to be robbing the gospel of its force in communities of believers" (*The Church with a Human Face,* 1).

In the face of these problems of contemporary praxis, Schillebeeckx looks for "contrast experiences" that will provide possibilities for diagnoses of present-day ills and point toward their solution for the future. He turns to the data of history for these contrast experiences—not to retrieve or repeat one particular historical solution, but to point to a pattern of response to changing social and cultural situations.

In line with a key principle of his theology—that revelation takes place through history—Schillebeeckx finds the normative principle for ministry in the variety of forms that it has taken through history. No one particular period should be considered the absolute norm, whether it be New Testament ministry or the modern image of the priest.

With today's questions in mind, Schillebeeckx looks back at the various manifestations of the church's understanding of its ministry in differing historical periods. He looks at the rootedness of ministry in the message of the life, death, and resurrection of Jesus, and at the messianic communities in which that message and ministry were continued. He then considers the practice and theology of ministry in the earliest communities, from both sociohistorical and theological perspectives. Finally, before turning once again to the contemporary questions that prompt the inquiry, he surveys the development of the organization and spirituality of ministry throughout the course of church history. In each of these periods, he finds the practice and understanding of ministry adapting to specific social, cultural, and spiritual needs of the time.

Schillebeeckx characterizes the changes in ministry that he observes as "legitimate but not necessary." In other words, ministerial responses arose out of the human choice to actualize some possibilities rather than others. There is a normativity in the sacramental nature of Christian ministry, but this cannot be abstracted from the concrete historical situation in which it is imbedded. Historical choices remain contingent and changeable. Later periods are not absolutely bound by any one historical solution, but by the principle that change and development are necessary if fidelity to the gospel message is to be preserved in different social and cultural situations.

These convictions rest on Schillebeeckx's absolute opposition to the dualism often assumed between "above" (that which comes directly from God through Jesus Christ) and "below" (that which is perceived to arise from the human choices of the Christian community). He overcomes this dualism through his resolutely sacramental understanding of the Christian community. The Christian community is the place where the Spirit of the risen Christ continues to dwell. Thus, there can be no talk of merely human or historical responses in the Christian community, nor of a purely functional ministry "from below." On the contrary, because of Schillebeeckx's profound conviction of the indwelling of the Spirit in the community, he is convinced that what comes from below at the same time comes from above. It is precisely through the decisions of the sacramental, human, historical community that God acts in the world.

This same conviction also leads him to critique a presupposition that, he says, lies behind what he calls the "classical" view of the priest. This view presumes, implicitly at least, that Jesus Christ was a priest, on the basis of his divine, not his human, nature. If the church's ministry is a sharing in the ministry of Christ, which Schillebeeckx regards as correct, this view has led to a problematic "sacral ontologizing" of the ministry. Schillebeeckx proposes that a view of ministry that takes seriously the humanity of Jesus as a basis for priesthood is truer to the nature of Christian sacramentalism and overcomes the dualism present in the classical view.

If Jesus is the primordial sacrament, it is precisely because *as human* he is fullest revelation of the divine. A true sacramentalism cannot bypass the humanity of Jesus. Once again, this underlines Schillebeeckx's emphasis on the fact that God's revelation comes to us *through* the human and historical. There is no dichotomy between a vertical and a horizontal understanding of revelation and, thus, there is none between an "above" and a "below" understanding of the development of ministry. And there is no dualism between a christological and a pneumatic-ecclesial understanding of ministry. It is in the pneumatic-ecclesial community that one finds the christological foundations of ministry.

In the light of this conviction, Schillebeeckx approaches the historical material from a sociohistorical as well as a theological perspective, and shows the interrelatedness of these approaches to the same data. Both are in service of the search for the manifestation of the grace of God in history. "There is no surplus of revelation above or in addition to specific historical forms" (*The Church with a Human Face,* 11).

The hermeneutical principle governing Schillebeeckx's use of the historical texts is that one goes to the texts with the questions raised by the contemporary practice of ministry, including what he refers to as "illegal practices." These questions provide the horizon for interrogating the texts. There is, thus, no such thing as an entirely neutral reading of history. This is not to say, however, that one approaches a text merely with the purpose of justifying a particular practice or church structure. Rather, one should read the texts with an openness to being illumined by the practice of the past, and particularly with the possibility of discovering there some forgotten truths that might help in the assessment of today's practice.

He advocates a dialectical process between past and present that allows one to investigate whether "the actual practice of Christians and Christian communities is for the time being simply a possible sign of faith . . . [or] whether it is a real sign of faith" (*The Church with a Human Face,* 11). In this dialectical process, one discovers in history "contrast experiences" that allow one to ask whether a particular exercise of ministry today is positive or negative. The praxis of contemporary Christian communities also serves a diagnostic purpose, in exposing possible ideology in existing systems of ministry. The fundamental question is: "Are the specific forms of ministry given in history liberating, or enslaving and alienating for the believing community?" (*The Church with a Human Face,* 12). This process can then illuminate and provide the basis for a critical assessment of today's practice of ministry, and point to some directions for the future exercise of ministry in the church.

THE DATA FROM HISTORY

Schillebeeckx begins his historical investigation with Jesus and the earliest messianic communities. In the life and ministry of Jesus, he finds the governing principle for Christian ministry. "The nucleus of the whole of this ministry is the God of human beings, concerned for humanity, who wants to make us people of God, in turn, like God, concerned for other people" (*The Church with a Human Face,* 24). Jesus' actions signaling the inbreaking of the kingdom reveal God's stance with regard to human beings. With a special concern for the poor, Jesus proclaims that the kingdom is "a new world in which suffering is done away with, a world of completely whole or healed people in a society no longer dominated by master servant relationships" (21). Christian ministry must be acting in service of the kingdom, as Jesus did. Fundamentally, ministry is the praxis of the kingdom of God, which Schillebeeckx defines as "salvation for human beings" (21).

In the earliest Christian missionary communities, which saw themselves as imbued with the Spirit through baptism in the name of Jesus, this concern for humanity was continued. It is Schillebeeckx's claim that these early, pre-Pauline communities were pneumatic and egalitarian. By virtue of the gift of the Spirit, each person had authority in the community according to his or her own charism. There was leadership and some structure in the community, but this was on the basis of the gift of the Spirit, from which no one was excluded, in principle. Galatians 3:26–28, which was probably used as part of a baptismal liturgy, epitomizes this earliest tradition. This text stands as a continuing challenge to the Christian community, as it evaluates its ministry.

Very early on in the missionary development of the church, it became necessary to make decisions about how the church would live its life in different social and cultural circumstances. Certain adaptations were made for reasons of what Schillebeeckx calls "pastoral strategy." In the interests of the good of the Christian mission, for example, Paul advocated some accommodation to the Graeco-Roman society in which Christians would have to live. This involved a certain weakening of the uncompromising egalitarianism of Galatians.

Without judging Paul's action, Schillebeeckx points out that this was a pastoral choice from among a number of options, and within a certain social cultural situation. It set a precedent for Christian communities continuing to make pastoral adaptations, when confronted with new social and cultural situations. The particular choices that Paul and the earliest Christians made were not binding norms, but the need to make such choices for the good of the gospel was and still is such a norm. This is an issue that Schillebeeckx takes up again in his later work, when he suggests that elements of democratic governance characteristic of the modern period would be a helpful corrective to church authoritarianism.

For Schillebeeckx, the earliest period in the church's history is enormously significant. As he follows the growth and development of the church's ministry, he sees this pattern of pastoral adaptation repeated. What should be remembered from these very early days of the church is that ministry, essentially, is in service of the message of Jesus, which is one of concern and liberation for all humanity. Ministry is carried on in a community in which all are empowered with the authority of the Spirit. Ministry goes wrong when the liberating message of the gospel is obscured by stratified ministerial structures that make particular legitimate choices divinely normative for all time, and when the fundamental fact of the Spirit-filled nature of the whole community is forgotten.

As the practice and theology of ministry evolves beyond the earliest communities, Schillebeeckx notes a tendency toward more institutionalization and uniformity in structure. This is characteristic of groups as they move beyond their foundation period and begin to face conflict situations. In this case, conflicts eventually led to the question of the locus of authority to resolve such disputes. There began to grow up in the early church a more uniform differentiation of ministries, an incipient church order, although with a good deal of variety remaining.

Ephesians 4:11 lists apostles, prophets, evangelists, pastors, and teachers as providing services consistently necessary for the building up of the community. It is generally agreed that the ministry of apostle, listed first and regarded as the highest authority, did not continue beyond this first constitutive phase of the Christian community. In the Pauline understanding, the apostle was a supralocal leader whose authority was connected to missionary activity. Paul himself was the premier example of the role of the apostle. His letters and many missionary journeys expressed a constant concern for and oversight of the communities he had founded. In this foundational period, the "more than local" leadership of the apostle was exercised alongside the other ministries, named in Ephesians, that served the local life of the community.

As is also normal in the organization of groups, the early Christians tended to adopt forms of organization familiar to them, either from their civic life in the Greco-Roman world or from their Jewish past. This led to some diversity in organization in the early communities, and eventually to a merging of patterns. In turn, this resulted in the consolidation and strengthening of the local leadership, in the persons of the presbyter-bishops, presbyters, and deacons. With the death of the apostles and the advent of heretical groups claiming to have the true doctrine of Jesus, the question of doctrinal authority in the community arose with even more urgency. By the time of the later New Testament, this authority was appropriated by the local leadership, albeit still with much fluidity in its exercise. By the time of Clement, the tripartite structure was seen as divinely intended and theologically legitimated.

With this theology, Schillebeeckx says, a system of authority and subjection becomes theologically and christologically legitimated. As a result, the authority and many ministries exercised by the Spirit-filled community ultimately become subsumed into the one ministry and authority of the bishop.

Certain historical and sociological choices, thus, led to a particular church structure. What was the theological significance of such choices? In a survey of New Testament texts, Schillebeeckx identifies a number of concerns related to these choices: first, preservation of the apostolic tradition in the postapostolic community; second, understanding the meaning of leadership in a Christian community; and third, recognition of certain characteristics that might be demanded of one who exercised such leadership *(The Church with a Human Face,* 92–93).

These issues color the presentation of ministry in the Matthean, Marcan, Lucan, and Johannine traditions reported in these gospels, as well as in the post-Pauline Letter to the Ephesians. They indicate that the development toward institutionalization during this New Testament period was seen as necessary for the survival and continued growth of the community, in what were often considered to be hostile surroundings. In response to changing circumstances, thus, certain of the ministries emerged as more permanent and stable functions in the community. In Ephesians, for example, proclamation, leadership, and building up the community are noted as central ministerial functions. Leadership is one among many necessary services. How people are appointed to these tasks, however, does not yet appear as a matter of concern. What *is* a concern is continuing fidelity to the community's apostolic origins. These tasks are in service to that goal.

It is important to mention Schillebeeckx's understanding of apostolicity, since his interpretation of apostolic succession, which has been a matter of some discussion, is grounded in this notion. In its earliest connotation, apostolicity characterized the self-understanding of the *whole* community, conscious of its roots in the apostolic proclamation of the gospel of Jesus Christ. By the time of the Pastoral epistles, apostolicity was more closely connected to the ministry of leadership in the community. This was connected, however, not with any concern for a certain structure or a mechanical or physical notion of succession, but rather with the central concern of the Pastorals for continuity or succession in authentic teaching. Thus the particular structure that had evolved by the time of the Pastorals is not normative, but rather their linkage of ministry with a concern for authentic doctrine. The laying on of hands, Schillebeeckx suggests, arose in the church as a way to ensure the permanent presence of ministry as well as a sign of that presence.

In response to criticism of his understanding of apostolic succession, Schillebeeckx outlines what he calls "four dimensions of apostolicity": (1) the churches are built on the apostles and prophets; (2) the apostolic tradition, of which the New Testament writings are a permanent foundation document; (3) the apostolicity of the whole community, which is signified by doing as Jesus did in his ministry; (4) the apostolicity of church ministries, which became known as apostolic succession (*The Church with a Human Face*, 116). For Schillebeeckx, all of these elements in relationship to one another are important in the characterization of the Christian community as apostolic. "Ministry is important, but it is only one of many authorities which are concerned to preserve and keep alive and intact the gospel of Jesus Christ" (117). Leadership ministry in the church is in service of the wider apostolicity of the whole community.

Within the general evolution toward more centralized structures, Schillebeeckx notes some countervailing trends. Both the Johannine and Marcan traditions, while accepting the need for some structure and authority, relativize these in face of the conviction of the continued presence of the risen Jesus through the indwelling of the Spirit. The Matthean tradition also witnesses to an earlier, more charismatic exercise of authority, and a suspicion toward office bearers. Schillebeeckx points out, however, a certain cautionary note in the early disappearance of communities that never made the pastoral accommodation of a certain institutionalizing of ministry. Some institutionalization, he says, is necessary for survival over the long term. The general experience of these early communities points to the ongoing tension that remains with us today, between the charism of all the believers and the "institutionalized limitation of this same charisma" (*The Church with a Human Face,* 92).

Also worth retrieving for today's discussions are certain essential characteristics of ministry and ministers that Schillebeeckx discovers in the testimonies of these early communities. In the Marcan corpus particularly, he finds a distinctive Christian reinterpretation of the exercise of power and authority. "Pagan leadership is based on power and ruling with an iron fist, but Christian leadership of a community must be service: ministers must be slaves, serve (10:42–44), as did Jesus (10:45)" (*The Church with a Human Face,* 87). This theme is, of course, also underlined in John in the foot-washing account.

In Luke, Schillebeeckx also sees some qualities that illumine the meaning of Christian ministry. The service of the minister is bearing witness to the gospel. The minister must devote him or herself to Jesus' cause, continued in the life of the community. This will involve suffering and even death, in some cases. Those who have been tested by suffering are, thus, candidates for the ministry. But suffering is not the whole picture; the minister is also one who should contribute to the joy of the community, by proclaiming the message of liberation and reconciliation

(*The Church with a Human Face,* 93). This is a recurrent theme in Schillebeeckx's later thinking. In a sermon delivered on the occasion of a papal visit to the Netherlands, Schillebeeckx exhorts the pope not to lord it over the people with authoritarian demands, but to listen to them and foster their spirit of joy and peace (*For the Sake of the Gospel,* 141–44).

Finally, Schillebeeckx's investigation of the New Testament data points out that ministry did not, in the first instance, develop exclusively in relation to the Eucharist. One presided at the Eucharist by virtue of one's leadership of the community. Leadership was a charism called forth by the community itself, for the service of the community. It would have been, thus, an anomaly in this earliest period of the church's history to have a Christian community without both Eucharist and authorized leaders.

THE ASSESSMENT OF DEVELOPMENT: CONTINUITY AND CHANGE

The witness of the New Testament clearly has particularly normative and illuminative possibilities for ministry today, in Schillebeeckx's view. He does, however, particularly in *The Church with a Human Face,* look seriously at post–New Testament developments in the structure and spirituality of ministry, searching for both positive and negative trends. In his view, today's situation must be confronted with the lessons of the whole tradition of ministry.

In the progress of history, for complex sociological as well as theological reasons, Schillebeeckx discerns a progressive narrowing of the rich understanding of ministry described in the pages of the New Testament. This narrowing began with certain directions that were already obvious, although not central, as early as the second century, and maybe earlier. Although there was a good deal of diversity among the various local churches in the first centuries, one can discern a gradual movement toward an increased focusing of the ministerial charisms—given to all through baptism—on the specific ministries of the bishops, presbyters (who eventually became identified as priests), and deacons. Gradually the central focus turned on the bishop and, ultimately, the pope.

Understandings of these ministerial roles changed and developed as the church became increasingly institutionalized, often taking on the civil structures of a particular culture or period. During these first centuries also, the liturgical rite of ordination, connected to laying on of hands, became more central, at first as a recognition of the call and missioning of the community that was considered to be the essential element of ordination.

In addition to the progressive hierarchialization of ministry that Schillebeeckx sees in these early centuries, he also notes an initial sacerdotalization of ministry. Two particular developments were central to this process. The advent by the fourth century of "country priests," presbyters who went out from the great urban centers of Christianity to celebrate the Eucharist for rural communities, led to viewing these men as "priests" whose functions were increasingly identified in relationship to the Eucharist. Second, the fourth-century declaration of Christianity as the state religion of the Roman Empire fostered the interpretation of Christianity as a cultic community, analogous to previous imperial religions. "As a result the priesthood itself was connected one-sidedly with the Eucharist as the highpoint of the cult" (*The Church with a Human Face,* 143). Schillebeeckx sees this development as a significant break with the New Testament understanding. The prohibition of the sixth canon of the Council of Chalcedon against absolute ordinations, however, attests to the fact that during this period, the link between the Eucharist and community leadership was not entirely broken.

By the early Middle Ages, a hierarchical, cultic understanding of the ministry was widespread. A pyramidal image of the church dominated, with the hierarchy at the top. A laity, who were the passive recipients of their ministry, formed the base. An increasingly sacrificial interpretation of the Eucharist reinforced the cultic identification of the priesthood. It is Schillebeeckx's contention that these clericalizing, hierarchializing, sacerdotalizing trends came to dominate the understanding of priesthood over the next centuries, eventually leading to what he calls the classical modern notion of the priest, which was legitimated, although not born, at the Council of Trent. This, of course, was not a unilateral development, and Schillebeeckx notes countervailing trends in the variety of images of the priest that have appeared through history.

Of particular importance to Schillebeeckx's thesis is the increasing tendency one finds from the eighth to the thirteenth century to identify ordination exclusively in relation to the cult of the Eucharist, and to separate this from jurisdiction, which related to pastoral responsibility for a community. The great monastic orders had many priests with no pastoral charge. This reality, as well as the rise of the mendicant orders, which saw their tasks as supraterritorial, contributed to the split between ordination and jurisdiction. New conceptions of law reinforced this separation. An ordained man possessed personally the priestly power to confect the Eucharist, even though he might not be assigned to any Christian community and, thus, did not have the power of jurisdiction. "If a man has been personally ordained priest, he has the 'power of the eucharist' and can therefore celebrate it on his own. For the early church this was inconceivable" (*The Church with a Human Face,* 193).

For Schillebeeckx, this split between ordination and jurisdiction, characteristic of second-millennium Christianity, is a second significant break in the history of ministry. Priesthood more and more was viewed as a personal state of life, rather than as service to the community: a priest was a higher-status Christian in a world where everyone was baptized. Priests became sacral persons. More emphasis was placed on the ritual as the locus of the conferral of the power of ordination (absolute ordination), even without specific reference to service of a particular Christian community. The priest was ordained more to confect the Eucharistic body of Christ than to preside over the ecclesial body of Christ.

An example of the consequences of this split between ordination and jurisdiction, with significance for today, is the medieval debate over lay preaching. The question was whether preaching was related to jurisdiction, that is, whether it was a function of leadership in the community or related to ordination, which would give it a sacramental base in the consecration to priesthood. Twelfth-century theology rooted preaching in ordination. The thirteenth-century solution was that the *missio canonica,* which granted jurisdiction, conferred the authority to preach. Theoretically this latter decision might have opened the door to lay preaching, but the hierarchical climate of the time led to a prohibition against such, and the reservation of preaching to the clergy.

Schillebeeckx illustrates the relevance of these medieval debates by inserting in this context his reflection on a similar contemporary discussion. Lay preaching is once again a major issue in the church. The 1983 code of canon law roots an implicit acceptance of lay preaching in the necessity of the church to grant jurisdiction to the nonordained for many ministerial functions where there is a shortage of priests. This maintains a separation of ordination and jurisdiction, which is hard to reconcile with the Vatican II assertion that the power of ordination is the sacramental basis of jurisdictional authority. Schillebeeckx suggests that this apparent discrepancy points to a perhaps unintentional implication, in the code, that the sacramental foundation of both jurisdiction and ordination is to be found in the common baptism of all Christians. This has important consequences for evaluating the increasing involvement of the nonordained in many aspects of leadership and pastoral care in the church. Such activity can be clearly evaluated as truly sacramental and ministerial. In his later work, Schillebeeckx continues to press his conviction that "laity" involved in such pastoral work should receive the appropriate ecclesial recognition.

THE "MODERN" PRIEST

The trends that Schillebeeckx traces through history as "legitimate although not necessary" responses to various social and theological situations eventually culminated in what he calls the modern, or classical, understanding of the priest. Starting with the period just prior to the Council of Trent (1545–63), he sees solidified a clear, though unintentional, break with earliest understandings of ministry. The council fathers, in attempting to remain in continuity with what they saw as the constant tradition of the church, served to canonize and make central the narrowing cultic trends whose gradual development Schillebeeckx traces through history. His contention is that from this gradual development, there has resulted a significant difference between early first-millennium and late-second-millennium interpretations of Christian ministry.

Hermeneutical studies of Trent have pointed out the complexity of this council and the necessity of understanding its historical context, as well as the need to probe the intentions of the fathers behind the texts. Schillebeeckx points out, however, that our modern understanding of the priest has been influenced by the texts themselves, and how they were received and transmitted. What has been characterized as the "Tridentine view" has been the central understanding of the priesthood to the present. This view has reinforced the split between ordination and jurisdiction, and solidified the tendency to identify priesthood one-sidedly with cultic activity, consecration, and absolution.

This narrowed priestly image led to the problematic assumption mentioned above, that Christ was a priest on the basis of his divinity rather than his humanity, and that priests were personally, mystically elevated above other baptized believers through their identification with Christ. This became a popular understanding of the meaning of the "character" associated with ordination. Thomas Aquinas, on the contrary, understood character to relate to the call and acceptance by the community for church service. The Council of Trent, although mentioning the character attached to priesthood, did not define the term.

Vatican II made some attempts to rethink the theological foundations of ministry. As mentioned above, it grounds jurisdiction sacramentally in ordination. It more often describes ministry as service than as power, and it does recognize the common baptism of all believers as the essential foundation of all ministry. But despite its ecclesiological emphasis, it does not completely separate itself from the direct christological approach to ordained ministry that Schillebeeckx sees as a source of contemporary problems.

Thus, at the end of his historical investigation, Schillebeeckx returns to the issue that is the leitmotif of his ministerial thinking. Ministry cannot be understood apart from community, and there can be no community without ministry. This connection has been obscured in modern understandings of priesthood, and it must be restored if the present-day crisis in ministry is to be resolved. The present-day situation, in which there are communities deprived of ordained ministers and, thus, of the Eucharist, would be an anomaly if the proper relationship between the christological and the ecclesiological were understood. Because it is the place where the Spirit dwells, "the church itself is the womb of the ministry, which is itself in the service of the community of believers" (*The Church with a Human Face,* 207).

There are, in fact, sufficient leaders in the Christian community today, but because of present structures growing out of contingent historical choices, such as mandatory celibacy and the exclusion of women, many of them are unable to preside at Eucharist. It is Schillebeeckx's conviction that once again, as has happened many times before, the understanding of ministry must adapt to changing needs. Antecedent to any existing structures, the Christian community has a right to leaders and to the Eucharist. If the important connection between ministry and service to the community were restored, it would be clear that those persons, male or female, who were called to the service of leadership by the Spirit-filled community should, by virtue of that role, preside at the community Eucharist. Leadership should be recognized by appropriate ritual, and communication and mutual critique with other Christian communities should be fostered.

It should be made clear that Schillebeeckx nowhere in his works on ministry defends the idea that "laypersons" should preside at the Eucharist. He in fact cites instances of this as among the negative experiences that prompt his reflections. He states clearly and unambiguously that his consistent position has been that "those faithful who in fact lead and animate a Christian community, such as 'lay ministers,' must be given an appropriate ecclesial recognition, and therefore the laying on of hands" (translation by R. J. Schreiter of "Verklaring Edward Schillebeeckx over de ambtsopvatting in zijn boeken," in *Tijdschrift voor Theologie* 25 [1985]: 180–81).

In *The Church with a Human Face,* Schillebeeckx lays out the history of the development of ministerial structures, raises some problematic issues, and concludes by "listening to the complaints of the people" (209–58). In these negative experiences of real people, he finds urgency for change. In this work, however, he does not focus on concrete suggestions for a more appropriate practice of ministry. He becomes more specific about his vision for the future shape of ministry in his later book *Church,* and in some more pastoral writings, for example, *For the Sake of the Gospel,* a collection of homilies, and *I Am a Happy Theologian,* a series of personal conversations. In these works, his thinking on office in the church continues in the direction of his earlier work, but becomes even more strongly critical of today's reified church structures.

Through these later works, Schillebeeckx plays the constant theme that church institutions, though necessary, are for the service of the legitimate freedom of the people of God. "The functioning of ministerial authority must . . . be organized in such a way that the liberating authority of the Lord Jesus, which is abidingly present, can come into effect time and again in the life of the Christian community of faith" (*Church,* 216).

Theology of the church and its ministry must, in fact, be radically decentered and contextualized within a broader focus on God, and on the world where God's saving activity is carried out. Turning the old dictum around, Schillebeeckx now says: "No salvation outside the world" (*Church,* 5–15). The church is not an end in itself or the sole locus of salvation, but its visible sign, or sacrament. Explicit attention to God and the world should always be the context, he says, in which a theology of the ministerial church is developed. "The church should be more of an appendix, a corollary to what is said of God" (*I Am a Happy Theologian,* 74).

In the later works, Schillebeeckx develops more extensively some implications of his historical work. Structures of ministry evolved in the past in response to pastoral need, and often they borrowed from governance paradigms of the time. In light of this, Schillebeeckx now suggests that a more democratic exercise of power in the church would be appropriate within today's ecclesial and social context. He finds it quite anomalous that the official church supports democracy as a preferred form of civil government, while holding that its own hierarchical organization prohibits the exercise of such democracy within the church. In fact, he suggests that a nuanced understanding of democracy is more faithful to the egalitarianism of the early church than is today's authoritarian exercise of power in the church.

Theologically, Schillebeeckx grounds his appeal for a more democratic church organization in the many mediations of the Holy Spirit. To restrict the illuminating activity of the Holy Spirit to church leadership and ignore the insights of believers, he maintains, denies the ecclesial conviction developed in his early work that the church as a whole is the Spirit-filled community. The voices of all are needed to decide important church matters, and the work of all for the building up of the community should be affirmed.

Schillebeeckx continues to insist that recognized ministries in this church, in service to the world, should no longer be restricted to the traditional triad, though the triad need not be abolished. The varied ministries of the many so-called lay workers in the church should be recognized by a kind of ordination, and incorporated into the church's understanding of ministry. The community must not be deprived of the dedicated leadership of these committed pastoral workers, male and female, who should, by virtue of that leadership, receive an official mandate, which would in effect be ordination. To maintain the present structure in face of the present needs of the Christian community, Schillebeeckx says, is ideology (*Testament,* 115–22).

In these later works, Schillebeeckx reiterates his conviction ever more strongly that official church ministry should be open to married and unmarried Catholics, and to both men and women. "There are no arguments against the ordination of women to the priesthood" (*I Am a Happy Theologian,* 76). The a priori exclusion of women, who are often the most dedicated and numerous pastoral workers, from those who may experience a call to official church ministry, he calls discrimination. (He cautions, though, that such a change in church practice would need careful preparation.)

This inclusive view of ministry goes back to Schillebeeckx's insistence that the experience of those who are at the base—the members of critical local faith communities, the poor and the suffering—is at the heart of an emerging and more expansive understanding of ministry. Their practice of ministerial service is the experience that should ground an authentic contemporary theology and praxis of ministry. The classical triad of bishop, priest, and deacon is no longer able to encompass fully the actual experience of ministry in a church that is at the service of real people and their urgent needs. But if this reality is to be the grounding of a renewed theology of ministry, it must be listened to.

Schillebeeckx is concerned that the present exercise of the papacy, epitomized by the practice of frequent papal visits, in fact infringes on the role of local bishops as leaders and articulators of the experience of the local church. He fears that Vatican II efforts at collegiality are once again being subsumed under the centralizing authority of the pope, symbolized by his many travels and addresses to local churches. Papal visits, he says, should be a two-way listening experience. "Any church province must listen to the Pope, certainly when he is addressing a particular church province directly *qua* pope. But the Pope must also listen to the church province: to the spirit which also blows there" (*For the Sake of the Gospel,* 143–44).

Throughout his work on ministry, Schillebeeckx's central conviction remains consistent: that a new theology and practice of ministry, or office in the church, is urgently needed. It must be arrived at "from below," from reflection on the concrete praxis of diverse, pluralistic Christian communities, brought into mutually critical dialogue with scripture and Christian history. The gospel understanding of ministry as active involvement in the cause of Jesus Christ, as well as the gospel characteristics of freedom, liberation, and joy, should serve as evaluative criteria for the authenticity of contemporary praxis. In critical reflection on present-day experience illumined by the lessons of the past, the Christian community will discover a practice and theology of ministry that will allow the church to be experienced as the human face of God for our time.

SUGGESTIONS FOR FURTHER READING

The fullest presentation of Schillebeeckx's thought on ministry may be found in *The Church with a Human Face: A New and Expanded Theology of Ministry* (New York: Crossroad, 1985). For a briefer and earlier discussion, see "The Christian Community and Its Office Bearers," in *Concilium* 133 ("The Right of the Community to a Priest"): 95–133 (also in *The Language of Faith: Essays on Jesus, Theology, and the Church,* Maryknoll, N.Y.: Orbis, 1995, 127–166). An interesting dialogue that highlights the role of critical communities may be found in "Critical Communities and Office in the Church," in *God Is New Each Moment: Edward Schillebeeckx in Conversation with Huub Oosterhuis and Piet Hoogeveen* (New York: Seabury, 1983), 79–90. "Offices in the Church of the Poor," in *The Language of Faith,* 211–24, also provides a brief presentation of the basic lines of Schillebeeckx's thought. For the discussion of democratic church governance, see *Church:The Human Story of God* (New York: Crossroad, 1990), 187–228. Very accessible presentations of common themes of Schillebeeckx's later work on ministry can be found in *I Am a Happy Theologian: Conversations with Francesco Strazzari* (New York: Crossroad, 1994), 72–78; *For the Sake of the Gospel* (New York: Crossroad, 1990), 141–47; and the untranslated *Theologisch testament: Notarieel nog niet verleden* (Baarn: Nelissen, 1994), 115–22.

10

Eschatology and Ethics

Bradford E. Hinze

THERE IS A TIME to be born and a time to die. There is a time for conversion and a time for commitment, a time for the stability of tradition and a time for criticism. There is a time for conflict and a time for reconciliation, a time for political action and a time for prayer. There is a time for every season under heaven.

Eschatology is about living within time. It is about the many dimensions of our temporal existence: our sense of direction, and what threatens and inspires our journey into the future. Our perspective on time can be distorted by the rut of routine, by cynicism and despair, and by the denial or suppression of our own finitude and death. We may grow stagnant and nostalgic, or become restless and filled with a sense of apocalyptic doom. Whatever temporal moods and attitudes may dominate our individual and communal lives, they influence many things—how we view continuity and change, prayer and political action, birth and death, sin and grace, and God's relation to human history.

Christian eschatology reflects on the tensions and fulfillment of time and history. Where do we find the presence and absence of God in the drama of our lives, the life of our community, and the history of the world? Through sacrament and prayer, the Christian life in the present is shaped and guided by our memories of the past. Yet we are not to repeat this past; instead, we are called continually into an unknown future. Our hope in God, the future of the human race, is rooted in a prayerful solidarity with all those who search for fullness of life and ethical resolve in a world marred by sin, pain, and grief.

Eschatology has been a constant concern for Edward Schillebeeckx. There has been, however, a most profound transition in his thinking about this subject. His earliest work (before 1967) contends that history must be understood in light of the mystery of the incarnation of Jesus Christ as "the sacrament of the encounter with God." Schillebeeckx's later work continues to affirm the early claim about Jesus as sacrament, but it is placed in a tensive and productive relationship to his growing conviction that history must be understood in relation to Jesus Christ as the decisive "eschatological prophet." As we shall explore, Schillebeeckx creatively combines these two themes in his eschatology, which provides the framework for understanding his contribution to ethics and the appropriation of liberation theology.

Early Sacramental Eschatology

Early in his career, Schillebeeckx employed the resources of phenomenology and personalism to reinterpret the dominant and classic vision of history bequeathed to the church by Augustine and reiterated by Thomas Aquinas. Following in this tradition, Schillebeeckx points out that since we are embodied spirits who learn through our senses, and since we are personal beings, we encounter the invisible God most clearly through Jesus Christ, the Word made flesh. The incarnate one is the decisive revelation of God to the human community, the source of reconciliation, and the perfect model of the worship of God through prayer and actions. The meaning of history is disclosed through this human encounter with Jesus Christ.

With his death, Jesus is no longer present as the physical mediator. This void is filled by the church, which becomes in history the earthly extension of the body of the risen Lord. History from the death of Christ to the parousia is all of one kind, the age of the church. It is through the church that Christ is mystically encountered and, within this community, worshipped and served.

Schillebeeckx has clearly shown to a new generation why this sacramental eschatology remains the dominant model within Christian theology. It provides a theological rationale for the saving presence of Christ and for the church's mission. A wide variety of issues about christology, soteriology, ecclesiology, and the mystical and ethical dimensions of Christianity are treated with impressive coherence and adequacy to human experience. Through Christ, the created order, which has been frustrated by sin, is brought to fulfillment. The experience of Christ's grace within the Christian community is the basis of our hope for eternal life in God.

This model of eschatology strongly affirms the importance of historical mediation—the making present of an invisible God through physical, human, and institutional forms, as well as the necessary mediation of the religious message down through history, with the aid of philosophical and other nontheological languages and insights. Moreover, a sacramental eschatology enables the church to acknowledge ambiguity and ambivalence within history: ambiguity because the mediation of God does take place outside of Christianity through the so-called sacraments of nature, history, and historical religions, even though they pale in comparison to the primary sacrament, Christ (*Christ the Sacrament of the Encounter with God,* 7–13); and ambivalence because ethical purity is not the prerequisite for participation in the Christian community, and the practical decisions that Christians make are seldom made with apodictic certainty.

A Prophetic Reformulation

Schillebeeckx in his later work has identified several deficiencies in the sacramental model of eschatology, while continuing to affirm its basic tenets about mediation, ambiguity, and ambivalence. A sacramental eschatology proves susceptible to criticism on two fronts. First, recent historical-critical study of the scripture clearly shows that prophetic and apocalyptic eschatologies are present in the Jewish milieu, in which the person and mission of Jesus must be understood. Second, liberation theologians—Latin American, African American, feminist theologians, among others—point out that the scandal of massive human suffering and oppression poses a religious question in need of response.

What both of these recent developments have in common is that, more than the sacramental approach, they focus on moments of crisis in history that call forth the divine judgment and vindication. The prophetic eschatology at work in the earliest New Testament testimony and in present-day communities of liberation fights against incipient dualistic, pietistic, other-worldly interpretations of history. Rather than speak about a history divided into the city of humankind and the city of God, a natural plane and a supernatural plane, or a secular history and a sacred history, there is an insistence upon the oneness of history (*Christ,* 561). As chapter 2 of this book indicates, Schillebeeckx's new prophetic orientation also reflects his engagement with the thought of critical theorists (Jürgen Habermas, Theodor Adorno, and Max Horkheimer) and postmodern philosophers (for example, Emmanuel Levinas). As a result, Schillebeeckx's phenomenological and hermeneutical approaches to theological topics often incorporate a prophetic critique of idolatrous worldviews that posit an identity between reality and thought, rather than acknowledge the refractoriness of reality, and that fail to examine the deleterious effects of ideologies.

In his historical-critical study of the New Testament, Schillebeeckx attempts to uncover "the human face of God" in Jesus. However, in the *Jesus* volume, this sacramental mediation is now transformed by a truly prophetic vision of history. Jesus has prophetic solidarity with the suffering and sinners, because the cause of God is intent on humanity and God does not will suffering. What Schillebeeckx discovers through his historical reconstruction of New Testament Christianity, he also finds displayed in the narrative of the Christian community's testimony: the community encounters Jesus as a prophet and more than a prophet. It is through this recollection that the church discovers again and again what it means to affirm that Jesus Christ is the Lord of history.

JESUS, THE ESCHATOLOGICAL PROPHET

That we find in Jesus' vision a prophetic and not an apocalyptic eschatology is very important for Schillebeeckx. There are clear indications of a prophetic quality in Jesus' teaching, ministry, and way of life. By bearing in his person the cries of the poor, the sick, the suffering, and by voicing the judgment of God against injustice and for human wholeness, Jesus stands clearly within the prophetic tradition that stretches from Moses down through the prophets Elijah, Amos, Hosea, Jeremiah, and Isaiah. In the face of historical tumult, apocalyptic eschatology, by contrast, accents the radical discontinuity between this age and the age to come; it stresses the stern divine judgment upon the human project.

Even though Jesus shares certain convictions with apocalyptic eschatology—especially its sense of crisis and divine judgment—he clearly rejects the two-aeons doctrine and the severity of the justice of God upon the human situation in condemning the evil of this age (*Jesus,* 148–54). Rather, in the face of this crisis and judgment, Jesus embodies the promise of God's graciousness and steadfast concern for human wholeness, a stance that requires the rejection of any dualistic vision of history or humanity.

At the heart of the New Testament narrative is Jesus' understanding of himself as the eschatological prophet. In the tradition of Moses and the prophets of Israel, he does good in the face of evil and suffering, and he sides with the marginalized, the sinner and the sufferer. His preaching announces the reign of God, which is God's intent for humanity, and he insists that people look to the future and prepare for the full presence of God's reign. When Jesus is faced with the rejection of his message and mode of life and his own possible death, the persecution and martyrdom of Israel's prophets provide him with an interpretive key. Jesus freely accepts the outcome of his life. The resurrection event precipitates the conversion of his followers and their constitution as a community. In this conversion event, God vindicates Jesus' life and ministry, and engenders a salvific interpretation of Jesus' life and death.

One of the lasting contributions of Schillebeeckx's christology is that it is based on a prophetic modification of a sacramental eschatology. The dominant tradition of christology focuses on the identify of Jesus Christ as the Word made flesh, the incarnation of God, which has long worked in concert with a sacramental eschatology. The councils of Nicaea and Chalcedon proclaim the church's judgment about the definitive mediation of salvation through Jesus Christ, who is one in being with the Father in his full divinity, and one with human beings in his full humanity. Schillebeeckx maintains that we dare not reject this tradition. However, he insists that must we recognize the earlier, prophetic tradition as the fundamental source of all christological claims.

The earliest prophetic christology stresses that Jesus is the one who brings approaching salvation. He is the Lord of the future and judge of the world, who recognizes the crisis of suffering in the world and the need for a fundamental change of vision. This christology ought to remain in a creative, if tensive, relationship with the later sacramental formulations. Seen from this marriage of viewpoints, Christ remains the sacrament of the encounter with God in history, but the understanding of history has changed. No longer is it tied to an assumption that the time from Christ to the end of the world is similar in that it provides countless occasions to encounter the risen and eternal Christ by means of sacramental mediation. Instead, historical experiences of individuals and communities, especially in their struggles against inhumanity and injustice, take on theological significance as historical episodes and movements where one encounters the sacramental mediation of the prophetic Jesus Christ calling people into God's future.

JESUS, THE NEW HUMANITY, AND SALVATION

The prophetic modification of the sacramental eschatology likewise transforms our understanding of soteriology and ethics. Christological formulations originate in Jesus' question, "Who do you say that I am?" But this question about Jesus always includes one about ourselves: "What is the saving significance of Jesus for me as an individual, and for us as a community?" Traditionally, this is spoken of as the inseparable relationship between the person of Christ and the work of Christ. Christological claims have always been guided by their soteriological impact (*Jesus,* 564–656; *Christ*).

In Schillebeeckx's mature formulation, the mystery of Jesus Christ continues to serve as the primal point of mediation for salvation. However, Jesus' mission is no longer spoken of in Thomistic terms as "a mystery of saving worship: a mystery of praise (the upward movement) and of salvation (the downward movement)," or as "the divine love for man and the human love for God: bestowal of grace and religious worship" (*Christ the Sacrament of the Encounter with God,* 17–20). Instead, Jesus' mediation is now imbued with a prophetic force: as the definitive eschatological prophet, Jesus is the parable of God and the paradigm of humanity (*Jesus,* 626–74).

Jesus, in his message and praxis, "identifies himself in person with the cause of God as that also of man (God's rule, which man has to seek first, before everything else), and with the cause of man as God's cause (the kingdom of God as a kingdom of peace and salvation among men)" (*Jesus,* 269). The transition is not simply from a worship-centered vision of salvation to an action-centered one, although the accent lies there. More importantly, there is a reconfiguration of salvation that leaves behind the theory of the supernatural, with its two-tiered view of history.

Jesus is the parable of God by showing God's concern for human wholeness. In every period in history, humans have craved "wholeness" (*Jesus,* 153, 621; *Christ,* 62–64). Jesus in the New Testament has solidarity with all those who hunger for wholeness, who are torn apart by the contrast experiences of sin, suffering, and oppression. Those who encounter Jesus have experienced God's absence and negative sacraments of exclusion and pain. These people cry out aloud or in silent tears for God's divine compassion and judgment. Here people experience the hiddenness of God and long for the sacramental presence, through body, touch, and commitment.

This longing for human wholeness that springs so vividly from the pages of the New Testament is ultimately the longing for salvation. But what constitutes human wholeness—what is meant by salvation—is articulated differently in different epochs: eternal life beyond death; freedom from internal bondage, sin, and guilt; courage in facing the anxiety of finitude. With this ongoing reconfiguration, the church's understanding of salvation has been deepened, broadened, and made more precise. Traditional Christian beliefs concerning personal accountability for the exercise of freedom and divine judgment at the moment of death, eternal life, and the resurrection of the body are indispensable. But in our own day, the social character and effects of sin are more explicitly recognized in patterns of economic, racial, and sexual injustice, perpetuated by institutions, social structures, traditions, and customs (*God Among Us,* 128–52). Accordingly, redemption must be clarified in relation to all the manifestations of the human longing for wholeness and release from oppression and suffering. Redemption includes the quest for human liberation as a manifestation of God's intent on humanity.

Jesus is the paradigm for humanity. His actions and person not only show God's concern for humanity; they also provide a model for our lives. Salvation is disclosed in the gracious working of the kingdom in our midst through conversion, as a gift and a task.

> Jesus makes a connection between a coming of God's rule and metanoia, that is, the actual praxis of the kingdom of God. . . . This connection between God's lordship and orthopraxis clearly derives from Jesus: in his 'going about, doing good,' in his taking sides with the dispossessed and

> outcast, which comes out especially in his parables and his associating with sinners. . . . Orthopraxis, right conduct, is the human manifestation or logical rendering of God's universal saving love, registered in practical human living (*Jesus,* 153).

Jesus is the parable of God and the paradigm of humanity, for through him we are freed from the powers of sin, death, and oppression that shackle the self in vital, personal, and social ways, and we are freed for ethical action in the world as an anticipation and furthering of the kingdom of God.

> Liberation from various forms of human slavery and the fear of death is both the consequence of the adoption of grace or birth from God and also the requirement of grace . . . Liberation is not only liberation from unjust conditions for something good; what persons are freed for is itself a command to free humans from unjust circumstances, for it is redemption within a world which is still damaged and sick. All this indicates that redemption and liberation in the New Testament are both a gift and a task to be realized (*Christ,* 513).

Schillebeeckx's shift to a prophetically oriented sacramental eschatology moves Christianity's center of gravity from the past and present into the future. Mediation still remains central, as we shall explore in more detail. But it is not mediation grounded in a theory of participation, so crucial for Greek and Latin thought in early Christian theology and handed on by medieval theologians, notably Thomas Aquinas. Nor is mediation warranted by a certain approach to the doctrine of creation that posits the divine disclosure of an unchanging order in the cosmos and in human nature. Rather, we are left only with an anticipation of a total meaning in the ongoing gift of creation, and with a patient hope and trust in the God of Jesus Christ (*Jesus,* 618).

For Schillebeeckx, the Christian belief in creation affirms the fecund love of God and the limitations, contingencies, and freedom of humans in the world of nature. The doctrine of creation (protology) must ultimately rule out not only dualism and pantheism, but also a static view of the created order, and yield instead to a restless eschatological vision of creation that accentuates the human longing for wholeness in God, and that accentuates the responsibility of humans for protecting the natural realm (*Church,* 229–32). It also follows that the universal meaning and unity of history is not grounded in an understanding of the divine providence of God that affirms a preordained plan, based on the being and order of nature and cosmos. Instead, since "the question of universal meaning [in history] *qua* question is given inevitably," then it may be affirmed that "history is only potentially one" (*Jesus,* 615).

The unity of history is not reducible to the significance of the human subject, just as theology and ethics are not reducible to anthropology. Schillebeeckx maintains that God remains the subject and the universal meaning of history, even if this is only understood in fragments now. The God of Jesus Christ is the Lord of history. The same can also be inferred about the unity of the created world: the God of Jesus Christ is the Lord of the cosmos, but this can only be appreciated through the particles and refractoriness of reality. While salvation as human wholeness may be the guiding theme within this history and created world, the quest for wholeness cannot be reduced to personal piety, ethical action, or social-political involvement (*Christ,* 717).

ETHICS

Important ethical ramifications follow from Schillebeeckx's dynamic sacramental and prophetic construal of history, Christ, and salvation. It is no longer possible to find a secure ethical foundation in any objectivistic construal of human nature or natural law available from the world of creation. Instead, the Christian finds socially and historically conditioned ethical models at work in the New Testament, and throughout the history of Christianity, that mediate Christian conversion to praxis. These concrete models are essential for understanding the ethical character of Christianity, but they can never provide "a *direct* answer to ethical questions which are posed in terms of a different cultural model" (*Christ,* 593).

Schillebeeckx concludes that the New Testament has no specific ethical principle, no ethic of the categorical imperative, no commandments or prohibitions, no virtues or values that are not socially and historically conditioned. Any attempt to make the concrete ethical models of the Bible into lasting determinate norms is susceptible to criticism. So, for instance, Paul's statements about the subordination of women, slaves, and citizens to their sexual, racial, and social-economic superiors cannot be viewed as transhistorically binding. Nor are his statements against divorce and in favor of virginity sacrosanct. Such models offer prototypes of ethical behavior, not archetypes. To grant these models transhistorical validity is hermeneutically misguided, since it ignores the social and historical location in which those ethical claims were made, and tends to accord norms absolute validity by way of an undialectical sacramental notion of history (*Christ,* 586–600).

An important problem poses itself here: Since we have denied that there is any clear moral objectivity rooted in a created order and a natural law, and have affirmed the historically and socially conditioned character of ethical judgments within the Bible and throughout Christianity, are we left with a radical moral relativism? There are several levels of response to this question.

It must first be recognized that everyone discerns ethical norms and is ethically motivated through historical models and communal narratives (*Christ,* 655, 658). This is true not only for Christians, but for Buddhists, Sikhs, Moslems, humanists, and all religious and historical traditions. A radically autonomous interpretation of the self rejects the mediation of ethical values and norms through traditions and communities, and consequently fails to understand the historical character of a community's ethos. There is no autonomous ethics (*Church,* 14, 29–33). And as a result, there is no point outside of history for addressing ethical questions and adjudicating ethical conflicts.

The biblical ethic does not offer Christians any eternal moral sureties, but at the center of this testimony, there is the conviction that "the New Testament will not separate ethics from religion" (*Christ,* 590). Though ethical discourse can take place outside of the sphere of religion, for Christians the religious quest and the ethical impulse are irrevocably fused. The mystical dimension of Christianity taps our human receptivity to the givenness and gift of reality. Mystical experience establishes a relationship to the reality of God, which grounds our meaningful and truthful discourse about the God of Jesus Christ and orients us to a way of being and acting in accordance with the divine reality.

"Ethics needs a God who is more than ethics. The more we are silent about, indeed hush up, this God who is 'above ethics,' the ultimate source and horizon of all ethics, the more we human beings deliver ourselves over to idols or self-made gods, to a faith which does not result in life but in the torture and death of many people" (*Church,* 32).

The mystical encounter brought about through Christian conversion yields an ethical lifestyle and commitment. An ethical way of life, for Schillebeeckx, is logically distinct yet inseparable from religion, especially within Christianity. "Ethics has a certain independence, but the believer or the religious person sees its deepest foundation, source, and ground in the reality of God" (*Christ,* 59). And in turn, "the religious manifests itself in the ethical, and as a result transforms the merely 'natural' significance of ethics" (599).

The Christian transformation of ethical discourse is tied to the twofold claim that "Christian ethics has a christological and eschatological foundation" (*Christ,* 600). The christological foundation is located in the life and teachings of Jesus. Christians are called to a continual metanoia, which means that we are called to make "our history, following Jesus" (*Christ,* 641). What this entails is only ascertainable by examining the prophetic quality of Jesus, presented in the gospel narratives through his teaching, in parables, about the kingdom of God, and most clearly manifest in the beatitudes and in his solidarity with the suffering and marginalized.

Jesus' life is to be imitated, but this must be reinterpreted into our own day and age. The traditional distinction between counsel and precept wrongly spiritualizes the meaning of the beatitudes and disintegrates their potency. However, neither are the beatitudes for legal codification. Rather, Jesus' words and actions in solidarity with the marginalized constitutes a utopian critical force, which evokes an ethical conversion and a commitment to the ethical task on behalf of the constantly threatened *humanum.* This is the metaphoric power of the parable, the symbolic force of the paradigm. Jesus reveals what is and what can be.

The eschatological foundation for Christian ethics is determined by the tensive relationship between the church and the world, between the kingdom of God and human history. The sacramental and prophetic character of this tension is embodied in the word and action of Jesus. A sacramental eschatology affirms the presence and power of God in the world and the church through creation and grace, but this model risks dissolving the ambiguity and ambivalence in history, by legitimating a "logic of triumph." Such a triumphalism has, at times, led the church to support an alliance between the ecclesial and secular authorities or values, failing to call into question the finitude and sinfulness of either the church or the world. The later Schillebeeckx certainly acknowledges the real, if fragmentary, mediation of God in creation and grace, through the church, for the wholeness of the human race. Yet this is now tempered by the prophetic awareness that the "reign of God," though truly anticipated in the church and the world, will only be fully manifest in the end. What results is a nuanced recognition of the ways that the eschatological kingdom of God is manifested in the historical gift and task of salvation in the church and the world.

> Ethical life . . . is the *recognizable* content of salvation, the historical manifestation or demonstration of the imminence of the kingdom of God. . . . Through its ethical effects, the kingdom of God is present in our history in non-definitive forms which keep on becoming obsolete. Ethical improvement of the world is *not* the kingdom of God (any more than it is the church), but it is an anticipation of that kingdom (*Christ,* 599).

Christians have too often been incapacitated for action in the world, especially political action, by their interpretation of this eschatological proviso. Schillebeeckx joins liberation theologies here in three ways. First, he points out that even the early Christians recognized the need for ethical action and for structural change, even though this was envisioned primarily within the confines of the church (*Christ,* 561–67). Second, as we have seen already, for Schillebeeckx, previous concrete ethical models are prototypes, not diachronic norms, instances of "human ethics" that are historically and socially conditioned and yet reevaluated and reinterpreted by Christianity. Third, while the fullness of redemption and human wholeness is never realized in history, the church's mission is to promote salvation and liberation within history, personally, communally, and politically.

An important question remains: is there a place for ethical discourse that is distinct from and transformed by religious discourse? Schillebeeckx explicitly rejects Thomas Aquinas's natural law method, and any other system that would find in nature an eternally binding ethical order. Yet he does stand with Thomas, and, presumably, with numerous revised natural law theorists, in affirming the "relative independence of ethics on a human basis" (*Christ,* 655). Schillebeeckx also differs from the tradition by insisting that there is no decisive disclosure of what the *humanum* is, either in creation or in historical revelation.

As an eschatological concept, the *humanum*—genuine humanity—will only be realized in the future.

> The humanum, threatened and in fact already damaged, leads specifically and historically to ethical demand and the ethical imperative, and thus to confrontation with quite definite, negative experiences of contrast. Therefore ethical invitation or demand is not an abstract norm, but historically, an event which *presents a challenge:* our concrete history itself, humans in need, humankind in need [*Christ,* 659].

> We do not have a pre-existing definition of humanity—indeed for Christians it is not only a future, but an eschatological reality [731].

Schillebeeckx's ethics is clearly based on a conversion to imitate Jesus by conforming to the biblical narrative as kept alive in the memory of the church. He is not concerned with the relationship between narrative and character, nor with identifying specific virtues in the gospel story. Rather, Schillebeeckx finds in the New Testament narrative a distinctively eschatological ethic. Christian conversion to a mystical and ethical way of life requires searching the possibilities for realizing the as-yet unrealized gift of humanity. The gift and task of humanity will be concretely determined differently in each period in history. However, the anchor of the church's ethics, in Schillebeeckx's view, must be the commitment to solidarity with the marginalized and the suffering, the praxis of justice and love. The preferential option for the poor provides the biblical basis for a Christian ethics of political responsibility; it is "a datum of revelation" (*The Language of Faith,* 260–63; *Church,* 80–99).

The Bible is more than a moral reminder of what we may also discover in the natural or human realm. The eschatological character of Christian witness in the New Testament shakes up our accustomed ways of looking at the world; it disturbs the patterns we have set in our lives. Humanity is revealed there as a threatened and unfinished task. The Bible's ongoing power to inspire conversion and commitment makes the utopian prophetic eschatology of its narrative a critical, motivating, and sustaining force within the church and world.

In working out an ethical agenda, Christians must be vigilant. While embracing the sacramental and the prophetic dimensions in an eschatological ethics, Christians must reject utopian extremes on either side. On the one hand, as excessive sacramental eschatology can legitimate a retrospective, conservative utopia that reveres the past as the binding norm and finds only homogeneity in time since Christ. On the other hand, an extreme prophetic vision, one should say apocalyptic, can lend itself to a progressive, futuristic utopia that rejects every historical maifestation—ethical, social, religious, and political. Ultimately, neither way is able to discern the spirits within history.

More insidious and prevalent in our own day is a certain kind of rationalistic utopia. Placing their trust in technical rationality, government and business elites make decisions based on efficiency, cost-benefit analysis, and profitability. This utilitarian calculus precludes discussions of the wider public good, and the results undercut the ability of those affected to decide their own destinies. The structures of power and the patterns of ownership and distribution too often remain unchallenged. The wheels of economic progress for the few seem regularly primed by the suffering of the oppressed. In Schillebeeckx's view, the practices generated by such rationalistic utopias fall especially under the judgment of the gospel's eschatological vision.

AN ETHICS OF PROPHETIC MEDIATION

Schillebeeckx's prophetic and utopian ethic remains sacramental, requiring the bodily, personal, and institutional mediation of God in Christ and through the church. Jesus Christ mediates salvation as the parable of God and the paradigm of humanity. The Christian church mediates this message within the world. The Christian community mediates salvation to the human race, not only by remaining faithful to the work of Christ through prayer, sacraments, and lifestyle, but also through work for human wholeness and against bondage.

The church fulfills this mission in this mystical ministry of the sacraments, and also by being involved in the public debate in the pluralistic society about ethical issues. There is a universalistic intent here, but it is neither absolutistic nor triumphalistic. We enter into the public conversation with the best rational arguments we can provide about the *humanum*, on behalf of all who search for wholeness. While we are motivated by the search for genuine consensus, we realize this is often jeopardized by distortion in language, power dynamics within conversation, individual or group interest, and bias.

The sacramental principle of mediation calls for historical, theoretical, and practical mediations of God's reign through the church's ethical reflection and conversation in the public arena (*On Christian Faith*, 64–65). Schillebeeckx distinguishes three levels of ethical reflection and mediation: anthropological constants, formal norms, and material, concrete moral norms. Ethical values and norms are only learned and mediated through concrete historical models. But while these historical models are indispensable in handing down the ethical impulse, they are not transhistorical. However, "anthropological constants" are disclosed throughout the history of Christianity and other narrative communities that supply a very general system of coordinates.

These constants, described more fully in chapter 6, may be summarized as follows: All persons are corporeal and, by nature, intersubjective, and religious; they are conditioned by social and institutional structures and by temporal and spatial determinants. They work out their destinies through theory and practice.

Formal norms are the "general, dynamic directions which tell us we must promote the *humanum* and not try to slow it down" (*The Schillebeeckx Reader,* 261). They emerge from anthropological constants and are always valid. For example, being just is a formal norm that requires that we promote the values of life, health, social well-being, and so on. Material norms specify formal norms within the relative conditions of history and culture. The abstract anthropological constants and formal norms are only discovered through the mediation of a concrete ethical matrix.

> In contrast to the absolutely valid "formal norms," all concrete material norms are therefore relative, historically conditioned and mutable. Although the formal norm only gains validity concretely in the material norms, which thereby participate in the absolute character of the formal norms, namely, promotion of the *humanum* and the checking and avoiding of all those things which do it damage, these material norms count only as conditioned (*The Schillebeeckx Reader,* 262).

This principle of ethical mediation finally requires that since there are no transhistorical material norms given in the Bible or in human nature, we need to remain open to insights from philosophical ethics, the natural sciences, and above all the social sciences. The pursuit of economic, racial, and gender justice requires that we learn from social theories in order to understand the dynamics of continuity and change, harmony and upheaval. And although he severely criticizes technical rationality, Schillebeeckx still insists upon a sober acknowledgment and assessment of the positive human purposes that technology may serve.

Christian discipleship requires being both sacramental and prophetic. For Schillebeeckx, this means we must live by the eschatological narrative of the gospel, act in solidarity with the suffering and the outcast, and work in hope for the further manifestation of the kingdom in history. Christian faith ultimately entails learning to live with ambiguity and ambivalence within history, for we are ignorant of the future, and in the present we find "flashes of light and clouds of impenetrable darkness." There is no blueprint, no cosmic plan in history that we can know or follow. The guided memories of Jesus' death and resurrection and our solidarity with those who suffer can shake up our expectations and inspire in us a new work. This remembrance and reunion leads to a mystical surrender to the Lord of history, and to an ethical imitation of Jesus as one who does good for those in need.

Within Christian theology, there remains a tension between the sacramental and the prophetic approaches to history, just as there is a constant strain between communal stability and the crisis that yields change, and between continuity and discontinuity in the church's life. Schillebeeckx neither dissolves these tensions, nor does he offer a simplistic haven against the vicissitudes of time. His sacramental and prophetic eschatology does require the use of practical reason and the practice of the discernment of spirits in order to work within this tension, drawing past and present toward God, the hope and future of humanity.

SUGGESTIONS FOR FURTHER READING

For Schillebeeckx's sacramental interpretation of history, see *Christ the Sacrament of the Encounter with God* (New York: Sheed and Ward, 1963). The shift to a more prophetic eschatology can be traced in three intersecting ways: (1) by examining his increasing reference to "negative and contrast experiences" and "the future," beginning with "The Church as the Sacrament of Dialogue," written in 1967 in *God the Future of Man* (New York: Sheed and Ward, 1968); (2) by investigating his treatment of Jesus as an eschatological prophet, distinct from apocalypticism, in the *Jesus* volume (*Jesus: An Experiment in Christology,* New York: Seabury, 1979); and (3) by exploring his engagement with critical theorists (see *The Understanding of Faith,* New York: Seabury, 1974; see also *The Language of Faith: Essays on Jesus, Theology, and the Church,* Maryknoll, N.Y.: Orbis, 1995, 71–82).

On issues of personal eschatology and their relationship to collective eschatology, see "Some Thoughts on the Interpretation of Eschatology" (1969), in *The Language of Faith,* 433–54; and *God Among Us: The Gospel Proclaimed* (New York: Crossroad, 1983), 128–152. For the sacramental and prophetic dimensions of his vision of salvation and liberation and his view of ethics, see *Christ: The Experience of Jesus As Lord* (New York: Crossroad, 1980), *On Christian Faith: The Spiritual, Ethical, and Political Dimensions* (New York: Crossroad, 1987), and *Church: The Human Story of God* (New York: Crossroad, 1990). The specifically ethical statements are scattered throughout his work, but can be especially located in part 4 of *Christ*; in *The Schillebeeckx Reader* (Robert J. Schreiter, ed., New York: Crossroad, 1984), 260–71; and in *Church,* 29–33, 80–99. The importance of the doctrine of creation (protology) in relation to his eschatology by way of christology and soteriology is sounded throughout his work. His awareness of the need for human solidarity not only with the poor and the marginalized, but also with the cosmic community that entails the protection of nature is more pronounced in *Church.* The eschatological and ethical character of Christian faith is accentuated in numerous sermons in *God Among Us* and *For the Sake of the Gospel* (New York: Crossroad, 1990).

11

Edward Schillebeeckx: His Continuing Significance

Robert J. Schreiter

THE ESSAYS in this volume explore a number of different aspects of the multifaceted corpus of Edward Schillebeeckx's theology. No single volume of such reflections could hope to exhaust the many avenues that his thought has opened up for a genuinely faithful Christian praxis. In this concluding section, therefore, no attempt will be made to summarize either his thought or the numerous connections and new prospects the contributors to this volume have suggested. The syntheses and ideas brought forward can stand on their own merit.

What might be more helpful is to return to some of the probings into Schillebeeckx's thought begun by William Hill in his chapter, and framed within the sociocultural context of the Low Countries by William Portier in his contribution. In other words, it might be useful to identify some key aspects of Schillebeeckx's thought that account for his continuing attractiveness to such a wide audience, especially in North America.

As both Hill and Portier point out, the attraction to Schillebeeckx does not derive from the symmetries of a carefully crafted system derived from first principles. Schillebeeckx does not share that kind of grand philosophical design with the transcendental Thomists. Nor does it derive from a powerful synthesis of the full range of dogmatic questions. As a number of contributors have pointed out, much of his writing has been incidental, occasioned by pastoral need.

What is it, then, that so fascinates an audience of professional theologians and ordinary believers alike? In his epilogue to *The Schillebeeckx Case,* Ted Schoof notes the outpouring of sentiment at the time of

Schillebeeckx's difficulties with the Congregation for the Doctrine of the Faith over his christology books. Many ordinary people wrote to Schillebeeckx, telling him that they had struggled to read those books, or that their pastors had "translated" the christology books for them, and how much this had meant to them. Is it possible to identify the sources of that attraction?

I would like to suggest that there are four focal points in Schillebeeckx's thought that contribute especially to his long-term significance for Christian theology. While his work is significant for many reasons, it seems to me that these four points tell us something about what it means to do theology at this time in history, under the socioeconomic and cultural circumstances of the First World. These four points reveal a series of commitments both to method and to fundamental issues. It is these commitments, then, that have shaped Schillebeeckx's theology since the 1960s, and that probably need to be attended to by anyone wishing to bring the gospel message into First World realities in the twenty-first century. The four focal points of commitment are: working inductively; the narrative character of experience; the mystery of suffering and contrast; and the primacy of the soteriological.

WORKING INDUCTIVELY

As was pointed out in the book's introduction and in Hill's and Portier's chapters, Schillebeeckx doubts that a great dogmatic system is possible anymore. This sentiment does not grow out of some melancholy about the impossibility of a plausible metaphysics ever undergirding a theological system. Rather, it would seem to represent an intuition into the basic pluralism that marked twentieth-century life and experience. For the gospel message to be heard in such a context of pluralism, it has to be able to touch the immediate and the concrete. It cannot be presumed that there is a common frame of reference. Schillebeeckx's work with critical theory and his awareness of the pervasiveness of human suffering bring with them also a sense of suspicion about frameworks that claim to be comprehensive, for such structures often turn oppressive in order to ensure conformity. His commitment to God's proviso, to the ultimate resolution in the eschatological realm, reflects the fact that all our action and effort cannot be seen as definitive, as well as the fact of how much human suffering is still with us.

This awareness gives his work that searching, tentative character that resonates so immediately with the experience of many who read it. As Hill points out, Schillebeeckx is concerned with the credibility of Christianity. And by adopting a wayfaring attitude, he can be seen as a guide—one very good guide, but hardly a definitive one—along the road of Christian discipleship today.

So his method represents an inductive, rather than deductive point of departure. "It began with an experience" is a phrase that echoes throughout his christological writings. Even his eclectic use of different methodologies in his theology reflects the need to meet the situation on its own terms, rather than force the data into a predetermined form. It is this willingness to confront the issues and the concerns of both the committed Christian and the doubting seeker that has made him so widely read and appreciated.

One phrase of his, explored by Janet O'Meara, Donald Goergen, Philip Kennedy, and others in the contributions here, is "mediated immediacy." It is Schillebeeckx's attempt to express how finite humans, caught in the vortex of competing claims to knowledge and experience, come to experience the transcendence of God. The pluralism within experience is not all that there is; God and God's grace remain primary. Yet that primacy of grace never manages, in the present age, to erase completely the scars of human suffering. Hence, the quest must continue until the eschatological age is fully upon us. And so there is a continuing need to do theology in an inductive fashion, closely wed to human experience.

With such an emphasis on the inductive and the experiential, Schillebeeckx's theology is clearly aligned with the modern period. And indeed, most of his working life has coincided with this phase of Western thought. Yet in his most recent work, he has made allusions to the postmodern situation in which the West now finds itself. While not reorienting his thought to deal with all the dimensions of this change, his work on suffering has continued to fascinate those who grapple with the postmodern situation. The primacy he gives to the notion of suffering and contrast experience in his soteriology remains a fertile field for those who ponder the fragmentation of the postmodern reality.

THE NARRATIVE CHARACTER OF EXPERIENCE

But does this mean that all we can have to guide us in Christian discipleship are fragments of experience that never come together? Does respect for the plurality of experiences mean that we end up sinking away in a morass of relativism? Schillebeeckx has given considerable thought, in recent years, to the meaning of experience and how it relates to Christian revelation and tradition, as Mary Catherine Hilkert points out. Experience can be organized conceptually, but it functions for us most powerfully when threaded together narratively. Concepts focus our experience, but it takes narrative to allow them to express their full range of meaning.

Narrative, however, is not understood naively. Narratives can mislead as well as guide. Hence a critical understanding is necessary. Schillebeeckx achieves that by reminding us of the subversive narratives of the memory of human suffering, an idea he has taken over from J. B. Metz. Those "dangerous memories" make us suspect narratives that seem too glib, do not recount the contrast experience of life, and do not portray the struggles toward a fuller *humanum*.

Nor, as Hilkert points out, does Schillebeeckx equate divine revelation with human experienced—a pitfall that some theologies dealing with experience do not manage to avoid. For Schillebeeckx, divine revelation falls within human experience but is not coextensive with it. His growing preoccupation with the prophetic dimension, examined in this book especially by Susan Ross and Bradford Hinze, assures that there will be no facile equation of the two. Revelation comes to us with the narrative of experience and history, but always opens us to something beyond that experience and history.

John Galvin captures accurately Schillebeeckx's attempt to see christology as narrative. The subtitle of *Jesus* in the original Dutch edition is *The Story of the Living One.* Jesus is indeed "the parable of God," a phrase a number of contributors here have explored. It is not just the drama of the death and resurrection of Jesus that tells us of God, but the entire life and ministry of Jesus, his "praxis of the reign of God." Only by following that narrative can one hope to enter into the parable of God in Jesus Christ. And only by allowing our own narratives to be engaged by that parable can we hope to understand the experience of what God has done for us in Jesus. Perhaps more than any other theologian, Schillebeeckx has helped restore the narrative of Jesus' life and praxis of the reign of God to this generation of Christians. His work on carefully reconstructing that story has been instrumental in the shift back to the synoptic gospels, away from the sometimes too exclusively Pauline view of the saving work of Jesus. This has certainly been one of the reasons for the widespread interest in his theology. Schillebeeckx has helped us engage our stories more intimately with the story of Jesus.

THE MYSTERY OF SUFFERING AND CONTRAST

As Portier points out, Schillebeeckx's focus upon the mystery of suffering and the experience of contrast that that evokes found its expression in his encounter with the work of the early Frankfurt School, especially in the work of Max Horkheimer and Theodor Adorno. And, as nearly all the authors in this volume note, that concern with the massiveness of human suffering has become a pervasive theme in all of Schillebeeckx's work since the late 1960s. It has colored deeply his understanding of soteriology, a theme O'Meara explores in considerable detail. It figured into Schillebeeckx's growing interest and involvement with the critical Christian communities (examined here by Susan Ross and Mary Hines) and his more recent interest in liberation theologies (discussed by Hinze).

There are a number of facets to this dimension of Schillebeeckx's thought. Certainly his commitment to concrete, historical experience leaves him little choice but to engage himself with the reality of suffering. But as Goergen points out, Schillebeeckx sees suffering as a mystery, and not a problem to be solved by technological rationality or some other means. He sees it in its wrenching depths and realizes that only God can give ultimate relief from it. At the same time, however, the reality of suffering means that any genuine holiness must be a political one, a form of sanctity that seeks not only the kingdom within but also forms bonds of solidarity with those who would seek a fuller humanum. True holiness has both an ethical dimension and practical consequences for living.

But awe before the mystery of suffering is not the only dimension in Schillebeeckx's understanding of it. He explores in a number of places the revelatory nature of the contrast experiences that the encounter with suffering provokes. The contrast opens up not just the opposite of the previously experienced reality, but often new, unexpected worlds as well. Histories that have been suppressed or submerged are allowed to reappear. Many people have come to new understandings of faith and their membership in the church, along this pathway. It is often distressing to church leaders, but it is a reality that cannot be denied.

The revelatory nature of contrast experiences raises a third point about Schillebeeckx's use of this idea. There is a profoundly methodological dimension to the utilization of contrast experience. It comes out especially in his discussion of the quest for a universal horizon of meaning, toward the end of *Jesus.* One cannot arrive, now, at a universally agreed-upon horizon of meaning that takes into account fully the plurality of legitimate experiences of meaning. One can only engage in a solidarity of struggle to achieve that anticipated horizon. Anticipation finds its place alongside participation, as a legitimate mode of experiencing meaning in the world.

By making that assertion, Schillebeeckx introduces an option for a certain asymmetry in his methodology. Deconstructionists especially have pointed out that asymmetry, rather than symmetry, lies at the basis of experience. Schillebeeckx explores this insight in his own way (and, generally, more lucidly than do the deconstructionists). The experience of suffering and evil is not simply the symmetrical opposite of experiencing meaning and the good, for if such symmetry were the case, suffering and evil would not be the mystery they are. Nor would pluralism be the reality it is: it would mean that difference is only superficial and ephemeral. For both meaning and nonmeaning to be appreciated in all their fullness, they need to be taken seriously in their difference, without one being reduced to the mirror image of the other. To accept symmetry, as the deconstructionists point out, is to accept the hegemony of the status quo imposed by the powerful upon society. Difference needs to be respected.

That insight has grown to be shared by many, especially by feminist thinkers who see how accepting the symmetries of complementarity leads to a return of male domination. Indeed, the experience of asymmetry is considered by many to be a characteristic of the postmodern world. It has long been an experience of oppressed peoples who have seen their worlds of meaning subsumed into a dominant worldview of the powerful. Schillebeeckx's insistence on the contrast experience means that suffering and the encounter with nonmeaning cannot be explained away easily. They must be confronted in all their reality, if they are to be overcome ultimately. It is this sense that has given Schillebeeckx's theology a special significance to postmodern people in the First World, and to oppressed peoples throughout the entire world who do not see meaning or relief from suffering in places they are told to look.

As has already been mentioned, Schillebeeckx's reflections on suffering hold considerable potential for understanding the postmodern situation. With the upsurge of identity-based violence in the 1990s, Schillebeeckx has also turned his attention to the relation of religion and violence, as was pointed out in the introduction. He has joined others in wondering aloud whether absolute claims made by monotheistic religions might not contribute to intolerance and violence. He struggles with the problem of seeking on the one hand, a universal horizon of meaning and, on the other hand, drawing a distinction between universality and absoluteness. This has been expressed most concretely in his reflection on the claims that Christians make about the soteriological significance of Christ. While some of these were hinted at already in the first volume of Schillebeeckx's trilogy, they find more cogent expression in *Church* and in a number of articles written around the same time, in the late 1980s and early 1990s.

THE PRIMACY OF THE SOTERIOLOGICAL

What keeps the concentrated focus upon suffering and contrast experiences from fragmenting the praxis of Christian faith? Certainly Schillebeeckx's lifelong insistence on the primacy of God contributes mightily to creating a sense of cohesion in the midst of such powerful centrifugal forces as suffering and contrast. Schillebeeckx never tires of reminding his readers that Christian praxis is not another form of technical rationality. It is the eschatological proviso, explored here in detail by Hinze, that alone assures the completion of the quest for the *humanum*. But on a more mundane basis, something else is needed to thread together human experience, if one is not going to accept the unifying premises of a more symmetrical methodology.

Schillebeeckx finds the answer to this by giving primacy to the soteriological. In an important way, his whole christological project is about discovering a new soteriology for a postmodern world. The Anselmian model of satisfaction, as venerable as its roots and history may be, does not relate adequately for people today the story of what God has done for us in Jesus. But even more than the need for a new soteriology, Schillebeeckx wishes to give a primacy to the soteriological over the more traditional christological part of the equation of the person and work of Christ.

Such a move is not without its problems or precedents. Emphasis on the soteriological can divorce the significance of Jesus for us from the historical Jesus, and reduce that saving meaning to a mere projection of our immediate needs. It can allow for a reduction of the revelatory experience of a saving God to simple human experience, something that happened in nineteenth-century liberal theology and something of which (though generally incorrectly) twentieth-century liberation theologians are accused.

Schillebeeckx eludes these pitfalls through his detailed examination of the historical Jesus and through his critical theory of experience. Schillebeeckx not only affirms the importance of the historical Jesus for his project, he also has done much to restore the life of Jesus to christological awareness. His emphasis on the historical Jesus as an eschatological prophet, and his mode of reconstructing the experience of the disciples' growth in resurrection faith, assure a solid linkage between the Jesus of history and the Christ of faith. And his critical understanding of the relation of human experience and revelation (explored extensively here by Hilkert) keep him clear of the liberal pitfall.

How does Schillebeeckx, then, affirm the primacy of the soteriological? It is shaped, in many places in his thought, by its tie to the prophetic and pneumatic traditions. The need to assert the soteriological dimension of christology becomes most apparent when the given explanation is found wanting. Then the prophetic and the pneumatic dimensions of the tradition come to rise over the ontological and the dogmatic. Three of the contributions in this volume have explored that move in Schillebeeckx's work: Ross, in Schillebeeckx's understanding of the church; Hines, in her understanding of ministry; and Hinze, in his understanding of eschatology and ethics. In many ways, Schillebeeckx's work in eschatology in the latter half of the 1960s prepared the way for the growing emphasis on the prophetic in the 1970s and 1980s. But he has been making that prophetic dimension a greater part of his preoccupations—so much so that at one point, he announced that the projected third volume of the christology would be on pneumatology.

That search for where the soteriological dimension of God's grace manifests itself in human history is certainly shaping his most recent theology. His search for that saving moment in history has changed his understanding of the church and its ministry. Schillebeeckx's soteriological interest in its prophetic dimensions portends to change much of the face of Christian theology and of the church, if it is followed through. The fact that there is a felt need for that change accounts, in some way, for the appeal to so many of his writings on Christ, church, and ministry.

It is the perceived threat of such a change that alarms others who read those same writings. But in a time when the Eurocentric church becomes a world church, and when the postmodern reality calls for a new and renewed understanding of Christian faith and praxis, must we not run the risk of examining that soteriological dimension more fully, precisely for the sake of fidelity in our discipleship?

Philip Kennedy takes up the important theme of creation in Schillebeeckx's work. There are, as Kennedy notes, scattered references to creation throughout the oeuvre. In the 1990s, Schillebeeckx has turned more directly to the theme of creation, in a number of articles focused upon ecology. He has made assertions about the foundational nature of creation for all of theology. These, however, have not been worked out in detail. In other instances, he has warned that this emphasis on creation should not eclipse the importance of eschatology to his thinking.

Does this emphasis on creation change Schillebeeckx's fundamental commitment to the soteriological? I think not. Soteriology is linked also to creation, and perhaps his emphasis on creation might best be seen in light of his larger soteriological plan. Perhaps this increasing emphasis on creation theology might be seen precisely as exploring how the soteriological dimension of God's grace is manifesting itself in human history.

THE PRAXIS OF THE REIGN OF GOD

Schillebeeckx continues his quest for new ways to help people come to the "point of saying 'yes' to the heart of the gospel." This final chapter has tried to point out some of the foundational dimensions of his thought that guide him in that quest and have made him such an important thinker to so many people, especially in North America, but elsewhere as well. Schillebeeckx remains profoundly concerned with the God bent toward the cause of humanity, and with the concrete experiences, sufferings, and hopes of those who would follow after Jesus.

When one reviews these four reasons for the continuing significance of Schillebeeckx's thought—the importance of inductive method, the narrative quality of experience, the place of suffering and contrast experience, the primacy of the soteriological—one might be struck by the almost commonplace nature of these assumptions for contemporary theology. That is particularly the case for the first two. Why does this make Schillebeeckx's contribution to theology distinctive? Assumed as these ideas might be today, one must remember that induction, experience, and concrete narrative were not so long ago suspect, and even absent from Catholic theology. Schillebeeckx, more than any other Catholic theologian, has through his work made them foundational to how theology is done today. While certain elements in his theology may come to be superseded by more recent reflection and research, these foundational elements remain. And for Schillebeeckx, who has committed himself so passionately to make the message of the gospel intelligible to modern women and men, it is not a concern that his theology be relevant to all times and places; his very commitment to the concrete precludes that. But even with his commitment to the concrete, one cannot escape the conclusion that so much of what he has written will echo in the human heart for a long time to come.

WORKS OF EDWARD SCHILLEBEECKX CITED

For a full listing of Schillebeeckx's writings from 1936 to 1996, see *Bibliography 1936–1996 of Edward Schillebeeckx O.P.*, compiled by Ted Schoof, O.P., and Jan van de Westelaken. Baarn: Nelissen, 1997.

"Breuken in christelijke dogma's," in E. Schillebeeckx et al., eds. *Breuklijnen Grenservaringen en zoektochten. Veertien essays voor Ted Schoof bij zijn afscheid van de theologische faculteit Nijmegen.* Baarn: Nelissen, 1994.

"Can Christology Be an Experiment?" in *Proceedings of the Catholic Theological Society of America* 35 (1980): 1–14.

Christ: The Experience of Jesus As Lord. New York: Crossroad, 1980.

Christ the Sacrament of the Encounter with God. New York: Sheed and Ward, 1963.

On Christian Faith: The Spiritual, Ethical, and Political Dimensions. New York: Crossroad, 1987.

"The Christian Community and Its Office Bearers," *Concilium* 133 (1980): 95–133 (in *The Language of Faith,* 127–66).

Church: The Human Story of God. New York: Crossroad, 1990.

The Church with a Human Face: A New and Expanded Theology of Ministry. New York: Crossroad, 1985.

"Critical Theories and Christian Political Commitment," *Concilium* 84 (1973): 48–61 (in *The Language of Faith,* 71–82).

"Documentation: Religion and Violence," *Concilium* 4 (1997): 129–42.

"Erfahrung und Glaube," in *Christlicher Glaube in moderner Gesellschaft,* Teilband vol. 25. Freiburg: Herder, 1980.

The Eucharist. New York: Sheed and Ward, 1968.

For the Sake of the Gospel. New York: Crossroad, 1990.

God and Man. New York: Sheed and Ward, 1969.

God Among Us: The Gospel Proclaimed. New York: Crossroad, 1983.

God Is New Each Moment: Edward Schillebeeckx in Conversation with Huub Oosterhuis and Piet Hoogeveen. New York: Seabury, 1983.

God the Future of Man. New York: Sheed and Ward, 1968.

I Am a Happy Theologian: Conversations with Francesco Strazzari. New York: Crossroad, 1994.

Interim Report on the Books "Jesus" and "Christ." New York: Crossroad, 1980.

Jesus: An Experiment in Christology. New York: Seabury, 1979.

The Language of Faith: Essays on Jesus, Theology, and the Church. Maryknoll, N.Y.: Orbis, 1995.

Marriage: Human Reality and Saving Mystery. New York: Sheed and Ward, 1965.

Mary, Mother of the Redemption. New York: Sheed and Ward, 1964.

Ministry: Leadership in the Community of Jesus Christ. New York: Crossroad, 1981.

"Naar een herontdekking van de christelijke sacramenten: Ritualisering van religieuze momenten in het alledaagse leven," *Tijdschrift voor Theologie* 40 (2000): 164–87.

"Offices in the Church of the Poor," *Concilium* 176 (1984): 98–107 (in The *Language of Faith,* 211–24).

"The Religious and the Human Ecumene," in M. H. Ellis and O. Maduro, eds., *The Future of Liberation Theology: Essays in Honor of Gustavo Gutierrez.* Maryknoll, N.Y.: Orbis, 1989 (in *The Language of Faith,* 249–64).

Revelation and Theology, 2 vols. New York: Sheed and Ward, 1967, 1968.

"The Role of History in What Is Called the New Paradigm," in H. Küng and D. Tracy, eds., *Paradigm Change in Theology: A Symposium for the Future.* New York: Crossroad, 1989 (in *The Language of Faith,* 237–47).

The Schillebeeckx Case, Ted Schoof, ed. New York: Paulist, 1984.

The Schillebeeckx Reader, Robert J. Schreiter, ed. New York: Crossroad, 1984.

"Some Thoughts on the Interpretation of Eschatology," *Concilium* 1 (1969): 42–56 (in *The Language of Faith,* 433–54).

Theologisch geloofsverstaan anno 1983. Baarn: Nelissen, 1983.

Theologisch testament: Notarieel nog niet verleden. Baarn: Nelissen, 1994.

The Understanding of Faith. New York: Seabury, 1974.

"Verklaring Edward Schillebeeckx over de ambtsopvatting in zijn boeken," *Tijdschrift voor Theologie* 25 (1985): 180–81.

"Verzet, engagement en viering," in *Nieuwsbrief Stichting Edward Schillebeeckx* 5 (October 1992): 1–3. Unpublished translation by Robert J. Schreiter, "Resistance, Engagement, and Celebration."

World and Church. New York: Sheed and Ward, 1971.

CONTRIBUTORS

John P. Galvin is professor of systematic theology at the Catholic University of America. He received his doctorate from the University of Innsbruck, and is a priest of the Archdiocese of Boston. He is coeditor, with Francis Schüssler Fiorenza, of *Systematic Theology: Roman Catholic Perspectives* (Minneapolis: Fortress Press, 1991), and has contributed articles to numerous theological books and journals.

Donald J. Goergen, O.P., is a preacher, teacher, lecturer, author, and theologian who has taught in the areas of christology and spirituality for many years. He received his doctorate in theology from the Aquinas Institute of Theology, now in St. Louis, where he has also taught. His dissertation was on Teilhard de Chardin. His publications include four volumes on the *Theology of Jesus* (Wilmington, Del.: M. Glazier, 1986, 1988; Collegeville, Minn.: Liturgical Press, 1992, 1995). He is presently a member and cofounder of the Friends of God, a Dominican Ashram, in Kenosha, Wisconsin.

Mary Catherine Hilkert, O.P., is associate professor of theology at the University of Notre Dame. She is the author of *Speaking with Authority: Catherine of Siena and the Voices of Women Today* (New York: Paulist, 2001); and *Naming Grace: Preaching and the Sacramental Imagination* (New York: Continuum, 1997). She received her doctorate from the Catholic University of America, with a dissertation on Schillebeeckx's hermeneutics of tradition as a foundation for a theology of preaching. Her articles on his theology have appeared in *A New Handbook of Christian Theologians, The Thomist, Spirituality Today*, and *U.S. Dominican*.

William J. Hill, O.P., was professor emeritus of systematic theology at the Catholic University of America, until his death in 2001. He was the author of *Search for the Absent God: Tradition and Modernity in Religious Understanding* (New York: Crossroad, 1992); *The Three-Personed God: The Trinity As a Mystery of Salvation* (Washington, D.C.: Catholic University of America Press, 1982); and *Knowing the Unknown God*

(New York: Philosophical Library, 1971). A past president of the Catholic Theological Society of America, he served as editor in chief of *The Thomist* from 1975 to 1983.

Mary E. Hines is professor of theology at Emmanuel College in Boston. She received her doctorate in systematic theology from the University of St. Michael's College, Toronto, and has taught at the Washington Theological Union. She is the author of *What Ever Happened to Mary?* (Notre Dame, Ind.: Ave Maria Press, 2001); *The Transformation of Dogma: An Introduction to Karl Rahner on Doctrine* (New York: Paulist, 1989); and numerous articles on ecclesiology, feminist theology, and theology of Mary.

Bradford E. Hinze is an associate professor at Marquette University. He is the author of *Narrating History, Developing Doctrine: Friedrich Schleiermacher and Johann Sebastian Drey* (Atlanta, Ga.: Scholars Press, 1993); and the editor, with D. Lyle Dabney, of *Advents of the Spirit: An Introduction to the Current Study of Pneumatology* (Milwaukee: Marquette University Press, 2001). *He* has published numerous articles advancing a trinitarian and dialogical approach to tradition, revelation, and the church.

Janet M. O'Meara is associate professor of religious studies at Clarke College, where she has chaired the department since 1989. She earned her Ph.D. from the Catholic University of America, with a dissertation on the soteriology of Edward Schillebeeckx. Her research interests are in the areas of christology and the soteriological implications of trinitarian theology for social justice.

Philip Kennedy, O.P., is a member of the faculty of theology in the University of Oxford. He received a doctorate in theology from the University of Fribourg, Switzerland, with a study of Edward Schillebeeckx's religious epistemology. He is the author of *Schillebeeckx, Deus Humanissimus: The Knowability of God in the Theology of Edward Schillebeeckx* (Fribourg, Switzerland: University Press, 1993); and of numerous articles on Schillebeeckx's theology. He is based at Blackfriars, the Dominican House of Studies at Oxford, where he lectures in twentieth-century theology and philosophy.

William L. Portier is Henry J. Knott Professor of Theology at Mount Saint Mary's College, Emmitsburg, Maryland. He is the author of *Isaac Hecker and the First Vatican Council* (Lewiston, N.Y.: E. Mellen Press, 1985); and *Tradition and Incarnation, Foundations of Christian*